WHEN SHE NAMED FIRE

WHEN SHE NAMED FIRE

An Anthology of Contemporary Poetry by American Women

edited by
ANDREA HOLLANDER BUDY

Autumn House Press
PITTSBURGH

ISBN: 978-1-932870-26-8
Library of Congress Control Number: 2008929875

All Autumn House books are printed on acid-free paper and meet the international standards of permanent books intended for purchase by libraries.

Generous funding for publication of this anthology was provided by The Heinz Endowments and by The A. W. Mellon Educational & Charitable Trust Fund at The Pittsburgh Foundation.

This project was supported by the Pennsylvania Council on the Arts, a state agency, through its regional arts funding partnership, Pennsylvania Partners in the Arts (PPA). State government funding comes through an annual appropriation by Pennsylvania's General Assembly. PPA is administered in Allegheny County by Greater Pittsburgh Arts Council.

Contents

Preface: Necessary Poetry

At a writers' conference some years ago I was asked to participate on a panel titled Why We Need Poetry. Of all the featured literary genres, which also included the novel, short story, memoir, essay, drama, and screenplay, only poetry evidently needed justification.

And yet poetry is our oldest form of verbal art. We have been creating, reciting, writing, and reading poems as long as there have been people. But even poets have difficulty defining it. Robert Frost, perhaps attempting to be droll, said that poetry is "what poets write," but he also called it "a way of remembering what it would impoverish us to forget." Samuel Taylor Coleridge defined it as "the best words in the best order." And Emily Dickinson famously denied that it could be defined at all, though she claimed she'd know a poem if she met one: "If I read a book and it makes my whole body so cold no fire can ever warm me, I know that is poetry. If I feel physically as if the top of my head were taken off, I know that is poetry. These are the only ways I know it. Is there any other way?"

When writer Nancy Willard saw the obituary for a friend in *The New York Times*, she remarked in her journal that she "understood why we need poems. Facts tell us everything and nothing."[1] When she mentioned this to another friend, he related a story his Irish grandfather had told him about the god Lir who "created the world by speaking the names of everything in it. Because he had only half a tongue, his words were only half understood. Half of creation, therefore, remained unspoken. That's why we need poets: to sing the hidden side of things."

If poetry, then, is the human voice singing the hidden side of things, an anthology of poetry presents a chorus of selected voices singing alongside one another. With the publication in 1973 of two women-only poetry anthologies, *No More Masks* and *Rising Tides*, readers were given the opportunity to hear

[1] Nancy Willard, "Telling Time," *The Bread Loaf Anthology of Contemporary American Essays*, eds. Robert Pack and Jay Parini (Hanover: UP of New England, 1989) 361.

the voices of American female poets writing at the dawn of the Women's Movement. What were the concerns of such writers? What were their aesthetics, their sensibilities? What did they have in common? How did they differ? Thirty-five years later, during this opening decade of the twenty-first century, the present anthology offers readers a parallel prospect.

When She Named Fire is the result of almost two years of reading and rereading hundreds of poetry collections by American women, along with scores of recent issues of literary journals, numerous anthologies, and recommendations of specific poems by other poets and poetry lovers. Disregarding a writer's reputation or lack thereof, I concentrated on the poems themselves. I let my body be the judge. If a poem made me at once forget myself and at the same time transported me deeply into my body, that poem was a keeper.

The anthology includes 461 poems by 96 women, the youngest born in 1976, the oldest in 1925. Some have won the most prestigious awards available to a writer; others are just at the start of their careers. The group is diverse in other ways as well. While they are all Americans, a few were born as far away as Hong Kong and Liberia. They were raised and have lived all over the United States and outside it. While many have earned positions as teachers of creative writing, some work or have worked in other capacities: cleaning lady, gas station attendant, vineyard manager, homemaker. Their poems, too, demonstrate excellence in various ways: while the bulk are written in what I prefer to call *discovered* form (rather than free verse, because I believe that all good poems exist in form, even if that form is discovered by the poet during the process of creating the poem), some are executed in traditional or experimental forms.

And the poems explore a variety of subjects—political, social, biological, ecological, cultural, anthropological, and, yes, domestic, but never do the speakers of the poems take for granted any relationship, be it with other human beings or animals or any member of the planetary kingdom. Subjects and situations may be familiar—a wife contemplates divorce, a child longs for her long-dead parent, an immigrant misses the odors of her country's landscapes—but the exploration is never obvious, and the journey always satisfying. And there is plenty of humor here. And much solace from the ordinary griefs that accompany a lived life.

Who is the intended audience for this book? Women, yes, but certainly not only women. The audience is one that cannot be characterized in terms of gender, age, class, race, occupation, education, or even experience. It consists of ordinary people who are curious and intelligent, who are often but not necessarily formally educated, and who enjoy a measure of literature, music, and art in their lives, men and women who occupy their time in a myriad of ways and who have—in the unlikely but appropriate words of Norman Mailer—"no tradition by which to measure their experience but the intensity and clarity of their inner lives."[2]

During the Great Depression, President Herbert Hoover made a surprising announcement: "What this country needs now is a good poem." The same could be said today. But what constitutes a good poem? As in any art, this is a matter of taste and duration. Poet Dave Smith has said that such a poem "has a single human voice . . . yet it is also the echoing voice of all men and women."[3] True enough. But a good poem must be more than a vehicle to speak for all of us. It must also be able to speak to us.

We human beings need reassurance that our heartfelt experience in the world has credibility, value, and some measure of authority. Good poems don't tell us anything we don't already know, but they deliver us to ourselves in a language we crave, a condensed and potent language we need because the air waves have been bleached by the language of commerce.

Necessary poetry—poetry that speaks memorably and authenticates experience as it sings "the hidden side of things"—is both *entertaining* and *useful*: *entertaining* in that it is grounded in the human traditions of telling stories and making music, and *useful* in that it disturbs our lives enough to reinforce our humanness by shaking us from complacency.

Some readers may question the necessity of music in poetry, but a poem is fundamentally a song played on the solo instrument of the human voice uttered in ordinary tones and natural cadences. Even when it is purposefully narrative, good poetry is also lyrical.

Others may object to my insisting upon storytelling. Certainly the nature of the human is to be interested in the human. Narrative is the essence of history, including personal history—and telling stories has always been a way to search for truth. Stories are the ingredients of memory, the firmament of culture. And although some of the poems in this anthology may not consciously focus on story, all have narrative elements, if only in their mimetic beginning-middle-end structure.

As for usefulness, I offer this: Poetry has enough competition from other genres and entertainments that if it is to last,

[2] David Denby, "The Contender," *The New Yorker* 20 April 1998: 62.
[3] Helen Vendler, *The Music of What Happens* (Cambridge: Harvard UP, 1988) 40.

if it is to be hauled off the shelf and read and reread, if it is to be hand-copied into a letter or typed into an e-mail or read aloud to a lover or friend, if it is to be committed to memory and uttered, it had better be useful. Poetry is not escapist literature. It reminds us how to live and how to cope with life's difficulties by stirring us in the places where what we feel and know but cannot express nevertheless exists. It provides one of life's few defenses against inevitable grief and intolerable, unfathomable disaster. Yet, as you will discover throughout this gathering of poems by contemporary American women, poetry is equally the language of celebration, of unexpected joy, and of human love as potent as it is invisible.

Our lives are complex and contradictory, fraught with unexpected turns that result in unruliness. Powerful poetry offers one way of expressing such complexity without being unruly itself. One of my fascinations—even obsessions—with such poems is that they are *made* things, artful devices crafted from the ordinary tools of language. When gifted writers wield these tools, giving form and providing words for the yet-to-be-uttered—*when they name fire*—their poems become vehicles of magic that can rouse us in the marrow of our lives and utterly change the way we interact with the world.

I am indebted to the many people who helped me during the completion of this project. Michael Simms, Editor-in-Chief of Autumn House Press, inspired its existence and helped guide its implementation. The only argument we had (and which he won) was the appropriateness of including a few of my own poems. Until he convinced me that readers would want to know what kind of poems the editor herself wrote, I held back, not wanting to occupy the limited space. My husband, Todd Budy, supported me daily and in innumerable ways, some of them as mundane as listening to me read aloud dozens of poems as I considered them for the volume, but also—and often—he rescued me from my desk when I'd been at the project for hours too long. He also suggested the anthology's title, remembering an appropriate and eponymous poem from my first book. Most of all, however, I am indebted to the poets themselves for writing these marvels and for granting me permission to reprint them, and to those generous publishers who understood the nature of my endeavor and made the acquisition of the poems easy.

Andrea Hollander Budy
Mountain View, Arkansas

Kim Addonizio

Born July 31, 1954, in Washington, DC. Kim Addonizio has authored four poetry collections, most recently *What Is This Thing Called Love* (W.W. Norton). *Lucifer at the Starlite* is forthcoming from Norton in 2009, along with *Ordinary Genius: A Guide for the Poet Within.* Addonizio also has two novels, *Little Beauties* and *My Dreams Out in the Street,* from Simon & Schuster. Her awards include two fellowships from the National Endowment for the Arts and one from the Guggenheim Foundation. She teaches privately in Oakland, California, and on-line, and also plays blues harmonica. Her website is www.kimaddonizio.com.

Collapsing Poem

The woman stands on the front steps, sobbing.
The man stays just inside the house,
leaning against the doorjamb. It's late, a wet
fog has left a sheer film over the windows
of cars along the street. The woman is drunk.
She begs the man, but he won't let her in.
Say it matters what happened between them;
say you can't judge whose fault this all is,
given the lack of context, given your own failures
with those you meant most to love.
Or maybe you don't care about them yet.
Maybe you need some way
to put yourself in this scene, some minor detail
that will make them seem so real you try to enter
this page to keep them from doing
to each other what you've done to someone,
somewhere: think about that for a minute,
while she keeps crying, and he speaks
in a voice so measured and calm he might be
talking to a child frightened by something
perfectly usual: darkness, thunder,
the coldness of the human heart.
But she's not listening, because now
she's hitting him, beating her fists against the chest
she laid her head on so many nights.
And by now, if you've been moved, it's because
you're thinking with regret of the person
this poem set out to remind you of,
and what you want more than anything is what
the man in the poem wants: for her to shut up.
And if you could only drive down that street
and emerge from the fog, maybe you

could get her to stop, but I can't do it.
All I can do is stand at that open door
making things worse. That's my talent,
that's why this poem won't get finished unless
you drag me from it, away from that man;
for Christ's sake, hurry, just pull up and keep
the motor running and take me wherever you're going.

The Moment

The way my mother bent to her car door, fumbling the keys, taking forever it seemed
to find the right one, line it up with the lock and feebly push it in and turn,
the way she opened the door so slowly, bending a bit more, easing herself finally into the leather seat—She'd hurt her ribs, she explained, but it wasn't injury
that I saw, not the temporary setback that's followed by healing, the body's tenacious renewal;
I saw for the first time old age, decline, the inevitable easing towards death. Once in the car, though,
settled behind the wheel, backing out and heading for the steady traffic on the highway,
she was herself again, my mother as I'd always known her: getting older, to be sure,
in her seventies now, but still vital, still the athlete she'd been all her life; jogging, golf,
tennis especially—the sport she'd excelled at, racking up championships—they were as natural
to her as breath. All my life she'd been the definition of grace, of a serenely unshakeable confidence
in the body; impossible ever to imagine her helpless, frail, confined to walker or wheelchair.
She was humming now as she drove, that momentary fumbling erased, no trace of it.
No acknowledgment of pain, of the ache she must still be feeling in her side. My mother
refused all that, she would go on refusing it. She peered ahead at the busy road, the past all but forgotten—
somewhere behind us griefs, losses, terrible knowledge, but ahead of us a day we'd spend together,
we were going there now, while there was still time, none of it was going to be wasted.

Onset

Watching that frenzy of insects above the bush of white flowers,
bush I see everywhere on hill after hill, all I can think of
is how terrifying spring is, in its tireless, mindless replications.
Everywhere emergence: seed case, chrysalis, uterus, endless manu-
  facturing.
And the wrapped stacks of styrofoam cups in the grocery, lately
I can't stand them, the shelves of canned beans and soups, freezers
of identical dinners; then the snowflake-diamond-snowflake of the rug
beneath my chair, rows of books turning their backs,
even my two feet, how they mirror each other oppresses me,
the way they fit so perfectly together, how I can nestle one big toe into the
  other
like little continents that have drifted; my God the unity of everything,
my hands and eyes, yours, doesn't that frighten you sometimes,
  remembering
the pleasure of nakedness in fresh sheets, all the lovers there before you,
beside you, crowding you out? And the scouring griefs,
don't look at them all or they'll kill you, you can barely encompass your
  own;
I'm saying I know all about you, whoever you are, it's spring
and it's starting again, the longing that begins, and begins, and begins.

My Heart

That Mississippi chicken shack.
That initial-scarred tabletop,
that tiny little dance floor to the left of the band.
That kiosk at the mall selling caramels and kitsch.
That tollbooth with its white-plastic-gloved worker
handing you your change.
That phone booth with the receiver ripped out.
That dressing room in the fetish boutique,
those curtains and mirrors.
That funhouse, that horror, that soundtrack of screams.
That putti-filled heaven raining gilt from the ceiling.
That haven for truckers, that bottomless cup.
That biome. That wilderness preserve.
That landing strip with no runway lights
where you are aiming your plane,
imagining a voice in the tower,
imagining a tower.

Ed Seling

Pamela Alexander

Born April 2, 1948, in Natick, Massachusetts. Pamela Alexander is a transplanted New Englander who now teaches creative writing at Oberlin College in Ohio. Her most recent book is *Slow Fire* (Ausable Press, 2006), her most recent award an Ohio Arts Council fellowship. Her work has appeared in many magazines and journals, including *Orion, Denver Quarterly, Tri-Quarterly* and *The Journal* and in more than twenty e-zines and anthologies. An associate editor of *FIELD,* Alexander divides her time between Ohio and Ontario, Canada. She has banded several hundred warblers, stroked the guard hairs of an armadillo, and disturbed a hibernating bear.

Letter Home

I can't write you because everything's
wrong. Before dawn, crows swim
from the cedars: black coffee calls them down,
its bitter taste in my throat as they circle,
raucous, huge. Questions with no
place to land, they cruise yellow air
above crickets snapping
like struck matches. My house on fire, crows

are the smoke. You've never left me.
When you crossed the river you did not
call my name. I stood in tall grass
a long time, listening to birds
hidden in reeds, their intricate songs.

The grass will burn, the wrens,
the river and the rain that falls on it.
I can go nowhere else: everything
I cannot bear is here.

I must listen deeper. Sharpen my knife.
Something has changed the angles
of trees, their color. Do not wait to hear
from me. I cannot write to you
because this is what I will say.

Look Here

Next time you walk by my place
in your bearcoat and mooseboots,
your hair all sticks and leaves
like an osprey's nest on a piling,

the next time you walk across my shadow
with those swamp-stumping galoshes
below that grizzly coat and your own whiskers
that look rumpled as if something's
been in them already this morning
mussing and growling and kissing,
the next time you pole the raft of you downriver
down River Street past my place
you could say *hello*, you canoe-footed fur-faced
musk ox, pockets full of cheese and acorns
and live fish and four-headed winds and sky, *hello*
is what human beings say when they meet each other
—if you can't say hello like a human don't
come down this street again and when you do don't
bring that she-bear and if you do I'll know
even if I'm not on the steps putting my shadow
down like a welcome mat, I'll know.

Crossing

Snow falls. A raven flies through it
and grates out the one curse he knows.
He sets his course above the boulder field
I'll cross soon, its thin track
highlighted with powder, the rest blown clear—
a granite slide, gray-green, steep.
Exposure, it's called, when what's above
is rock and what's below, air.

A tall, sharp place. I need it. One path,
clean of guilt and second-guessing—

I'm on it. The wind hasn't left
much snow but my skis float
along the narrow ledge that cuts
straight as a piece of tape. The hard part
is forgetting all else is cocked—
vast tilt of rock above right ear, deep nothing
at left ankle. The hard part's forgetting.

In the middle of something I glide
to a stop. I'm an edge, a balance of going
and going against. I hold the storm down
by one corner, ground it with my weight.
I wear it.

In the woods the snow wanted
to complicate me: everywhere I looked
looked like trail. Now I know
where I have to go and the knowing stings
like anger. I am a stone
at the bottom of a blizzard, eye
of a raven flying through it. I am rock
and sky and the seam that marries them.

What We Need

A roof over
three squares.
Warmth to wear,
something to burn

in winter. Water
music: sheets
of rain hung out
to dry. Time, or

the habits of light.
A road that thins
in hills. Hills.
Once an image

sufficed; now I see
we must speak.

Manners

Sit, she said. The wolf sat. Shake, she said.
He held his face and tail still
and shook everything in between. His fur
stood out in all directions. Sparks flew.
Dear sister, she wrote. His yellow eyes
followed the words discreetly. I have imagined
a wolf. He smells bad. He pants, and his long tongue
drips onto the rug, my favorite rug. It has arrows
and urns and diamonds in it. The wolf sits
where I've stared all morning hoping
for a heron: statuesque, aloof,
enigmatic. Be that way, the wolf said.
There are other poets.

Ginger Andrews

Born May 16, 1956, in North Bend, Oregon. Ginger Andrews runs a small housecleaning business with her sisters, who all live within walking distance. Her first collection of poems, *An Honest Answer*, won the Nicholas Roerich Poetry Prize. Her second book, *Hurricane Sisters*, has been praised by Garrison Keillor, who has featured her work more than twenty times on National Public Radio's "The Writer's Almanac." Most recently her work has appeared in *The Literary Experience* (Thompson Wadsworth) and in *Long Journey* (Oregon State University Press). She teaches a children's Bible class on Wednesday nights, and when she's not crazy busy, she loves to take walks near the ocean.

What the Cleaning Lady Knows

Cleanliness is not and never has been next to godliness.

White carpets are hell.

You can get by without Comet, Spic and Span or lemon oil,
but Windex is mandatory.

Ammonia can cause pneumonia.

People who pay to have clean houses cleaned are lonely.

Children whose parents work full-time will fall in love with you.

Rich people splatter diarrhea
on the inside rim of their toilet seats, just like the rest of us.

Cleaning rags should always be washed separately with bleach.

Cash is better than checks.

The Housewife

sits on her carefully made bed.
Her blue curtains are more than half drawn.
All household members are acting perfectly rational.
So everyone is a little boring.
So everyone is a little crazy.
She could pick up
her somewhat expensive marble-based candelabra—
and throw it out her window
because she's bored,
because she's just a little crazy.

For any one of a hundred reasons,
she could throw it.
But she won't.
She'll straighten the bed covers
and, maybe, later,
she'll burn the hell out of dinner.

O That Summer

my sister and I
both wound up back in Coos Bay,
basket cases, lonely as hell.
She was recovering from drugs and alcohol,
I was newly divorced, a Sunday School teacher
with no job skills whatsoever
and two little boys to feed,
praying for a maid job at Best Western.
Lord how we prayed

walking from one end
of Sunset Beach to the other, barefoot,
freezing in tank tops and cutoffs,
hair and makeup perfect,
fingernails painted with three coats
of Wet'n Wild, hoping
some good-looking single doctor
was walking his dog nearby
should one of us happen
to slice our foot on beach glass.

How to Talk about Jesus

It's easy to tell your sister she's got a black thing
in the corner of her eye, some mascara, a little bug,
maybe an eyelash or something. It's not quite as easy
to tell her she's got a booger hanging. Nobody likes
to mention boogers. If you're driving down the road,
you can dig Kleenex out of your purse, say, Hon,
you got a booger. She'll maybe ask, Which nose hole?
You'll tell her. She'll get it with the Kleenex you offered,
check in the rearview to make sure, and on you'll go
to work, wherever. But how about a stranger, a pretty lady
in the grocery line with pink lipstick on her front teeth
as she smiles, offering to let you go ahead
because you only have a loaf of French bread?

I once pointed a finger toward my next door neighbor's crotch
when we were talking at our mailboxes.
Two big green praying mantises were mating
right there on his button fly. We laughed. I really don't
know how to throw Shadrach, Meshach or Abednego
into a casual chat with my pharmacist about the weather,
but I've learned it's best to talk apples before Eve,
to start with little things.

Home Alone

Cigarette smokers,
sweet tooths,
alcoholics, teetotalers,
bad cooks, good cooks,
food stamp recipients,
low blood sugar and type 2 diabetes,
depression, codependency, cancer,
high energy, low self-esteem,
nap takers, neat freaks, control freaks,
carpal tunnel syndrome,
strong arms, skinny ankles, pot bellies,
public speakers, introverts, braggers,
blue eyes, long legs, red necks,
enablers, naggers, whiners,
pride, guilt and honesty all run in my family.
We have an out of work long haul truck driver,
a race car driver, a certified pesticide applicator,
an Olympic decathlon pole vault record breaker,
Sunday School teachers, a politician, a poet,
professional house cleaners, a dishwasher who
works in a dive for dimes, and an Environmental
Services worker who mops floors at the local hospital
and recently moved in with me because
paying off her ex's bills put her in a real bind and
even though she comes in from work exhausted
she manages to vacuum my carpets and Comet my toilets.
There's never a dull moment, though I'm praying for one,
that my sister will get her own place soon,
that my brilliant, eighteen-year-old needs-to-get-a-job son
will snap out of it, that my in-laws' place will hurry up and sell,
that they'll pack up and move to Arkansas already . . . . I see myself
home alone writing a poem in a quiet house, smoking one cigarette
after another, eating candy, flicking
my ashes on the floor.

David G.W. Scott

Julianna Baggott

Born September 30, 1969, in Wilmington, Delaware. Julianna Baggott is the author of four novels, *Girl Talk, The Miss America Family, The Madam*, and *Which Brings Me to You* (co-written with Steve Almond), and three books of poems, *This Country of Mothers, Lizzie Borden in Love*, and *Compulsions of Silkworms and Bees.* She also writes novels for younger readers under the pen name N.E. Bode—*The Anybodies* trilogy, *The Slippery Map*, the prequel to *Mr. Magorium's Wonder Emporium*, and *The Prince of Fenway Park.* Her work appears in *The Best American Poetry, Glamour, Ms., Poetry, TriQuarterly*, and has been read on National Public Radio's "Here and Now" and "Talk of the Nation." She teaches at Florida State University's Creative Writing Program and lives in Tallahassee with her husband and their four children. She has no hobbies.

Marie Laurent Pasteur Addresses Louis in Her Mind While She Scalds the Sheets

Without you, I would know nothing
about what festers—germs,
their heated breeding,
their love without exhaustion.
What does death look like, Louis,
held by your microscope for inspection?
I know it intimately
worn on our children's faces—
the scalding of typhoid fever, the wrung mouth,
the loosened eyes. I would recognize it anywhere.
It charmed me that you forgot our wedding,
instead dithering in the laboratory,
bent to your microscope, living among
the unseen.
But now my sin is a weak desire
for ignorance. I adore the boy at the market
with the cleft in his skull,
a dent from a shovel.
He believes the world of bushels,
onions and seed,
what can be held in his giant fists
and seen by his wide-set, pitching eyes.

Helen Keller Dying in Her Sleep

"Suddenly I felt a misty consciousness as of something forgotten, a thrill of returning thought, and somehow the mystery of language was revealed to me."
—Helen Keller

Here is the pump again, its cool neck,
the well house draped in honeysuckle.

This is before the vaudeville rendition of my miracle,
before the newspapermen took photographs of me
petting the dog, reading Shakespeare,
before I met President Cleveland.
My parents haven't yet talked to Alexander Graham Bell
about my ragged fate.
                                        I am walking backward,
reaching into my own mouth
for the world's dark syllables.
Anne has returned to me, forever spelling water.
But there isn't a word in my hand
                                        only a hand in my hand, turning.
It is a mist again, but this time of unknowing.
The returning thought is thought leaving,
escaping, pumped eagerly from my body.
Brain fever, I recall it now,
                                        my supple mind afire.
Rain water fills a bucket mother left out in the yard.
The doctor is made of rough hands and camphor.
And now it smells like night.

For Sylvia: Come Winter. Come, Winter.

I would give you back to yourself
                                        if I could—
here, before you knew much—
Sylvia Plath, Fulbright Scholar modeling
the latest fashion: a white swimsuit
with black polka dots, high heels,
long legs
as stiff and posed as two young soldiers.
I thought of you this morning,
the oven, the lush unceasing offers
                                        of death.
And how I long, today,
to stall in the yard, the mail flipping
in my hands while the house parts
                                        a field of wind.
Look! Leaves build at the door.
Here, in the dirt, bulbs.
                    The crocuses keep patient time—
                    those blind eyes, buried—
but the sun will cause
                              an inner ticking
that only the bulbs can hear
dim as a fragile pulse in the ear.

Blurbs

I don't want to be *a national treasure,*
too old codgery, something wheeled out
of a closet to cut ribbon. I prefer
resident genius, or for the genius
to be at least *undeniable.*
I'd like to steer away from the declaration
by far her best. Too easily I read,
The predecessors were weary immigrant stock.
The same goes for *working at the height*
of her powers, as if it's obvious
I'm teetering on the edge of senility.
I don't want to have to look things up:
lapidary style? I'd prefer not to be *a talent;*
as if my mother has dressed me
in a spangled leotard, tap shoes,
my hair in Bo-Peep pin curls.
But I like *sexy,* even if unearned.
I like *elegance, bite.* I want someone
to confess he's fallen in love with me,
and another to say, *No, she's mine.*
And a third to just come out with it:
She will go directly to heaven.

Ruth E. Hendricks

Jan Beatty

Born November 27, 1952, in Pittsburgh, Pennsylvania. Jan Beatty's most recent poetry collection is *Red Sugar* (University of Pittsburgh Press, 2008). Her previous books include *Boneshaker* and *Mad River*, winner of the 1994 Agnes Lynch Starrett Prize. She is director of creative writing at Carlow University, where she teaches the Madwomen in the Attic workshops and in the MFA program. For the past twelve years, Beatty has co-hosted and produced "Prosody," a public radio show on which she interviews national writers. She is a Pittsburgh Steelers fan and likes muscle cars.

Cruising with the Check-out Girls

Aisle 6 at Giant Eagle, I slap
my bananas on the conveyor, a six-
pack of Ho-Ho's, three bottles of water,
and a *People* magazine with Tina Turner's
legs on the cover. I'm trying to be
anonymous, I glance at her name tag—
Marcy—she's staring into nowhere.
She calls to the checker in 7: *Shari, did ya*
see him? He's checkin out in 10 right now.
Oh yeah, Shari says, *I saw him.*
I have to ask, *Who are you talking about?*
Marcy says, *This hot guy, the one*
in the leather jacket, comes in every
Thursday, he's hot, go ahead and look.
I look over my shoulder: *Not bad—*
have you talked to him? Marcy twists
her face like I've been frozen for years:
I ain't talking 'bout no talkin, as she
drags my Ho-Ho's over the computer window,
never looking down. I say, *I knew that,*
but it's her I'm interested in—not him,
and I'm looking at her eyes looking at him—
she's got a look like the first time she tasted
chocolate—and now *I'm* gone too, wondering
if her lips are as soft as they look—
till Marcy says, *Here he comes!* and we are
forever bonded, me & the check-out girls,
in our head-down-sideways-glance
tracking his long, slow stride out
the automatic door—
Marcy, inches from me,
lets out the breath she's been holding,

Shari proclaims: *That is one hot man!*
and we're laughing, and Marcy is flushed
& resplendent and I don't want to
leave, I want more! More talk! More sex!
But I smile at her, say, *Hey,*
good luck, and I'm walking out thinking
about velocity on a hot night, a
thousand small heavens, my long
ride home.

Procession

Little wren, your body is breaking down into air.
I find you under my desk,
—how long dead?—
What do the hollowed black cones of your eyes
and your tiny claws have to tell me about home?
Your small patch of city yard,
droop of telephone wire on your daily flight,
the wind draft over the Allegheny?

I pray to the four directions
then put your body in the trash, cover you
with typewriter ribbons and calendar days and press down.
Ten minutes later I dig you out,
carry you outside in the styrofoam box
and we walk the streets of Etna
while big-haired women watch from their porches.

Across Butler Street,
the workers of the Tippins Machinery Plant
break open their lunch buckets on the stone wall.
At the churchyard I dig behind the hydrangea
with my father's tack-hammer and cast-iron awl.
Everything goes on without us.

If I could see the cities inside you,
if I could find my own ocean of light—

In the hole:
paper with a stamp of an orange sun on it
and the word: */FINISHED/*
a piece of carnelian and last words:
I am sorry. I know you were alone in this room of poems.
I tried to hide your death.
RIP May 29th Calvert United Presbyterian Church.

The Long White

I think it was a Lincoln, the man's hand
coming from the open door: *c'mere,*
in front of my house, I was 9, I stood still.
I want to talk to you. I started walking
towards school the long white beside me
and I wasn't really scared—just in another
separate place of my own, I wasn't wishing
for anything, just watching my feet walking fast,
the hand reaching out, could they see
a fresh girl who didn't know
her real parents: the wide-open face
with no protection, the paleness that says,
I'm lonely, I'm wandering and could be
scooped up in a minute if you insist—
I just want to talk to you,
and after a while I just jumped in.
I thought of this twenty years later when
the cab pulled up and there was fog and
three ravens sitting on the wooden totem of
the ashes of dead Inuit, I stepped into
the long white outside the closed train station,
5 am Prince Rupert, British Columbia
the cab pulled up, the same man's hand
threw open the passenger door, the same
question: *need a ride?*
Yes, yes, I climbed in
but this time I told about it:
blurted my story to this stranger, a father
who I never knew, never knew where
he was from, someone said a hockey player
from Canada and he said *yes, yes,* and I told him
I always wondered about my father,
and his head swung around and he insisted:
you need to look for him, you need to do this,
I didn't know I had been getting in cars
with men all my life looking for him,
a passenger in the long white, until then.

Dreaming Door

for Don

You brought donuts in the morning of our first days and
we watched the great rivers through my South Side windows/everything
swelling, we ate in the turquoise kitchen and opened the dreaming door:
our Pittsburgh rolling by on the coal barges, the P&LE carting steel
to the still-rising cities of the West, a couple speedboats
running the dirty summer Monongahela,
you on your way to work. I said *no one's ever*
been this nice to me as I walked you the 52 steps down
from my third floor apartment, you tilted your head,
looking at me in a way I'd never seen:
like I was the most sublime person,
your blue eyes seeming truly puzzled:
I haven't even started to love you yet,
and at the door the world barreling through—
this time with gifts, fierce fires,
and planets of luck.

Claudia Carlson

Jeanne Marie Beaumont

Born June 15, 1954, in Darby, Pennsylvania. Jeanne Marie Beaumont is the author of *Curious Conduct* (BOA Editions, 2004) and *Placebo Effects* (Norton, 1997), winner of the National Poetry Series. With Claudia Carlson, she co-edited *The Poets' Grimm: 20th Century Poems from Grimm Fairy Tales.* Her poems are included in *The Year's Best Fantasy and Horror 2007, Good Poems for Hard Times*, and many other anthologies. She teaches in the Stonecoast MFA Program and at the Unterberg Poetry Center of the 92nd Street Y, and she is director of the Frost Place Seminar. Jeanne Marie lives in Manhattan with her husband and two Cornish Rex cats, and studies jazz dance with Luigi.

Going by Taxi

I wear gloves to my elbows; you wear herringbone trousers.
It starts to snow; the streetlights haven't switched on yet.
I lack ordinary patience; where's the towne crier?
  You say correction; I say retraction.
The citrus look exacting; they make calm orange pyramids.
Let me buy alstroemeria; you choose the beer.
Wood bundles whiten near the awning; remember our fireplace?
Life takes things away from you; the snow gives way to sleet.
  You say umbrella; I say imbroglio.
Tuesday's best for sleuthing; we pursue the stubborn missing.
When I'm needy, I'm rude; keep an eye down the avenue.
We don't want to let that taxi go by; we don't.
All this time yields no evidence; all this time gives no clue.
  I say angry; you say ennui.
Let's kiss when the meter starts; ah, here come the lights.
I've forgotten the address; you've a claim check in your pocket.
We stocked our coat closet with wood; it was ten, eleven years ago.
Bugs crept out under the door; carried far from earthy homes.
  You say step on it; I say no stop.

We don't know the tune on the radio, and the street's turned black
    with snow.

Rock Said

I only dance when I'm thrown.
I was baptized in the riverbed but lost my faith underground.
It is darker inside me than it is inside you.
I am a member of a vast society.
I have recently disentangled myself from smothering roots.

I am celibate because of gravity.
I can describe you perfectly because I was here first.
I meant the scissors no harm.
I apologize to the person I tripped yesterday.
Has anyone told you your hands are warm as the desert?
You're not as fluent in Rock as I'd hoped.
I am small for my age and getting smaller.
Call me the companion of last resort.
When I grow up I'd rather be a mountain than a statue.
But I'd rather be a pest than a pet.
My fellow travelers prefer not to make my acquaintance.
I torture each moment until it reveals its secret.
I am the witness's witness.
I stare deliriously all winter at winter.
I am knocking on a door, O who will answer?
I've got folks in my bed, folks in my bed.
Do you know your feet are as cold as the lake's bottom?
Don't get caught up with pathetic fallacy.
We are destined to lie together.
Leave me by a thousand dense and fragrant gardens.

Chapter One

It was a dark and stormy night
in the dog's mind, therefore
he chopped the air into bits
and pieces with furious barking.
Shaddup!—his master's voice.
Sound of a tin can tossed down
like stage thunder and lightning
or it was the real thing as it was
indeed a dark and stormy—No,
the master protests the opening cliché
so it's the writer in the doghouse
hunching over the full mouth of keys.
Here's the hunger that devours all the days.
What will the mouth say now?
Click click, click, click click . . .
A dark night it was. It truly was, but
that's not the beginning, that's a mind
emptying itself, soul scouring itself.
It was a white and scary blank.
That *was* the truth, but the very truth
one had to hide, was hired to hide.

Try other keys. Three false starts
and you could be out for good.
The spotlight turns.
"For several dark years, I spent my nights in a doghouse . . ."
Now a silence
in which a scent may be picked up,
a hook may be placed on which
the dear, rare, unsuspecting Reader
can be hung out to soak
on a stormy night,
at the head of a brambled trail
with—now, who erased the dog?—
with not even a damp dog to lead the way.

Bonnard

Surely paradise has
a table by a window

that looks out
on a garden

dark apple
in the compote

a dog
happy in shadow

happy in red and gold
mosaic of air

not the way we see
objects

but the way we
know them to be there

Miriam Goodman

Robin Becker

Born March 7, 1951, in Philadelphia, Pennsylvania. Robin Becker has published six poetry collections including *All-American Girl* (1996), *The Horse Fair* (2000), and *Domain of Perfect Affection* (2006), all in the Pitt Poetry Series. Professor of English and Women's Studies at the Pennsylvania State University, she has received fellowships from the Bunting Institute, the Massachusetts Cultural Council and the National Endowment for the Arts. In 2000, she won the George Atherton Award for Excellence in Teaching from Penn State. Becker serves as Contributing and Poetry Editor for *The Women's Review of Books*, for which she writes the poetry column "Field Notes." Becker teaches in Provincetown's Fine Arts Work Center Poetry Program each summer.

Salon

Acolyte at the font, my mother
bends before basin and hose
where Jackie soaps her fine head,
adjusting pressure and temperature.
How many times has she
bared her throat, her clavicle,
beside the other old women?
How many times the regular
cleansing and surrender to the cold chair,
the sink, the detergents, the lights,
the slick of water down the nape?
Turbaned and ready,
she forgoes the tray of sliced bagels
and donuts, a small, private dignity.

Vivienne, the manicurist, dispels despair,
takes my mother's old hands into her swift
hands and soaks them to soften
the cuticles before the rounding and shaping.
As they talk my mother attends
to the lifelong business of revealing
and withholding, careful to frame each story
while Vivienne lacquers each nail
and then inspects each slender finger,
rubbing my mother's hands
with the fragrant, thin lotion,
each summarizing her week, each
condemning that which must be condemned,
each celebrating the manicure and the tip.

Sometimes in pain, sometimes broken
with grief in the parking lot,
my mother keeps her Friday appointment
time protected now by ritual and tradition.

The fine cotton of Michael's white shirt
brushes against her cheek as they stare
into the mirror at one another.
Ennobled by his gaze, she accepts
her diminishment, she who knows herself
his favorite. In their cryptic language
they confide and converse, his hands busy
in her hair, her hands quiet in her lap.
Barrel-chested, Italian, a lover of opera,
he husbands his money and his lover, Ethan;
only with him may she discuss my lover and me,
and in this way intimacy takes the shape
of the afternoon she passes in the salon,
in the domain of perfect affection.

The New Egypt

I think of my father who believes
a Jew can outwit fate by owning land.
Slave to property now, I mow
and mow, my destiny the new Egypt.
From his father, the tailor, he learned not
to rent but to own; to borrow to buy.
To conform, I disguise myself and drag
the mower into the drive, where I ponder
the silky oil, the plastic casing, the choke.
From my father, I learned the dignity
of exile and the fire of acquisition,
not to live in places lightly, but to plant
the self like an orange tree in the desert
and irrigate, irrigate, irrigate.

The Lover of Fruit Trees

in memory of Henry Sauerwein

The desert of northern New Mexico
stretches behind the garden,
punishing cactus in a hot blue bed.
Civilization begins with the Russian olive
and the Chinese elm.

This year all the trees are full.
Early apricots cluster, and greengage

plums dapple the adobe wall.
We walk what you call your English garden
for its wild and unlikely flowers.

You call them by their Latin names
like the strict uncle who wants to be firm
but loves his brother's children for their flaws.
One blazes bright in the morning and wilts by noon;
another flowers before its time.

We turn to the orchard, your prize,
and I think of the stubborn Jews
who, throughout my childhood, made oranges
grow in the desert. *A miracle*, my father would say.
You understand? A miracle.

Twilight. You reach for your hose
and water disappears into the sandy soil.
Inside, you show me an oversized book
of photographs taken in the Warsaw ghetto
before everything beautiful burned.

The Return

At night he is returned to me—
a small dog with black eyes—
and his tongue stripes my face
pink, the color of his tender
underbelly. We laugh, we weep,
to find each other again.

Cobwebs shine bright as stars
in the forest. I kneel to feel
his fur against my skin, his satin ears,
the fine bones of his skull
returned to me.

In the Sangre de Cristo we run
through paintbrush and columbine.
I follow him into streams where small stones
glitter in his wake. Past larkspur and penstemon,
he fills the woods with his happiness.

When he lies down, I take him into my arms,
a small stillness returned to me, my everlasting stone.

A shovel is waiting. I dig, again, in the dark wood,
as this is my share, to dig and make a place for him
before the light divides us again.

Hold Back

Like afternoon shadows on October adobes, she will fall
and fall on me, wind fluttering white at the window,
smell of piñon fires and first snow

on the mountain. Cool blue altitudes we drive,
down here we burn, let silence rain its quiet
weather, let her suntanned arm graze mine

with its peachbloom glaze; I know how to walk away
and come back shining. In time she will open her shirt,
she will show me her neck, she will close her eyes.

But we're not yet lovers, we're seekers from the valleys,
laden with turquoise and silver, interested
in each other the way traders fall in love

with a beautiful bracelet, the one they haven't had
and still think will make a difference. But we're not
thinking of the future—that's one of the conditions—

I'm tracing her palm with my finger and feeling
the Rio Grande rush over autumn stones. I'm kissing
the inside of her elbow, the moccasin-soft skin

is a song I heard at the pueblo when the women
danced together the small, mysterious movements.
Soon she'll lie on her stomach with her chest pressed

into the thin sheet and I'll climb
to her back, freckled with summer
light. Impatient, she throws her head left and right,

she wants me to begin, she's been waiting
all afternoon for my hand
at the base of her spine,

so I hold back. All we know of pleasure
is pleasure delayed, the fine
restraint which once given over is gone.

Roger Crowley

Robin Behn

Born June 15, 1958, in Bay Shore, New York. Robin Behn is the author of three poetry collections, most recently *Horizon Note*, winner of the Brittingham Prize from University of Wisconsin Press, and co-editor of *The Practice of Poetry: Writing Exercises from Poets who Teach* (HarperCollins). The recipient of awards from the National Endowment for the Arts and the Guggenheim Foundation, she lives in Birmingham, Alabama, with her son and teaches in the MFA Program at the University of Alabama and for the Vermont College of Fine Arts. A trained musician, Behn plays flute, recorder, and penny whistle. She often collaborates with other artists, most recently the Chicago painter Mirjana Ugrinov, with whom she launched an installation called "Naked Writing."

My Hair

When I gather my long
leaf-colored hair
and make of it a stem

and twist the handle of my head
and join it back to me
with metal pins

I'm on your lap again
my hands are in the air
my view is mile upon mile

I feel you fashioning the serpent
on my head and the thick braid
of you inside me

I'm ready now to enter
a prim public place
where I am the teacher the police a saint

I turn my back
and everyone I command
sees what it can be to be commanded

Unabashed

for my men

All of my life I had been moving toward this word,

bashing things aside,
hoping not to cause harm,

but causing, in the earthly ways,
my female share.

Sometimes I was running through
the scorched, familiar distance—
a flickering face and seaweed beard

floating to the surface of a prairie's wildflower pixels,
breathing again, laughing again,
hot wind on my sex,

and sometimes I was ploughing inexorable red mud,
admixture of earth and birth,
grunt by grunt down
to infant-sound of suck and scythe

and for a time I was lost
at the bottom of all reckoning
and for a long time it transpired
that I stood before my selves,

unadorned. Unadored. Undulating. Aflame.
And from that flame, you, dear one, toward me,
and in that flame, I, toward you, unabashed, became.

Three Horses

Henceforth, three horses.
Dust- or rain-bedazzled.
Hot days or cool, days of wind
or merciful stillness, three, now, here,

three horses you must take
as long to look at as it took them
to become this triangle you could balance
a camera or lifetime or your suffering upon,

never just one horse anymore,
and never two woefully parallel horses,
but three, now, yes, three horses.
One called My Body and one called Your Body
and one called My Hooves in Your Hair.

Hydrangea

Peel the petals back, the spillage back,
the fists of paleness back from smoldering blue

to the color of fire to the color of fire burnt to time.
Now, by holding the stem and backing a long way off,

all the way out of your life to a ledge
above a dry pool, you could own the flower.

But the Other has set out a vase.
So now it is a charcoal sketch

of how rain wishes, crookedly, to fall.
Tenderness in the junctures.

Stemming from a pool into which the skater vanishes.
As into the lion's eye tameness.

As into the body with your voice inside it,
water-in-a-vase,

and into the body with O's voice inside it,
water-in-a-vase,

finally goes the flower.
The single blackened eyestalk.

What seeing did.
What desire wants to be shriven to the shape of.

Why in the world
this flower.

Elegy: Cook County

driving through the county
suburban urbane urban ban
my red car beats a path
across the quick plotted plots

big box sweatshops

my galloping hood ornament
hoping
like the Great Wall and kindness
to be seen from space

red dot take stock

underwheel's the underfeel
of farms'
bare ruined shoulders, corn's bumpy hunkered
husks

dumb stalks knock knock

over which a thousand picturesque invader geese
dip their oily heads
kaching into the motherlode of revved-green
corporate chem-ponds

squawk sop ill got

I come to hunt a woods
I haunted long ago
and that house unbalconied,
unbuxom, unbedecked

skid stocks quadruple locks

but where I did on two wheels and three gears
seek truth is paved and the forests
where I went to weep
are parceled, cutely named

sap slit gist gilt

I take thee and I dial in to thy
commingled signals,
thy filament and firmament,
I ride thy girth and grid,

post pasture lost rapture

O Plenteous, O Proud, O Fast Asleep
Ingenious Sprawl,
Hog Butcher, Self Butcher,
mall to shining mall.

Katrina Carter

Terry Blackhawk

Born February 5, 1945, in Glendale, California. Terry Blackhawk is author of two chapbooks and three full-length poetry collections, most recently *The Dropped Hand* from Marick Press. Her poems have appeared in journals such as *Marlboro Review, Michigan Quarterly Review, Florida Review* and *Nimrod*, with reviews of her books in *Calyx, Poet Lore, ForeWord* and elsewhere. A proud alumna of Antioch College, Terry is the founder of InsideOut Literary Arts Project (www.insideoutdetroit.org) and serves on the boards of the Associated Writing Programs and the National Writers in the Schools Alliance. She lives and writes not far from the river in Detroit, Michigan.

Leda

All day long I twisted
and turned
like a cat in heat
so my prayers were easy
and I was not surprised
at how quickly he came
with his hissing glide
across the smooth waters.
It was a sight all right—
the arc of his wing,
that snaking neck—
but there was no trick to it.
I always knew he'd pick
me, glib mortal
girl, target
for his flimsy passion.

How he flashed and preened.
It was laughable really,
that self-importance,
those ludicrous pinions
beating the air around me.
He was strong,
but I held him, breast
buttock and thigh
before brushing off
the sweat-stained feathers.
What these gods wouldn't give
for some solid flesh.

But still, I liked
his costume and anyway
it wasn't half bad
for a small devotion.

Little Red

Imagine her not hooded or coy.
No inadvertent blush
to stamp her victim forever.
But let us take her
as she was in the old story
having chosen the path of needles
over the path of pins.
Not a child, no father ahead
or mother behind
to frame her journey with admonition
or reward. None of this
prettification, simpering
rose petal baskets or little feet,
but a child-woman on the verge
of learning her own utility,
how to resist, be strong.
Needles, not pins.
Wit will be her weapon,
and flesh—so when she lies
naked next to the wolf, even there
bawdiness will save her
and she will tell him
she needs to dump a load.
How can he argue the body's truth?
What to do but wait and say go?
Imagine the darkness, the orchard
outside Grandmother's cabin,
fruit trees clouding above her
as she slips free of his bonds,
escapes into the apple-cool night,
and leaves him lying there, slathering,
stupid and confused, pulling
the rope he tied her to, finding it limp
in his hands.

The Dawn of the Navajo Woman

for Evan

The Navajo medicine woman gets up early
to greet the sun. So my radio tells me
and so I stay tuned, though you already showed
the way of greeting: simply to hold
this winter the hickory nut brushed free
of snow, the plain prize beneath the season's tree.

Perhaps it's the way your arch fits my instep,
my instep curves over your arch, but we've kept
at it these years, our limbs linking and unlinking deep
in the quilting, and still a hunger for skin, not sleep,
leads me on to you, your hand on my breast or
your calm talk of death and the ghosts of our ancestors,

all of them gone into the crowded earth. Such
comfort and ease I can almost consider becoming mulch
myself. Or ash. And I wonder at how a rush of heat can
disperse into something so much bigger than I am
that it leaves me pulsing, ignoring what's beyond,
daring to dispute the frozen ground.

The predawn sky offers an arctic green
below a blanket of flaming clouds. I try to imagine
the devotions of that Navajo woman but get only as far
as yesterday when we detoured through a graveyard
seeking, after shopping, a more quiet crowd.
The sun dazzled us: stark trunks thrusting upward

in the polar air, a batch of mallards in a bubbled
pool and all around the bright untroubled
snow. In the granite names I read the luck and rhythm
of even this hair's-breadth of a life, your breath with mine,
the branches swirling by, and the bobbing ducks, their
emerald heads flashing a green and palpable fire.

At Silver Creek Presbyterian Church

Lindale, Georgia 1953

We tossed sticks from the bridge
that spanned the creek, my brother and I,
draped ourselves over iron railings,
or counted rings from stones we dropped
and we did not think about redemption.

The creek circled the church
and we crossed it Sundays to sit on pews
itching to run through tall grass
to the Confederate Soldier's grave
at wood's edge where the churchyard ended.

We'd flip through hymnals,
sing along with the simpler tunes
and just once was worship broken
by the songs of a Negro congregation
wading in the water.

I craned to see whole bodies
dressed in robes being dunked under,
heard only unaccompanied tongues,
a harmony from beneath the bridge
where we played our idle games.

It was baptism, full immersion
in a minor key, a vibration
crossing the yard, reaching
through open windows, filling us
with sound, and my body

trembling with resonance
at the suddenness of their joyful noise,
the stern nudge not to look,
to be still, sit polite
under the rafters of Our Lord.

Margaretta K. Mitchell

Chana Bloch

Born March 15, 1940, in New York, New York. Chana Bloch is the author of three books of poems, including *Mrs. Dumpty* (University of Wisconsin Press, 1998), winner of the Felix Pollak Prize in Poetry. She is co-translator of Yehuda Amichai's *Open Closed Open* (Harcourt, 2000), *The Song of Songs* (Modern Library Classic, 2006), and *Hovering at a Low Altitude: The Collected Poetry of Dahlia Ravikovitch* (Norton, 2009). Among her many awards are fellowships from the National Endowment for the Arts in poetry and translation, the National Endowment for the Humanities, and the Rockefeller Foundation, as well as the Poetry Society of America's Di Castagnola Award for a manuscript-in-progress, and two Pushcart Prizes. A poetry junkie and weekend hiker, she lives in Berkeley, California.

Act One

Hedda Gabler is lighting the lamps in a fury.
From the front row center
we see the makeup streaking her neck,
little tassels of sweat
that stain her bodice. She says *Yes* to Tesman
and it's like spitting.

We are just-married,
feeling lucky. Between the acts
we stop to admire ourselves in the lobby mirror.

But Hedda—how misery
curdles her face!
She opens the letters with a knife
and her husband stands there
shuffling, the obliging child
waiting to be loved.

Yes, she says, fluffing the pillows
on the sofa, *yes dear*, stoking
the fire. And Tesman smiles. A shudder
jolts through her body to
lodge in mine, and
                                        oh yes, I can feel that
blurt of knowledge
no bride should know.

Twenty-Fourth Anniversary

I hung my wedding dress
in the attic. I had a woolen

shoulder to lean against,
a wake-up kiss, plush words
I loved to stroke:
My husband. We.

You hung the portraits of your great-
grandparents from Stuttgart
over the sofa—boiled collar,
fashionable shawl. The yellow
shellac of marriage
coats our faces too.

We're like the neoclassical facade
on a post office. Every small town
has such a building.
Pillars forget they used to be
tree trunks, their sap congealed

into staying put. I can feel it
happening in every cell—that gradual
cooling and drying.
There is that other law of nature
which lets the dead thing stand.

"And the darkness he called night"

I was trying to keep things neat and shiny.
I had two sets of dishes—one for love,
one for hate. I kept them in separate cupboards.
Eat love and hate at the same meal
and you'll get punished.

The rabbis taught us the mathematics of keeping
this from that. They divined
the micro-moment when day flips over
into night: *When the third star presents itself in the sky.*
They drew a line through that eye of light, a longitude.
You've got to navigate the evening blessing
with precision, not one star too soon.
But night comes on slowly.
It takes all day.

When I couldn't love what I thought
I would love forever,
it was shame that punished me:
the god of *Thou Shalt Not.*

My friend's father was killed
in a car crash. She hated him,
hadn't seen him in years.
When the police called, she drove to the ditch
where his wrecked Chevy waited for the tow truck.

The body was gone. On the dashboard, broken glasses,
an open notebook splotched with his blood.
Then she was crying, not knowing why.
She tore out a stain on the blue-ruled paper,
his ragged last breath,
and took it into her mouth.

The New World

My uncle killed a man and was proud of it.
Some punk with a knife came at him in Flatbush
and he knocked the sucker to the ground.
The sidewalk finished the job.

By then he'd survived two wives
and a triple bypass. He carried
a bit of the plastic tubing in his pocket
and would show it to anyone.
He'd unbutton his shirt right there on the street
and show off the scar.

As a boy, he watched a drunken Cossack
go after his father with an axe.
His sister tried to staunch the bleeding
with a hunk of dry bread.

That's the old country for you:
they ate with their hands, went hungry to bed,
slept in their stink. When pain knocked,
they opened the door.

The bitter drive to Brooklyn every Sunday
when I was a child—
Uncle George in the doorway snorting and laughing,
I'm gonna take a bite of your little behind.

He was a good-looker in a pin-striped suit
and shoeshine shoes.
This is America, we don't live
in the Dark Ages anymore, he liked to say.
This is a free country.

The Lesson

When she played
those veins
glittered and jumped.

That's what I saw
from the piano bench
under the tasselled lamp—

and in the back room that scarecrow
her mother, dirty rouge
on the cheekbones, the hooded eyes
staring.

Each Tuesday I'd come back,
tugging at my music:
Will I have veins like that
when I learn to play?

The ugliness of the adult world,
how I craved it—
not knowing but wanting.

"What a man
does to a lady"—whatever I dreamed
that mystery would be like,

the brutal music
of a real life,

bent over kissing
hair, breastbone, thigh,

whatever could make her blood
stand up like that.

Gloria Vando

Michelle Boisseau

Born October 26, 1955, in Cincinnati, Ohio. Michelle Boisseau's most recent books are *Trembling Air* (University of Arkansas Press, 2003), a PEN USA award finalist, and *Understory*, winner of the Morse Prize (Northeastern University Press, 1996). She is also co-author of *Writing Poems* (Longman). Her work has appeared in *The Yale Review, Kenyon Review, Ploughshares, Shenandoah,* and *Poetry.* She won a National Endowment for the Arts fellowship and two Poetry Society of America awards. A professor of English and director of Creative Writing at the University of Missouri-Kansas, Boisseau is also an editor for BkMk Press. She and her husband, linguist Tom Stroik, have a daughter, Anna. Each summer the larcenous squirrels in her neighborhood rob her garden. Last year one of her tomatoes fell from a sweetgum tree.

Counting

After a while, remembering the men you loved
is like counting stars.
From the arbitrary constellations
you pick out those the brightest. Then the others,
dimmer and dimmer until you can't tell
if they're real or only reflections
from your eyes watering with the strain.
The body's memory is a poor thing. Ask the adopted child
who falls asleep against any steady heart,
to a lullaby in any language.
Between my first lover who was thin
and my second who was warm and nostalgic,
my arms remember little. Though, yes,
there was one who had that sweet smell in his skin
of a child who still drinks nothing
but milk. A milk ladled out
by the Big and Little Dippers. If you look up
long enough into the night sky,
it becomes surer of itself and you less sure
whether you're lying on the lawn, skirt tucked
against mosquitoes, a cigarette
about to burn your fingers,
or if you're falling and the sky
is a net that can't catch you
since, like everyone else, you are water
nothing can stop. So you lie on your bed,
all night staring at the cracks
in the ceiling, terrified of falling through.

Eavesdropping

It was Mrs. Garvin, the doctor's wife,
who told my mother, Well if you're that broke
put the kids up for adoption.
Out under the porch light that summer
we slapped at mosquitoes and invented
our brave escape—luminous sheets
knotted out the window
were the lines of a highway down the house.
We would know the way,
like ingenious animals, to go
quietly toward the river,
but we could imagine no further
than the shacks on stilts
shivering the water,
the Kentucky hills on the other side.
Denise, the youngest, took to sleepwalking,
wading room to room for the place
one of us—curled up in a bed's corner—
might have left her. I'd wake
with her face pressed against my back,
her hands reining the edges of my nightgown.
I didn't tuck her into my shoulder
but loosened her fingers and led her
back to her own bed, her fear
already seeping into me like water
or like the light spilling
from the milk truck
as it backfired down the street.

Tariff

It takes time to appreciate how I once
made a friend so unhappy the next night
on the road from Chauncey to Amesville, Ohio,
she steered her Fiat Spyder head-on
into an oncoming truck. Her boyfriend
identified her waitress uniform.
She's been dead now for more than twenty years.
What I did to hurt her I won't tell you—
so you're free to imagine any vicious,
self-indulgent, hapless blunder or crime

while I go about turning this into a poem again,
turning over heavy marl, the garden
in spring, and the wind picks up, flinging soil
against my neck, behind my ears, into my teeth.
You have to get dirty: what *appreciate*
means is *to price*. After living a while
you understand the ways you have to pay.

Dog's Ars Poetica

Though its whiskers take the air's temperature, and its gritty tongue tastes
        the marrow of pleasure,
though it's rightly proud of its skill in the stalk, how camouflaged
        as a collapsed staircase, it catapults at a twitching wing,
though all grace and cunning,
a cat is no good at poetry.
It spits at water and brings you only a dumb tangle of tendon.

No, it requires me. Slobbery and faithful,
strictly disciplined yet eager and modest,
I can enter a lake without a wrinkle
and what I bring back, secure in my black
mouth, is unbloodied—alive and terrified.

Will Dunlap

Marianne Boruch

Born June 19, 1950, in Chicago, Illinois. Marianne Boruch's six poetry collections include *Grace, Fallen from* (Wesleyan, 2008) and *Poems: New and Selected* (Oberlin, 2004). Her essay collections are *In the Blue Pharmacy* (Trinity, 2005) and *Poetry's Old Air* (Michigan, 1995). Her awards include fellowships from the Guggenheim Foundation and the National Endowment for the Arts. Since the late 1980s, Boruch has taught at Purdue University and, semi-regularly, in the Warren Wilson College Program for Writers. For years she's been learning, almost successfully, to identify birdsong so she can lie in bed in the morning and hear who's out there. She's lived for two decades in a TV-free house.

The Garden

So many ways to call shapes
out of a dying world. Be a snake,
said the snake to the girl
drawn out of the rib, the garden
too beautiful to be noticed as she
stands there still, long enough
to want something, something
else. So the beginning
of all stories, the culling

of expanse and rest, quick
rise in wind then
the hush of *about*
to happen. Digression isn't
always evasion. She digressed
in wonder, watching that snake, such
intelligence, I suppose.
There are options, the snake said,
to this beauty. What

beauty? she thought, or felt in her chest.
Did Eve have language? Did she say that
out loud? Aren't words the curse
that comes later, our daily gruel, mouthful
by mouthful, a little milk, some sugar
to please ourselves, to think ourselves
so astonishing? But she
knew it. To be exact, she wanted
to know, sudden
heat and stirring: police tape
cordoning off where blood makes
a trail to suggest
the last breath, a small

stained fascination. Eve
hypnotized: oh, the strange and not-here,
not-of-this-garden, not really. I could be,
she thought, or simply *me* and *my hands*
moving toward something, a wish
all at once to be
covered, to be secret, to have
a thought like no other.

And what did the snake
dream, this snake that could talk
in this garden that never was
but marks our fate? Before falling into dust,
forced to love filthy water
and the highest grass concealing bright
as the moon its cold side, its
dark side, the snake was
dazzling. Story
that never happened. The snake was
human. *Over here, closer*, he said
to the girl come out of the rib.

O Gods of Smallest Clarity

If only those perennial opposites, the bully
and the sweet worried one
slept, kept sleeping. Not side by side,
not the lion and the lamb, just that most
ordinary blind passage, brief
and profound, as it happens
all over the planet. I mean the prince
who's happy with gardening, and the other kind
plotting someone's downfall, each
going under for the night. Which is to say, not
our usual taking turns at it, not Greenwich
or daylight savings or eight flight hours from here
equals five hours early or late but right now,
this minute, by my marvelous powers
of desperation and delusion, it's
soldier and monk, Sunni and Shiite,
Republican, Democrat, all Muslims and Christians
and Jews and those of us quietly
not anything to speak of, no reason or rhyme or
respectively about it, no tit for tat
but every one sleeping. And the president

curled fetal, his aides and think-tankers
all twitching in their dreams as dogs do,
on the scent or the chase, hours,
many hours to come. For that matter, the Pope is
drifting off and the greeter
from Wal-Mart, and the magician come out
of a long day's practice in a sword-crossed box
rests now, exactly like the oldest woman
asleep on her side, empty as the young docent
at Ellis Island already certain
it's robot-work, telling the country's vast sad story
of promise and trouble. And I think so many
miners home from their dark to this
gladder one, sprawled out
on their beds where exhaustion is fierce, no longer
patient. Every child in the world sleeping too,
hunger, *once there was,* but not here
in this dream, no gunflash, no flood.
Every mother minus panic. Every father
finding his daughters, his sons right where
they should be. Even
the torturers gone into that place they might
nightmare what they've done.
But not yet, not for a moment. And of those
who were done *to,* for them the rope and hood
and diamond-toothed wire, all banished
a few hours, forgotten
as dream is, in this, the real dream
to ink it out, beyond reach.
Believe me, I want to see
the despicable go down as much
as you do, and the innocent shine. But that's
sleeping too. Or so I try,
an experiment which may be stupid,
full of *less* not more, as in *pointless,* as in
hopeless, as in *less than nothing*
because—o gods of the smallest
clarity, let nothing happen
for an hour, for six hours. Rage.
Let that sleep too, its sorrow
no longer a brilliant rant, no longer anything,
a wash, a confluence of great waters
seen from a distance, the horizon a matter of
on and on where a speck out there
might well be a boat, the figure at the oars

untangling and stretching out. One eye
closed, then the other: welcome
no moon, no stars.

Elegy

Before the basil blackened. Before plates
slept in their cupboard. Before the streets
were snow. Before the song started in the throat
or crept sideways into the hands that hold the cello
or the moon spilled to nonsense all
over the floor. Before color composed itself
to twenty names for blue, or was it green or was it
red? Before seeds entered the ground
to transform themselves. Before cake was eaten, before
the icing bubbled up and crystallized. Before
all that sugar. Before shells
when things were moving in them and the sea
made a noise. Before our son grew so eye
to eye. Before worms made their fiefdom
in the compost. Before sleep refused the night
and the clock kept ticking. Before the hospital
took the soul from the body, dark
from dark, and the long drive home. Before the dog
stopped mid-bark to bark and the cat rose
from her stretch, unblinking. Before every moth
in the flour stilled its wings. Before the stain,
before its memory in the wood
grew wider. Before the garden gave everything
to weeds. Remember that, O charm
to forget, to go back, to vanish? Before
the dead appeared at the edge of my vision. Before
the grace to be broken was broken.

Double Double

Where my son once slept, now
I write. These stick-on stars
flood the ceiling's slant, take in
light all day. It's a glowing night of it
at night. *Double double,* my brother
scribbled awkwardly up there, in pencil. His doing.
He put the constellations here. Below these twins—
whatever *double double* means—four stars

make a box. And then the pale green bits trail off.
Heaven's shapes are weird.
                                        Low, odd-angled room.
My son dreamt here—what?
Not even he remembers, his bedroom now
my old study, a trade
we made when he got too tall. In the house
next door, a baby cried non-stop
for years; older, that neighbor kid
still cries. And won't get in the car. Won't.
Never. And then he does.
And the car door slams.
                                        I wait at this. And wait,
to clicks of sparrow, the tuneless
finch—my window's up. *Write write!* because—
I don't know. Birds close down
for a fine few seconds.
                                        My brother's love was for
distant, burning places, my son's, simply
that the dark light up. But these stars
aren't stars. The ceiling
lies about it. This isn't endless space,
isn't the upper register of time where
timelessness is famous. Take a room.
Then quiet the world in there.
First, it's small.

The Driveway

next door. A mother to her
children *put that down*, and *I
said*, and *Did you hear what
I said?* And the small voices like
flowers blown back by wind
rise up, not really music,
not words, a high pitch of shrug,
and looking away, and looking
down where the ground is
suddenly interesting. The day
is summer, passing without
any weight at all, like water
loves the hose, and stains
its dark channel.

Star Black

Laure-Anne Bosselaar

Born November 17, 1943, in New York, New York. Laure-Anne Bosselaar grew up in Belgium and moved to the United States in 1987. Her books are *The Hour Between Dog and Wolf* (BOA Editions, 1997), *Small Gods of Grief* (BOA Editions, 2001), winner of the Isabella Gardner Prize for Poetry, and *A New Hunger* (Ausable, 2007). She is also editor of four anthologies and translator, with her husband, poet Kurt Brown, of a book by Flemish poet Herman de Coninck. Recipient of a 2007 Pushcart Prize, Bosselaar teaches at Sarah Lawrence College and at the low-residency MFA Program of Pine Manor College. Her best stews are simmered in Flemish beers, and she loves to take long walks along the Hudson.

The Pleasures of Hating

I hate Mozart. Hate him with that healthy
pleasure one feels when exasperation has

crescendoed, when lungs, heart, throat,
and voice explode at once: *I hate that!*—

there's bliss in this, rapture. My shrink
tried to disabuse me, convinced I use Amadeus

as a prop: *Think further, your father perhaps?*
I won't go back, think of the shrink

with a powdered wig, pinched lips, mole:
a transference, he'd say, *a relapse*: so be it.

I hate broccoli, chain saws, patchouli, bra-
clasps that draw dents in your back, roadblocks,

men in black kneesocks, sandals and shorts—
I *love* hating that. Loathe stickers on tomatoes,

jerky, deconstruction, nazis, doilies. I delight
in detesting. And love loving so much after that.

English Flavors

I love to lick English the way I licked the hard
round licorice sticks the Belgian nuns gave me for six
good conduct points on Sundays after mass.

Love it when *plethora, indolence, damask,*
or my new word, *lasciviousness,* stain my tongue,
thicken my saliva, sweet as those sticks—black

and slick with every lick it took to make daggers
out of them: sticky spikes I brandished straight up
to the ebony crucifix in the dorm, with the pride

of a child more often punished than praised.
Amuck, awkward, or *knuckles,* have jaw-
breaker flavors; there's honey in *hunter's moon,*

hot pepper in *hunk,* and *mellifluous* has aromas
of almonds and milk. Those tastes of recompense
still bittersweet today as I roll, bend and shape

English in my mouth, repeating its syllables
like acts of contrition, then sticking out my new tongue—
flavored and sharp—to the ambiguities of meaning.

Belong

for Kurt

Here are boughs snow broke
from our birch, metal-blue berries
bending a twig, two frozen buds:

for you—take them, my hands
are cold, I worked in the yard too long,
wearing the brown

shoes you left by the shed.
The word *belong* hummed in my head,
and—while crows screeched and police

cars keened through dawn—
I cleared our garden of winter's waste:
all those broken limbs to gather,

they didn't hang on, *belong*
any longer. What a word: the heft in it,
dare and weight. It defies: *Hold on,*

belong, and *be—for long.*
So let's keep this ugly bunch, like I
kept that shred of stained window

blown apart in the convent chapel—
Sister Kelleen gone mad again, lighting
all the candles she could find,

heaping chairs loaded with her flames
all the way up to St. Bosco's face,
longing to see him lit, be-

longing to her as she stacked
her scaffold up to his chin, broke
candles in two for more fire until it

scorched his throat, reached his locked
face, and she saw his gaze soften. That's when
the music started—faint

glassy notes, *ping, ding, ping*:
the window behind Bosco split with heat,
and burst, sucking in snow—heavy,

dousing snow—the sudden draft
collapsing him to the floor. Kelleen
screamed his name through the halls,

then walls, when they locked
her up again. Then it stopped. They said
she'd snapped, was taken

away, she didn't *belong*.
That's when I understood what that word
meant—it burst a window in me

I thought nothing could mend.
It all came back to me this morning. That's
why I brought in these twigs—for you.

Taller, Wider

What is it I feel: this odd fusion
of elation and sadness that makes me
stop weeding and stand this way, hands
on hips, knee-deep in lavender?

The air, zealous with aromas
and swirls of bees, lisps in the breeze.
The willow I planted by the pond
five years ago in May, no longer

needs that stake I hammered
deep in dense, moist clay. It sways,
strokes the water with nimble limbs,
and will grow fuller still—taller, wider.

Bouncing off the granite
back of Sainte-Victoire, the dull
timbre of church bells. A quiet noon.
My hands sting with nettles and dirt.

On my wrist, the bracelet
love locked around it, long ago,
on a winter night. A wilted leaf
now caught between its links—

I leave it there: I am learning happiness.

Jerry Stockdale

Cathy Smith Bowers

Born November 15, 1949, in Lancaster, South Carolina. Cathy Smith Bowers teaches in the low-residency MFA Program in Creative Writing at Queens University of Charlotte. She also does private consultation and teaches at writers' conferences throughout the United States and Canada. Her collections include *The Love That Ended Yesterday in Texas* (Texas Tech University Press, 1992), *Traveling in Time of Danger* (Iris Press, 1997), *A Book of Minutes* (Iris Press, 2004), and *The Candle I Hold Up to See You* (Iris Press, 2008). Cathy hides out in the Appalachian foothill town of Tryon, North Carolina, with her gifted and talented Border collie, Manna.

Learning How to Pray

When I heard my brother
was dying   youngest
of the six of us   our
lovely boy   I who in matters
of the spirit
had been always suspect
who even as a child
snubbed Mama's mealtime ritual
began finally to
pray   and fearing
I would offend
or miss completely
the rightful target of my pleas
went knocking everywhere
the Buddha's huge
and starry churning   Shiva
Vishnu   Isis   the worn
and ragged god of Ishmael
I bowed to the Druid reverence
of trees   to water   fire
and wind   prayed to weather
to carbon   that sole link
to all things
this and other worldly
our carbon who art in heaven
prayed to rake and plow
the sweet acid stench of dung
to fly   to the fly's soiled
wing   and to the soil
I could not stop
myself   I like a nymphomaniac
the dark promiscuity

of my spirit there
for the taking whore
of my breaking heart willing
to lie down with anything.

The Napkin

One night in a pub
on the outskirts of Roanoke,
I sat with my husband

at a table lit only
by the candle's mute flickering
and the small waning moons

of our drinks. I was writing
in my journal, journaling
a journey soon coming

to its end when suddenly,
at the table to our left,
a soft commotion of arms

and hands. I looked
at my husband, lost in some
lost moment of the now

lost day, and then at them,
a subtle, peripheral glance
I had long ago perfected.

I could easily have touched
them—they were that close—lovers,
perhaps, signing to each other

their tongueless words. Each
in turn, their hands rose, bright
wings above the flame's dim

corona, secret negotiations
of finger and thumb.
I was stunned to see

how beautiful he was, as if
in the convoluted logic
of my mind, those devoid

of sound and speech must, too,
be devoid of loveliness.
I could see the silvery sheen

of her nails, glimmer of bracelets
and rings as they mounted the air,
lifting then falling, strafing

the crumbed and waxy
landscape of the table below.
When they left, something

fluttered to the floor, the napkin
they had at intervals been scribbling
on, passing back and forth,

the sweet lexicon of their
hands eluding even them.
My husband reached down,

handed it to me. Slowly
I began to read,
unfolding like lingerie

the delicate layers,
each boneless,
fleshless

syllable
naked before
my eyes: *She*

should be talking
to him, it said, *not writing*
in that book. Poor guy,

he looks so lonely.

Easter

"Orrys," Allen says and laughs
when he drips gravy from Mama's
porcelain dish onto the table.
It is Easter and we are speaking,
as we do at all our family gatherings,
the old language of childhood, the way
my niece began rolling the world
into words, dropping the initial "s"
and grafting it to the end
like an awkward branch from
some other family's tree.

So "sorry" is what he meant.
"Sorry" for the stain blossoming
brown as the tips of dogwood
on the lace cloth used only
for holidays. All day this language
more obtuse than the Rosetta Stone
as my niece cringes in her seat,
too old now, she believes, for such silliness.
She is just thirteen and waiting
for the blood to begin. "Anitarys,"
my sister whispers, speaking of the small napkin
she has begun to carry in her purse
and we laugh.

Later, because he is so far
away, we will phone our youngest brother
and how's "Ausalitos" our mother will ask
before passing the phone to each of us
who will speak to him of weather,
the profusion of daffodils lighting
the far pasture of the farm, though
no one will mention the disease
he carries inside him, a language
we can't yet speak, and no stone,
no stone to help us understand.

Last Day

for Kate Berryman

Readying for the morning errands, you bundled
baby Sarah, Martha off already
to her daily dose of history, language arts.
You won't have to worry about me
anymore, he said, donning a coat and scarf.
You'd heard it all before, who'd born him to exhaustion, loved him well.

I, too, shopped that morning, met my husband
later at KFC—two wing deals, two sweet teas—
where beyond the rippling window that sudden first white.
It's snowing! I gasped. *Spitting*, he corrected. Like
a school girl lured from the day's unfinished lessons,
I pressed my nose to the glass.

That night, wine and the gas logs blazing, Keillor on the radio
reading your husband's poem. How had he done it, my
husband wanted to know when I mentioned the suicide.
And in my happy ignorance so
began the stunning last revision
of his plan.

The Notes

for Nick Flynn

You dreamt your mother's,
scrawled in pencil on a brown paper bag,
and in the bag, huddled at the bottom, six baby mice.
Ah, but the care my husband took!
Classic font laid meticulously down
against the finest bond,
brandished,
even,
with epigraphs.
Twice that week he'd interrupted the morning's work
to solicit my better memory—a couplet
of rich prosody, resonant line of prose. Words,
throughout the single decade of our love,
the two of us had cherished, I unwitting
collaborator of his final masterpiece.

You dreamt the bag
smoldering
from the top down
as your mother's voice
released into the night.
Dreamt the mice growing wilder
as it burned,
their only way out,
if ever,
through the fire.

Kathryn Harris

Fleda Brown

Born July 20, 1944, in Columbia, Missouri. Fleda Brown is the author of six poetry collections, most recently *Reunion* (University of Wisconsin, 2007), which won the Felix Pollak Prize, *The Women Who Loved Elvis All Their Lives* (Carnegie Mellon University Press, 2004), and *Breathing In, Breathing Out* (Anhinga Press, 2002), winner of the Philip Levine Prize. She is Professor Emerita at the University of Delaware, where she taught for twenty-seven years and directed the Poets in the Schools program. She was poet laureate of Delaware from 2001–07. She now lives in Traverse City, Michigan, with her husband Jerry, and is on the faculty of the Rainier Writing Workshops.

Language

One day Adam said "Adam"
and found out he was standing
across the field from everything
else. It scared him half to death.
He lifted his arms as if they
could help. The air felt cool.
So he said "air" and "cool":
a population of not-Adams
sprouted everywhere. One
of them was Eve, a wild card.
He heard her clearly, distinct
from his internal voice, his
private naming. She was singing
"In time, the Rockies may crumble,
Gibraltar may tumble . . . "
and sure enough, it was
something o'clock already.
He saw that her mouth was pink.
"Pink," he said, because it was
small and had lips to push the air
away. And there was something
else, he was sure of it, a softening
of the air between them,
a spell. Nothing could be the word
for it. He was reeling
with the wound of it, the chink
between subject and object.
Light entered, memory followed
and began to tell its own story.
He felt himself held in it,

traveling *within* it, now,
driving toward a particular town.
"Something's happened,"
he said to her, but she'd guessed
the doom of it already, the wooden
signs along the highway
bravely standing for everything
that matters: *Burma Shave,*
Kollectibles Kottage, The Cock
& Bull. She ran a finger delicately
along the window as if she could
trace what it was that had
broken loose from the two
of them, that was running crazy
out there, never looking back.

Knot Tying Lessons: The Slip Knot

—the most useful temporary knot or noose

What can I say? I turned a corner. No matter
that I doubled back, there was still progress. I was lying
low, crossing under both my coming and going,
and when I rose to see where I was, felt the cool
air on my face, I skidded like a skater, wrapped around
myself again, burrowing back up through the small
figure-eight I'd made of myself. How secure it all seemed,
how sure to result in something unfaltering—patriotic,
even. But the way things have gone, I'm left with
a looseness through the center.
There's been this tendency to let things drop.
It's the opposites I have trouble with,
the way my attention begins expanding as if
the richness has eased past the borders, no longer
lives in this constriction, this lump in my throat.
I drew you to me with such firmness, you were sure
of the implications. The exact point at which I began
to be disappointed, who knows? The more I gave myself
room to work it out, the more I felt the movement
of possibilities within me. I should have felt relieved
when all fell through, but I only felt what I am,
how I'm made. "Open your mouth," my mother used to
say, coming at me with a bar of soap because of some
word I'd said. I opened, as I do now, willing to take
the bitterness, to have done what I did.

Makeup Regimen

I've developed complicated pores, I need radiance, more beauty steps,
more ice-colored bottles, the old me exfoliated so the young one can emerge

dewy, daily. As if I could see my own face, as if the mirror reflected me
by the shortest route instead of at crazy angles, all probabilities adding up

to my face, as if it weren't our ignorance that makes things appear in their
classical forms. When the Newtonian God went away, what took His place

acts more like rain, mist, sunshine, bounded by horizons du jour. Enter
clarifying lotion, like the crisp, high range of stars. The face of night's

supposed to be naked and spread from ear to ear, but at dawn the workmen
arrive with their electric saws, their hydraulic hammers; everything's to be

built again. The sum of it is complex: for example, my mother's mouth
in her coffin was all wrong. They made her look mature, confident.

Their mistake was concentrating on the flesh, trying to fill the emptiness
with it. She had her red suit on. They took her jewelry off when all we asked

for was her ring, leaving her not quite put together forever. I like to think,
though, that dying is like falling all the way back to where everything's

held to itself by memory. Two old men I knew in Arkansas would pass
each other Mondays on their country road, driving so slowly they had time

to ask after each other's family. "Mr. Caid," one would say, and nod.
"Mr. Kimball," the other would say, and nod. The main thing was to come

along looking as much as possible like somebody same as the week before.

No Heron

Herons are bigger than egrets, though they have the same long legs.
My father said one with an eight-foot wingspan flew over his boat.
I would like to be shadowed by something that big. It would seem

like poetry, just out of reach, moving and making a bare flush
of wings, and I would think of it long after, the way it was heading
away from me. My longing would not be satisfied even if I could

grab its scrawny legs in my hand, even if it nuzzled up to me.
I would be looking up the origin of *heron* with my free hand, and
when I read Greek, *to creak*, and Old High German, *to scream*,

I would wait for it to begin, but it would not say anything to me
in this boat which I am not in, but at my desk hoping for the heron,
a big one, as I said, so I can say, "Wow, look at that!" as if I were

getting up a circus. Out there are herons white and blue, not really
blue but smoky, with wings bigger than their bodies, dipping and
standing motionless beside lakes and rivers. Out there are universes

expanding until the space between atoms is too far to do anyone
any good. Thus, somewhere this minute one heron is calculating
the distance between his beak and a fish, the way it shifts. It is

as if he travels in space until heron and fish are swallowed into
each other. There is no heron at my desk. In fact, the absence
of heron is how I would define my study: no heron on the ceiling,

no heron on the floor, no heron on the wall, so that of course
I think of nothing but heron, how it floats its weight on one leg,
for example, flying that way even when it's not.

Red Paint

Here is my father, lying sideways on the dock
trying to scrub off blood-red marine paint.
Here are his old hands and forearms, bloody,
everything he touches, bloody. My words
are so bloody, as usual, I try not to say them.
I could be ten years old, mopping up
my brother's blood after another seizure.
My father's acting like he's ten, as usual,
smearing paint everywhere. If you knew
the history. I drive to the lumberyard
after paint thinner. "Don't move," I say.
I douse the dock with thinner, too.
"Oh, for heaven's sake," he says.
"In World War II, they used to splash red paint
on the decks to get the men used to blood."

"Oh, well," I say, because he will die
sooner than later, because the sun is a white eye,
and I've cleaned up the dock under the willow,

because the water's sloshing, gone and permanent
in its way. Because his sailboat's sleek with red,
a missile cradled on sawhorses.

"Merely cosmetic," my father says
about my cleaning, as if I've wasted
my life. *A body doesn't like to spill,* I think.
Not even light spills. Look at the sun, stopped
by leaves, trunks of trees. There are sorrows
like hot stones, they give birth in silence.

There is my mother scrubbing a bathroom
in heaven, folding sheets, getting to have
her version of nice. "Mother," I say, to remind
the universe I'm here, holding back with my
bare hands what still needs holding back.

Kevin Kinnebrew

Debra Bruce

Born April 4, 1951, in Bristol, Connecticut. Debra Bruce's poetry collections are *What Wind Will Do, Pure Daughter*, and *Sudden Hunger*, which won the Chicago Public Library Carl Sandburg Award. Her work appears in *The Atlantic, Poetry, Ploughshares, Prairie Schooner, Shenandoah, The Virginia Quarterly Review*, and other journals. She has been the recipient of grants and awards from the National Endowment for the Arts, the National Endowment for the Humanities, the Illinois Arts Council, the Poetry Society of America, and *Poetry* magazine. Originally from Albany, New York, she lives in Chicago, where she is a professor of English at Northeastern Illinois University.

Divorced Men

She was the best one
on the beach, but what a bitch
she was later. Summer after summer
she tossed, she twisted the sheets
on her side, she burnt the edges
of everything to spite you. The small
kitchen sweated grease, babies stuck
to her hip until they finally slipped
away from her and dropped, one
by one, into your arms in the backyard.
Like other fathers you knew, you
played ball with your boys
on a homemade diamond. You played
until your trick knee gave, until she
called through the screen for you
to bring them in. But it was just dusk,
you slapped your catcher's mitt
and shouted. You could still see the perfect
arc of your son's pitch, you thought
you could see everything.

Divorced Women

The bedroom mirrors reflect
from all angles that you've
trimmed down since him to the slim
size you used to be. Turning again,
you turn to yourself. The hip-hugging
fit fits, and dusky blue is the right
shadow for tonight.

Cosmetic kit, car keys, and the quarter moon
like a key-ring trinket. Your whole life
you've known only one man. Now
you will know how all men
are one, when their muscles melt
in motion, hips curve into waves.
But you won't drown. Just dry
your thighs and drive home, alone,
alive, with time for the first time
to notice how the September crepe myrtle
strips off its bark. Its petals
are so pink, too pink, and a late
summer storm has torn them up
and smeared them on the lawn
of your apartment complex.

Fasting

My father could eat eggs Sunday morning
because he didn't believe.
He dipped warm bread in the yolk,
and we scraped his plate with our stares
but still had to wait three hours
before Communion. We held our veils
down with bobby pins, and followed
my mother up the winding steps
to the choir loft. Long pipes
on a wall warmed with music as she sang
by an organ with pedals as big
as the man who played them.
I loved the sun pouring in through
the saints' bright robes, and my mother's
red hair, her long red hair. I saw him touch it—
the organist, where the stairs curve
into the church basement,
but I didn't care. Mass was over.
We were going down there
for sweet rolls, sweet rolls with butter.

Infertility

Often it begins in bliss, like this:
Her husband piles the good dry wood higher
at dusk, and as the dark gets deep their fire
acquires authority. As if a wish
had been acknowledged there and must be given,
she lets the flames' heat beat against her skin,
watches their wild light. As for him,
even from himself it stays hidden—
his joy—like the next day's sun still stashed
behind the pines. Now off this couple goes,
insanely early along the beach, splashing,
talking, sleepless. She shakes a shell. He knows
that she can't wait to tell and tell. (And will.)
The bay is calm; the bell-buoys, all, are still.

Prognosis

I hold my breath and balance on a cliff,
instructed not to focus on the edge.
Instead of *when*, my sentence starts with *if*,

though surreptitiously I spot a cleft
of rock and tiptoe toward the hope I can wedge
myself inside, be safe upon this cliff.

But what I'm searching for is what I've left
behind—the snug, sunlit privilege
of making plans with *when* instead of *if*.

Some climb the years, and in their sixty-fifth,
join Tuesday's book club, take a course in French,
while others, younger, balance on a cliff

listening for news whose wild relief
allows them one more step, one increment
of *now*, not *then*. My sentence starts with *if*

and plummets easily—if one streaked leaf
descends to circle at my feet, I clench—
hold my breath, balance on this cliff
where everything I think begins with *if*.

Sharon Bryan

Born February 10, 1943, in Salt Lake City, Utah. Sharon Bryan's fourth collection of poems, *Stardust*, will published by BOA Editions in 2009. Her third book, *Flying Blind*, was published by Sarabande Books in 2006. She is also the editor of *Where We Stand: Women Poets on Literary Tradition*, and co-editor, with William Olsen, of *Planet on the Table: Poets on the Reading Life*. The recipient of two National Endowment for the Arts Fellowships in poetry, and awarded an Artist Trust Fellowship from the Seattle Arts Council and the Washington State Arts Commission, she is currently Visiting Professor of Poetry at the University of Connecticut/Storrs. Bryan also serves as fulltime staff for her two cats, Gracie and Spencer.

Weird Niece

Or is it *weird neice*?
as soon as you write it
wrong you can tell

by the way it makes you
queasy, like putting on
someone else's glasses:

the world is out there
but askew, you're aware
of what you're looking through,

a filigree of letters
that opens and discloses
a point of view, a scenic

turnout—or in this case
a wrong turn, a cul-de-sac,
a brief glimpse of possibilities

pulled back from, little
slipups, a gawky girl
almost the spitting image

of the one you meant
to write about, summoned
in error, abandoned

by the side of the road,
faint but unforgettable
in the rearview mirror.

Be-

A begat B begat C
and here we are at the depot,
surrounded by more baggage

than we could ever carry
alone, begirt, a little bedraggled,
but beguiled by what lies

before behind beyond us
and the power of a prefix
to make a noun a star:

bedecked, bedizened, bejeweled,
there must be something special
under all that finery, if only

a swirl of longing we've given
a name to, and a voice—why not,
we're all born ventriloquists,

so good we feel betrayed
when the world won't speak
for itself—but nothing escapes us,

no matter how far we fling it,
and we're never entirely taken in
by *trompe l'oeil* and *trompe l'oreille,*

we're proud of our double vision,
our ability to see and see through
the illusion—it's just that

sometimes we'd like to close one eye
and believe wholeheartedly in objects
that don't depend on us

for their definition, not a world
of absence but one in which
we'd have everything to lose.

-esque

As wonderfully ornate and un-
necessary as a handlebar
moustache, or a handkerchief

just so in an old man's
breast pocket, not an empty
decoration but a ruffle

and flourish, a flair
for the dramatic, blesséd
excess—like the white-haired

gentleman who has shined his shoes
and put on a coat and tie
to buy groceries—

and like the intricate
orthography that spells out
our history with such pomp

and circumstance, reveals
the most delicate and indelicate
details of where we've been—

silent letters are as crucial as air
in a soufflé: imagine a ballet
dancer caught flat-footed

in an *arabesk*, or the jokes
like lead balloons if the show
were only *burlesk*—the echoes

we hear in *grotesque*,
the ancient caves we painted
our way out of,

are the voices of those
so eager for us to hear
what they had to say

they invented the alphabet
to carry their words light-
years into the heavens, here.

Todd Budy

Andrea Hollander Budy

Born April 28, 1947, in Berlin, Germany. Andrea Hollander Budy is the author of three full-length poetry collections, including *Woman in the Painting* (Autumn House Press, 2006), *The Other Life* (Story Line Press, 2001), and *House Without a Dreamer* (Story Line Press, 1993), which won the Nicholas Roerich Poetry Prize. Other honors include the D. H. Lawrence Fellowship, a Pushcart Prize for prose memoir, two poetry fellowships from the National Endowment for the Arts, and two from the Arkansas Arts Council. Budy lives in the Arkansas Ozark Mountains near Mountain View, where she and her husband and son ran a bed-and-breakfast inn for fifteen years. Since 1991 she has been the Writer-in-Residence at Lyon College.

When She Named Fire

it was a sound
she uttered, not a considered thing, nothing
her mind did. It was a sound
which burned her throat to come out
and announce itself for the thing
that was burning outside her
where the trees had been down
for years and which lit the sky
then disappeared and changed
to something black.

When she named the sun, she didn't think
of fire at all. *Sun*, she claimed,
because it was huge and unexplainable,
a oneness that she loved
for its ability to command
the whole sky and the earth, too;
and because it was the warmest thing
she knew, and she sang
its tunes and missed it every night.

She didn't name the moon at all. That was
the name it gave itself. At night she heard
it call. To her it was
another kind of sun, still white
but cold, an icy light
that narrows as it grows, that is not
light at all.

She thought she gave love's name
to love, that beating thing she could not
still. She might have called it

bird. Or *fire* again
for fire inside that gives no light
but burns and burns and does not
stop until she touches
what she loves, and then it only burns
again and makes her want
to name it something more.

Firmly Married

is what he said but as he said it
swayed a little in my direction,
the hair on his neck so like
my son's, barely there, but golden
if you bothered looking.

He was looking at me anyway
no matter what he said,
a benefit of having spoken
his excuses so I'd excuse
anything he did thereafter.

I walked away.

And afterwards I thought
how easily he'd escaped
whatever I may have taken
from that look, that he wanted
it to be *my* invention, the way

I used to pull my stockings up
pretending not to notice Richie
watching, when I was nineteen
and wanted secretly my first time
to happen already, but wanted it

to be *his* doing, this undoing
I longed for desperately,
the way this man wants
some blameless ruin.

Nineteen-Thirty-Eight

I remember the way my mother
answered when people asked
where she'd gone to school:

South Side High, 1938,
adding the year in the same breath
though I knew

she never graduated,
yanked out
when her father lost his job.

Now it was her turn
to make herself
useful, he told her.

Hadn't he put
food on the table
all her life and all her little sister's?

How necessary
to tell a lie like hers, to answer
South Side High, 1938, and smile

without betraying
the blaze in her chest, her envy
for the questioner who likely met

her own husband at some university.
But wasn't my mother *the lucky one,*
my grandfather was fond of telling her

even into my childhood, sometimes
in front of my friends, lucky
to have got my father, a college man

who sat beside her at a ballgame
in 1939? *Just look at her*
who didn't finish high school!

Didn't I tell her then it wouldn't matter?

My Grandmother Taking Off My Grandfather's Shoes

Every day after work he'd sit in his armchair
with its antimacassar and its plush burgundy velour
and she'd kneel on the floor to unfasten the laces,
loosen the tongues, and lift out his feet.
When I was ten I stayed for a week
and did it for her. He thought I did it
for him.

Living Room

In the cave of memory my father
crawls now, his small carbide light
fixed to his forehead, his kneepads
so worn from the journey they're barely
useful, but he adjusts them
again and again. Sometimes
he arches up, stands, reaches, measures
himself against the wayward height
of the ceiling, which in this part of the cave
is at best uneven. He often hits his head.
Other times he suddenly
stoops, winces, calls out a name,
sometimes the pet name he had
for my long-dead mother
or the name he called his own.

That's when my stepmother tries
to call him back. *Honeyman,* she says,
one hand on his cheek, the other
his shoulder, settling him
into the one chair he sometimes stays in.

There are days she discovers him
curled beneath the baby grand,
and she's learned to lie down with him.
I am here, she says, her body caved
against this man who every day
deserts her. *Bats,* he says, or maybe,
field glasses. Perhaps he's back
in France, 1944, she doesn't know.
But soon he's up again on his knees,

shushing her, checking his headlamp,
adjusting his kneepads, and she rises
to her own knees, she doesn't know
what else to do, the two of them
explorers, one whose thinning
pin of light leads them, making
their slow way through this room
named for the living.

Kelly Cherry

Born December 21, 1940, in Baton Rouge, Louisiana. Kelly Cherry is the author of seventeen books, eight chapbooks, and two translations. Recent titles include *Hazard and Prospect: New and Selected Poems* (Louisiana State University Press, 2007), *History, Passion, Freedom, Death, and Hope: Prose about Poetry* (University of Tampa, 2005), *In the Wink of an Eye*, a novel (Louisiana State University Press, 2004), *Welsh Table Talk*, a poetic sequence (Book Arts Conservatory, 2004), and *We Can Still Be Friends*, a novel (Soho Press, 2003, 2004). She is Eudora Welty Professor Emerita of English and Evjue-Bascom Professor Emerita in the Humanities at the University of Wisconsin-Madison. She and her husband live on a small Virginia farm that belongs to their small dog Pippin.

First Marriage

I held you, or I never held you, or I held you briefly, once, long ago, and you kissed me while my heart kept time.

Or perhaps not, perhaps it was your heart beating, so hard I mistook it for my own.

But surely the paint was new in the floor-through in the Brooklyn brownstone. And I know there was music.

White walls. Books everywhere.

And I remember how the still rooms filled with sun.

You may have taken me into your arms as the music (something by Schoenberg, all twelve tones as sweetly reserved and mysterious as a sundial), beginning in a place of peril and possibility, found its way home.

You may have loved me.

Or perhaps not, perhaps it was my heart beating like a metronome.

Fair Is Fair: A Dialogue Between Husband and Wife

I was incensed. "Even if it's true
that the best things in life are free, there are not
enough of them. Or else some damn idiot
got a good deal more than any fool is due.
Meanwhile, the poor cannot afford to sue
Congress for a chicken in every pot.
Justice? I guess it's just that hell is hot.
In death the poor can live on Supply Side Stew."

My gentle husband said, "Suppose justice
isn't a balancing of scales, an equation
between terms, but rather a singular gorgeous thing
to be weighed against sheerest emptiness?"

"Plato's metaphysics is out of fashion."

"So what?" he said. "Has the North Star stopped shining?"

Truth and Tolerance

"As there's no truth, or none that we can know,
We must be tolerant of one another."
This is how the argument should go,
According to today's philosopher
Or literary theorist. One might reply,
"Without belief in truth, the concept of
Tolerance is meaningless. Anarchy
Does not work well as a substitute for love,
And who can love who does not think she knows
A reason for the choices that she makes?
Or must she love the worm that sickens the rose
With its own secret love?" William Blake's
Dark apostrophe to a dying rose
Is so true and tolerant that her heart aches.

On the Soul

By "soul" I mean the self described by passion,
For passion shapes us. We are carved and hollowed
By what we love—love irrationally,
Perhaps, and yet we think our hearts hallowed
By love that acquaints us with the contours of
Ourselves, until we know ourselves as well
As the arms and legs and back and knees of love,
The body of it, sweat and salt and smell.
The love of thought is as identifying
As any other passion and survives
Time's despoliation—love undying,
For as long as the sense of oneself lives,
And then the soul departs, leaving behind
The record of an open, responsive mind.

Welsh Song

Rain blew against the window pane.
The kestrel's shadow quartered the air.
A rooster crowed. The drainpipe banged
Against stone. The child brushed her hair

And sang a song. The gas fire burned.
The gas lamp glowed. The rain fell faster.
Blue became black in the window.
The wind pulled the sea up to the pasture.

The child brushed her hair and sang songs.
The lost pigeon sheltered alone
In the chapel rafters. The red
Glass on the sill gleamed in gaslight.

A winged darkness crossed the dark night,
And the drainpipe banged against stone.

San Diego State University

Marilyn Chin

Born January 14, 1955, in Hong Kong, People's Republic of China. Marilyn Chin's books include *Rhapsody in Plain Yellow* (Norton, 2002), *The Phoenix Gone, the Terrace Empty* (Milkweed, 1994), and *Dwarf Bamboo* (Greenfield Review Press, 1987). She has also published two books of translations. Her work has been widely anthologized, most recently in *The Norton Anthology of Literature by Women* and *The Norton Anthology of Modern and Contemporary Poetry.* Her numerous awards include a USA Artist Foundation Grant, the Radcliffe Institute Fellowship at Harvard, two National Endowment for the Arts fellowships, and a Rockefeller Fellowship at Bellagio. Chin teaches in the MFA program at San Diego State University. Presently she is writing a book of tales.

Family Restaurant #1 (from *Bad Date Polytich*)

Empty Lotus Room, no patrons
 Only a telephone rings and rings
Muffled by an adjoining wall
 He murmurs to a distant lover
His wife head-bent peeling shrimp
 Hums an ancient tune about magpies
His daughter wide-eyed, little fists
 Vows to never forgive him
His shadow enters the deep forest
 Blackening the shimmering moss

Family Restaurant #2 (from *Bad Date Polytich*)

The old neon flickers and hums.
The grandmother turns it off.
The boy empties the last of the trash,
Eager to return to the prom.
The grandmother gestures him back,
Fan loy, fan loy, waving both arms.
He curses *Goddam old hag,*
Rolls up his tux sleeves gingerly,
Sorts out the bones from the glass.

Moon and Oatgrass

The moon is not over the water,
as you would have it,
but one with it, and the house
is on the precipice
overlooking a green meadow.

And you—an *eye* and not an *I*—
are walking through it.

And whether you live here
or are visiting
in your long pilgrimage—
is my prerogative.
Whether she is your acolyte,
the Pearl Concubine,
or a mere beggarwoman—
is also my invention.

Only I know where
terrace ends and house begins,
whether the country is lost,
whether rivers and mountains
will continue. And finally,

after the inkstone is dry,
we shall be together
high in a corner bedroom
with a pale view of hills.
Without pleasure or transcendence
we penetrate this landscape.

And what *is* this landscape?
The moon in oatgrass,
the oatgrass moon.
A woman pacing
the linoleum floor,
contemplating a poem.
A man dissolving
into the dailiness of rain

and the red eye of morning.

Blues on Yellow #2

for Charles

Twilight castes a blue pall on the green grass
  The moon hangs herself on the sickly date palm near the garage

Song birds assault a bare jacaranda, then boogie toward Arizona
  They are fewer this year than last

Sadness makes you haggard and me fat
 Last night you bolted the refrigerator shut

X-tra, X-tra, read all about it
 Chinese girl eats herself to death

Kiss a cold banquet and purge the rest
 There's room in the sarcophagus if you want it

I keep my hair up in a bereavement knot
 Yours grows thinner, whiter, a pink skullcap

My Levis hang loosely and unzipped
 You won't wash, won't shave or dress

I am your rib, your apple, your adder
 You are my father, my confessor, my ox, my draft

Heartbreak comes, again, when does it come?
 When your lamp is half dim and my moon is half dark

That Half Is Almost Gone

That half is almost gone,
 the Chinese half,
the fair side of a peach,
 darkened by the knife of time,
fades like a cruel sun.

In my thirtieth year
 I wrote a letter to my mother.

I had forgotten the character
 for "love." I remember vaguely
the radical "heart."
 The ancestors won't fail to remind you

the vital and vestigial organs
 where the emotions come from.

 But the rest is fading.
 A slash dissects in midair,
ai, ai, ai, ai,
 more of a cry than a sigh

(and no help from the phoneticist).

You are a Chinese!
My mother was adamant.

You *are* a Chinese?
My mother less convinced.

Are you *not* Chinese?
My mother now accepting.

As a cataract clouds her vision,
and her third daughter marries
A Protestant West Virginian

who is "very handsome and very kind."

The mystery is still unsolved—

the landscape looms

over man. And the gaffer-hatted fishmonger—

sings to his cormorant.

And the maiden behind the curtain

is somebody's courtesan.

Or, merely Rose Wong's aging daughter

pondering the blue void.

You are a Chinese—said my mother
who once walked the fields of her dead—

Today, on the 36th anniversary of my birth,

I have problems now
even with the salutation.

Sortino

Judith Ortiz Cofer

Born February 24, 1952, in Hormigueros, Peurto Rico. Judith Ortiz Cofer is the author of ten books, most recently *A Love Story Beginning in Spanish: Poems* (2005); *Call Me Maria* (2006), a young adult novel; *The Meaning of Consuelo* (2003), a novel; and *Woman in Front of the Sun: On Becoming a Writer* (2000), a collection of essays. Her work appears in numerous journals, textbooks, and anthologies, including *The Georgia Review, Kenyon Review, Glamour, Best American Essays, The Norton Book of Women's Lives, The Heath Anthology of American Literature,* and the *O. Henry Prize Stories.* She is the Regents' and Franklin Professor of English and Creative Writing at the University of Georgia.

Beans: An Apologia for Not Loving to Cook

for Tanya

For me memory turns on the cloying smell of boiling beans
in a house of women waiting, waiting for wars, affairs, periods
of grieving, the rains, *el mal tiempo*, to end, the phrase
used both for inclement weather and to abbreviate the aftermath
of personal tragedies. And they waited for beans to boil.
My grandmother would put a pot on the slow fire
at dawn, and all day long, the stones she had dropped in, hard
and dry as a betrayed woman's eyes, slowly softened, scenting
the house with the essence of waiting. Beans.
I grew to hate them.
Red kidney beans whose name echoes of blood, and are shaped
like inner organs, I hated them in their jaw-breaking rawness
and I hated them as they yielded to the fire.

The women waited in turns by the stove
rapt by the alchemy of unmaking. The mothers turned hard
at the stove, resisting our calls with the ultimate threat
of burned beans. The vigil made them statues, rivulets
of sweat coursing down their faces, pooling at their collarbones.
They turned hard away from our demands for attention and love,
their eyes and hands making sure beans would not burn
and rice would not stick, unaware of our longing
for our mothers' spirits to return back to the soft sac
that once held us, safely tucked among their inner organs,
smelling the beans they cooked for others,
through their pores.

The beans took half a child's lifetime to cook,
and when they were ready
to bring to table in soup bowls, the women called the men first
in high voices like whistles pitched above our range,
food offered like sacred, steaming sacrifice to *los hombres*.

El hambre entered the room with them, hunger
as a spectral presence, called forth from whatever other realm
the women visited when they cooked, their bodies
remaining on earth to watch the beans
while they flew away from us for hours.

As others fed,
I watched the dog at the screen door, legs trembling,
who whimpered and waited for the scrap. I hated
the growling of pleasure when at last it got its gory bone.
I resisted the lessons of the kitchen then, fearing
the Faustian exchanges of adults, the shape-shifting nature
of women by the fire.

Now it is my daughter who keeps a voluntary vigil by the stove.
She loves the idea of cooking as chemistry, and the Tao
of making food. Her waiting for the beans to boil is a meditation
on the transformative properties of matter; a gift of memory food
from my island. And I come out of my poem to partake, to share
her delight in the art of feeding, like a recently freed captive
of a long-ago war, capable at last of a peaceful surrender
to my old nemesis, *el hambre.*

Notes for My Daughter Studying Math on the Morning of a New Year

Mira, mira, our Spanish-speaking kin
are always saying. Look and look again. It amuses us,
this insistence on seeing, even when they mean listen.
Could it be that they keep the world less at bay
than we their exiled children? That they can see
emotions in color? Anger is the scarlet
hibiscus, joy, the blue of the Puerto Rican sky
after a July rainstorm, and grief,
a black mantilla on the head of the woman
sitting alone in the last pew of an empty church.
Mira, Hija, I say to you in my mother's voice,
when I mean listen, and you may turn your eyes
in the direction of some unexpected bit of wonder:
the dull gray city pigeon is iridescent
in a certain slant of light, and she perches
at *your* window. If this is not enough, *pues, mira,*
the sun shines indiscriminately over everything. *Mira, Hija.*
Even the shadows make interesting designs on the concrete.

Listen: whatever the weather, when you step outside
and breathe deeply, you inhale the history

of our race in each molecule: Eve's desire,
Cleopatra's ambition, Magdalene's guilt,
the New World of Isabel of Castile,
the fierce conquests of Elizabeth, and the genius
of Sor Juana and Virginia Woolf; here too remains
the labored breath of an old woman
fishing a day's meal at the dumpster,
and the fears of the fourteen-year-old run-away
who will soon run out of breath; my own relief
as the nurse settled you in my arms
on the day you arrived
into the breathless world.

Try to speak
in Spanish in your dreams. Say *sol,*
día, sueños, as you fall asleep. See
if you can believe that tomorrow
may be the day you have been designing in the dark,
an algebra from particles of light
swirling behind your eyelids—
your own private theory of relativity.

The Calculus of Freedom

The rescued eagle hates his aviary,
an expansive habitat according to the sign
directing visitors to keep a safe distance. He is restive
in his tree-lined cage. His glittering eyes,
diamond-tip precision instruments
in the mathematics of attack and survival,
dart from one angle to another, taking the
measure of his territory.
I watch him as he studies the sky ,
which he must see through wire mesh
as fractals of hexagonal blue, points of reference
he seems to count in quick clicks
of eye and neck movements, until he fixes
upon the longest branch of the spreading oak tree,
supporting axis of his enclosure.
Even with a broken wing, he is elegant
with purpose, exploding into flight.
Listing at 45 degrees to pain, he keeps his eyes
on one point—the point of greatest resistance—
and alights in perfect equilibrium, testing the limb
like the bow of a violin, having calculated precisely
the dimensions of his captivity.

The Poet's Work

Inside this old movie house still open for retrospectives,
I first savored the cool dark knowing of not having to watch
a film half as interesting as my life. My first kiss, last row,
Saturday matinee. That parking lot across the street was once
a playground for the dust-and-sweaty summer children
of the city. At fourteen, two on a swing
after a sudden August downpour emptied the lot,
an inspiration of long slender legs locked together in perfect synchrony:
the dizzying motion, rush of blood, desire etching its name
into bone. I knew nothing like this would ever happen again
in Paris or in Rome. Church bells, how right the metaphor,
church bells sent me running home, wet skirt clinging
to my body like newfound faith, blood rising
toward a Pentecost. I knew I had to write the poem.
I don't remember his name. His name did not matter even then.
I was working on the poem.

Ted Space

Martha Collins

Born November 25, 1940, in Omaha, Nebraska. Martha Collins is the author of the book-length poem *Blue Front* (Graywolf, 2006), which won an Anisfield-Wolf Book Award and was chosen as one of "25 Books to Remember from 2006" by the New York Public Library. Other recent awards include a Laurence Goldstein Poetry Prize and a Lannan Residency Grant. Collins has also published four collections of poems, two collections of co-translations of Vietnamese poetry, and two chapbooks. Currently editor-at-large for *FIELD* magazine and an editor of the Oberlin College Press, she lives in Cambridge, Massachusetts, and commutes to Bloomfield, Connecticut, where her husband lives.

After

After the scattering, after the nights of shattered
glass, broken stones, scrawls, marked
houses, chalked walls, after the counter-
threats, shouts, shots against the scattered
unhoused stones, after the bombs from over
the ocean, the desert, after oil has mixed
with blood, after the blossoming desert is bombed
to sand and risen again to blossom, though this
is more than the story tells, the story, simply
begun with the scattering, ends with the gathering
in again from distant cities, countries, corners,
basements, caves where children were hidden, graves
whose bones were moved to be burned, ashes that would
not burn, from earth, from air, the people will come
together, they will ride in carts and trains
and cars, they will walk and run, and this
is the story, the people will cross the oceans,
they will cross the rivers on bridges made
of paper, blank and inked and printed and painted
paper bridges will bring them together, over
the waters the borders the wars will be over, under
the paper bridges that bridge the most the best we can.

Likes

There was like this guy she said with really
great hair long and blond just like
a girl's you know and I had on this dress
he liked and he had on these running shorts
and shirt which he took off and I took off

the dress which he put on and I put on
the running shorts and shirt I liked the way
they felt like silk against my skin and soon
the shorts were on the floor but not the shirt
my hands were in his hair my hands were like
beneath my dress my hands were his were find-
ing me no her no him no both of us like
he was she and I was he and we and they
were both in both of us two like to like

Alone, One Must Be Careful

Alone means finding stranger ways to get
through longer hours, days: to slice the bread
around until a perfect square is left,
to fill a cordial glass with wine, to set
the cluttered table so it seems it's meant
for only one, to make the double bed
from just one side, and always pay the rent
on time, and never never get in debt.

I heard about a woman, how she died
alone, they brought her in, she bled
and bled, a broken orange juice glass, my mother said,
between her legs. I shut my eyes, saw red
inside. My father, sighing, went to bed.
I live alone. My mother never did.

Three Selections from ***Blue Front***

There were trees on those streets that were named
for trees: Sycamore, Cedar, Poplar, Pine,
Elm, where the woman's body was found,
where the man's body was taken and burned—

There must have been trees, there were trees
on Seventh Street, in front of the house that stands
in the picture behind the carriage that holds
the boy's mother, the boy's cousin, the boy—

And of course there were trees on Washington
Avenue, wide boulevard lined with *exotic*
ginkgoes, stately magnolias, there were trees
on that street that are still on that street,

trees that shaded the fenced-in yards of the large
Victorian houses, the mansion built by the man
who sold flour to Grant for the Union troops,
trees that were known to the crowd that saw

the victim hanged, though not on a tree, this
was not the country, they used a steel arch
with electric lights, and later a lamppost, this
was a modern event, the trees were not involved.

*
*
*

Birmingham

Because after I'd seen the church where it
was bombed where the four bodies were stacked
on top of each other said Josephine Marshall
Tuskegee '33 she saw nothing
but bloody sheets

laundry couldn't be washed
in the same machines

and read about this City of Churches this Magic
City this Bombingham where Shuttlesworth's
church and house had been bombed where Chambliss
before that Sunday had bombed homes for twenty
years where because of *Brown* the Klan castrated
a man who'd done nothing not even looked
at a white woman in '57

couldn't read a book
about black and white rabbits

because after I'd seen the two fountains the
replicated streetcar classroom courtroom the actual
door of that Birmingham Jail cell and followed
the tapes of the sit-ins the kneel-ins the marches
the students the children the hoses the dogs
and listened again to the famous speech

couldn't be sworn in
on the same Bible

the museum led to a hall they called it
Procession Hall where simply to walk was to join
the life-sized marchers because I had sat in a classroom
had only read the papers when it happened

*
*
*

drag

a woman this time, to haul down the street, the alley,
before or after, with friction, resistance, but less
if the killer was large, like this one, could have, must
have, therefore not prolonged, like a story, but right
now, a trail, a scent, to pull or otherwise move
with force from the house, the shack, the barn,
the woods, the city or county jail, the one
who slowly, painfully, maybe in chains, the mob
itself, along by itself, moved into this, and this
one now, along the ground, down the street, up
to the place where, rope in their hands, to force
the truth, they said, and when it was done, down
the street to that alley, a mile away, this
one, now, its great weight, with great effort

Motophoto Studios

Deborah Cummins

Born November 3, 1949. Deborah Cummins's most recent poetry collections are *Counting the Waves* (Word Press, 2006) and *Beyond the Reach* (BkMk Press, 2002). Cummins is winner of James Michener and Donald Barthelme fellowships, the Washington Prize in Fiction, the Headwaters Literary Prize, and fellowships from the Illinois Arts Council. Her work has been featured on Garrison Keillor's radio program "The Writer's Almanac" and Ted Kooser's "American Life in Poetry" newspaper column. Cummins was the first Chair of the Board of The Poetry Foundation, on which she continues to serve. Recently she began work as a hospice patient-care volunteer. She resides with her husband in Evanston, Illinois, and in summers on an island in Down East Maine.

The Bisbee Donkeys

Lowered in by pulleys and belts, donkeys were once used in the Bisbee Mine to haul carts of ore. Some lived as long as seventeen years in the mine. Most went blind.

Going down, they must've kicked,
fighting for a last breath of real air, a final
glimpse of light. Below,
they must've stumbled over iron-rutted tracks
until darkness thickened, shadows disappeared.

Here I should remind myself
animals don't reason, can't differentiate
between justice and fate,
have no knowledge of dust,
how it packs lungs, smothers desire.

They have no memories
of wet, green grass. Still,
beneath bright planets, a dispassionate moon,
if only for an afternoon, an occasional night,
the miners could've hauled the donkeys out.

And here, I could change the story,
write that they did. But I prefer to think
of those men as incapable
of such cruelty. They wouldn't haul
the donkeys out, only to drag them back,

considering, especially, the newest arrivals
who knew only a mother's shaggy flanks,
her black milk, born
into the palpable pitch
out of whatever instincts that, even if hobbled,

nevertheless break free.
How blinding all that sudden light would be,
the unfathomable blue.
A kindness then. By the men
who day after day had to coldly

ratchet themselves down, descend,
stygian, with shovel and axe,
the pinpricks of their lanterned miners' hats
a constellated sky brought underground:
distant celestial animals, fixed, wheeling.

Passage

Once more, in their dumb unknowing,
sandhill cranes are pulled to a place
they must again and again get back to.
I lean on a rake and scan the sky
for their small Chinese brushstrokes arrowing blue.
But it's their wild, wondrous sound
that pierces me, their high trill
more thrilling than the two young deer that at dawn
incised our lawn with their slender hooves,
lured by the dwarf apples' windfall.

Wherever the cranes' journey ends,
some shoreline probed by assiduous tides,
my garden's just another particular
and less important than the prairies, hills
or rivers the cranes clamor over,
all breath and bellow and creaking pinions,
their passage as compelled and unyielding
as the thump a ripe apple makes
falling. And quick
as that sound, the cranes are here, then not.
I'm left with dirt and rake.

As a child, I lay awake
in the colorless dark and waited for dawn's oncoming
freight, its whistle's single mournful whine.
How that last reverberating note,
especially when it was cold, hung
in the air of my room, our house,
above the river thick with ice, the hills beyond.
I didn't understand but knew.
Not the sound, but the ache of after.

Before It's Too Late

So at last I tell her to come out of the trees,
that I can't believe she's followed me
this time to central Virginia, to these hardwoods
at the edge of a hayfield overlooking a valley,
the Blue Ridge hunkered against the horizon.
Her voice of bitter complaint weaves in and out
of the leaves.
                    Before she gets to what-might've-been
had she married a smarter man,
and how of course I'd never understand
with my fatter wallet, my bigger house, I call
Come on, it isn't, as you always insist, too cold.
If the wind musses your hair, that, at least,
is easily fixed.
                    And though I never get back
whatever she must've said—or sung perhaps?—
withdrawing from my room, sleep hovering near,
the door ajar, a light in the hall reassuring,
I promise not to invent, again, another mother
who reads the classics or is happy
to walk the beach alone, stay up late with Mozart.
Before it's too late, I tell her
                                        Come feel
the sun on your face. Watch how wind,
climbing this slope of unmown hay, carves absence.
Let's agree that hawk, looping the thermals,
fools no one it's just on a joy ride.
Here's a log mapped with lichen
light hasn't touched yet. We can sit
at an easy distance, nothing between us.

"Tidy"

after Rhina P. Espaillat

my friend's new lover says
of my house, my garden,
but meaning, I'm certain, me.
I might've endured "neat" or "orderly"
but "tidy" reeks of age, with desire
limned by duty and discretion,
is the roadblock to genius,
the cause behind disorder, syndrome, behind,

his look suggests, sexual repression.
Does a tidy person, he might as well ask,
ever get laid?

So, un-tidy-fy my life?
Unset the table, unmend the upholstery,
unplant the basil in its soldierly row
of pots on the sill? And if I were to toss
the sliced bread to the scavenging possums,
smash the clock's face, let trumpet vine
claim the porch, would someone—
he, for example—find me more appealing?

Tidily put, screw him.
I gladly live with the potential hazards
of stitched hems, matching socks,
of framed glossy photos, washed coffee cups,
the whir of wings against a snug screen.
I love to walk my discreet path
into the dark spruce of my hidden life
as clean sheets flap wetly on the line.

Don J. Usner

Toi Derricotte

Born April 12, 1941, in Hamtramck, Michigan. Toi Derricotte's recent poetry books include *Tender*, winner of the Paterson Poetry Prize, and *Captivity*. Her memoir, *The Black Notebooks*, published by W.W. Norton, won the 1998 Annisfield-Wolf Book Award for Nonfiction. An essay is included in *The Best American Essays 2006*. Her honors include the Lucille Medwick Memorial Award from the Poetry Society of America, two Pushcart Prizes, the Distinguished Pioneering of the Arts Award from the United Black Artists, and fellowships from the National Endowment for the Arts, the Rockefeller Foundation, and the Guggenheim Foundation. She is a Professor of English at the University of Pittsburgh.

Shoe Repair Business

"This shoe is shiny
as a nigger's heel,"
his customer bursts out
approvingly. Then, remembering
the shop owner is black, he
tactfully amends, "I mean
shiny as a *Negro's* heel."

After Reading at a Black College

Maybe one day we will have
written about this color thing
until we've solved it. Tonight
when I read my poems about
looking white, the audience strains
forward with their whole colored
bodies—a part of each person praying
that my poems will make sense.
Poems do that sometimes—take
the craziness and salvage some
small clear part of the soul,
and that is why, though frightened,
I don't stop the spirit. After,
though some people come
to speak to me, some
seem to step away,
as if I've hurt them once
too often and they have

no forgiveness left. I feel myself
hurry from person to person, begging.
Hold steady, Harriet Tubman whispers,
Don't flop around.
Oh my people,
sometimes you look at me
with such unwillingness—
as I look at *you*!
I keep trying to prove
I am not what I think you think.

Black Boys Play the Classics

The most popular "act" in
Penn Station
is the three black kids in ratty
sneakers & T-shirts playing
two violins and a cello—Brahms.
White men in business suits
have already dug into their pockets
as they pass and they toss in
a dollar or two without stopping.
Brown men in work-soiled khakis
stand with their mouths open,
arms crossed on their bellies
as if they themselves have always
wanted to attempt those bars.
One white boy, three, sits
cross-legged in front of his
idols—in ecstasy—
their slick, dark faces,
their thin, wiry arms,
who must begin to look
like angels!
Why does this trembling
pull us?
A: *Beneath the surface we are one.*
B: *Amazing! I did not think that they could speak this tongue.*

For Black Women Who Are Afraid

A black woman comes up to me at break in the writing
workshop and reads me her poem, but she says she
can't read it out loud because
there's a woman in a car on her way
to work and her hair is blowing in the breeze
and, since her hair is blowing, the woman must be
white, and she shouldn't write about a white woman
whose hair is blowing, because
maybe the black poets will think she wants to be
that woman and be mad at her and say she hates herself,
and maybe they won't let her explain
that she grew up in a white neighborhood
and it's not her fault, it's just what she sees.
But she has to be so careful. I tell her to write
the poem about being afraid to write,
and we stand for a long time like that,
respecting each other's silence.

Bird

The secret is
not to be afraid, to
pour the salt, letting your wrist
be free—there is almost
never too much; it sits on top of the skin like a
little crystal casket. Under it the bird might
imagine another life, one in which it is grateful
for pleasing, can smell
itself cooking—the taste
of carrots, onions, potatoes stewed
in its own juice—and forget
the dreams of blood
coursing out of its throat like a river.

Not Forgotten

I love the way black ants use their dead.
They carry them off like warriors on their steel
backs. They spend hours struggling, lifting,
dragging (it is not grisly as it would be for us,
to carry them back to be eaten),
so that every part will be of service. I think of
my husband at his father's grave—
the grass had closed
over the headstone, and the name had disappeared. He took out
his pocket knife and cut the grass away, he swept it
with his handkerchief to make it clear. "Is this the way
we'll be forgotten?" And he bent down over the grave and wept.

Fred Viebahn

Rita Dove

Born August 28, 1952, in Akron, Ohio. Rita Dove served as Poet Laureate of the United States from 1993 to 1995. Other honors include the Commonwealth Award for Distinguished Service, the Heinz Award, the National Humanities Medal, and the Pulitzer Prize for *Thomas and Beulah* (1986). Her most recent poetry collection—her eighth—is *American Smooth* (2004). She is also the author of a book of short stories, a novel, a play, and several musical collaborations. Ms. Dove is Commonwealth Professor of English at the University of Virginia. In her spare time, Rita Dove plays the viola da gamba, sings classical and contemporary music, and dances ballroom as well as Argentine tango.

Testimonial

Back when the earth was new
and heaven just a whisper,
back when the names of things
hadn't had time to stick;

back when the smallest breezes
melted summer into autumn,
when all the poplars quivered
sweetly in rank and file . . .

the world called, and I answered.
Each glance ignited to a gaze.
I caught my breath and called that life,
swooned between spoonfuls of lemon sorbet.

I was pirouette and flourish,
I was filigree and flame.
How could I count my blessings
when I didn't know their names?

Back when everything was still to come,
luck leaked out everywhere.
I gave my promise to the world,
and the world followed me here.

Soprano

When you hit
the center

of a note, spin
through and off

the bell lip
into heaven,

the soul dies
for an instant—

but you don't need
its thin

resistance
nor the room

(piano shawl,
mirror, hyacinth)

dissolving
as one note

pours into
the next, pebbles

clean as moonspill
seeding a path . . .

and which is it,
body or mind,

which rises, which
gives up at last

and goes home?

Ö

Shape the lips to an *o*, say *a*.
That's *island*.

One word of Swedish has changed the whole neighborhood.
When I look up, the yellow house on the corner
is a galleon stranded in flowers. Around it

the wind. Even the high roar of a leaf-mulcher
could be the horn-blast from a ship
as it skirts the misted shoals.

We don't need much more to keep things going.
Families complete themselves
and refuse to budge from the present,
the present extends its glass forehead to sea
(backyard breezes, scattered cardinals)

and if, one evening, the house on the corner
took off over the marshland,
neither I nor my neighbor
would be amazed. Sometimes

a word is found so right it trembles
at the slightest explanation.
You start out with one thing, end
up with another, and nothing's
like it used to be, not even the future.

Geometry

I prove a theorem and the house expands:
the windows jerk free to hover near the ceiling,
the ceiling floats away with a sigh.

As the walls clear themselves of everything
but transparency, the scent of carnations
leaves with them. I am out in the open

and above the windows have hinged into butterflies,
sunlight glinting where they've intersected.
They are going to some point true and unproven.

Daystar

She wanted a little room for thinking:
but she saw diapers steaming on the line,
a doll slumped behind the door.

So she lugged a chair behind the garage
to sit out the children's naps.

Sometimes there were things to watch—
the pinched armor of a vanished cricket,
a floating maple leaf. Other days
she stared until she was assured
when she closed her eyes
she'd see only her own vivid blood.

She had an hour, at best, before Liza appeared
pouting from the top of the stairs.
And just *what* was mother doing
out back with the field mice? Why,

building a palace. Later
that night when Thomas rolled over and
lurched into her, she would open her eyes
and think of the place that was hers
for an hour—where
she was nothing,
pure nothing, in the middle of the day.

Nick Carbo

Denise Duhamel

Born June 13, 1961, in Providence, Rhode Island. Denise Duhamel's most recent book, *Two and Two* (University of Pittsburgh Press, 2005), is the winner of Binghamton University's Milt Kessler Book Award. Her other titles include *Mille et un Sentiments* (Firewheel, 2005); *Queen for a Day: Selected and New Poems* (Pittsburgh, 2001); *The Star-Spangled Banner* (Southern Illinois University Press, 1999); and *Kinky* (Orchises Press, 1997). A recipient of a National Endowment for the Arts fellowship, she is an associate professor at Florida International University in Miami. She enjoys karaoke and a fierce game of Scrabble.

Noah and Joan

It's not that I'm proud of the fact
that twenty percent of Americans believe
that Noah (of Noah's Ark) was married
to Joan of Arc. It's true. I'll admit it—
Americans are pretty dumb and forgetful
when it comes to history. And they're notorious
for interpreting the Bible to suit themselves.
You don't have to tell me we can't spell anymore—
Ark or Arc, it's all the same to us.

But think about it, just a second, time line aside,
it's not such an awful mistake. The real Noah's Missus
was never even given a name. She was sort of milquetoasty,
a shadowy figure lugging sacks of oats up a plank.
I mean, Joan could have helped Noah *build* that ark
in her sensible slacks and hiking boots. She was good with swords
and, presumably, power tools. I think Noah and Joan
might have been a good match, visionaries
once mistaken for flood-obsessed and heretic.

Never mind France wasn't France yet—
all the continents probably blended together,
one big mush. Those Bible days would have been
good for Joan, those early times when premonitions
were common, when animals popped up
out of nowhere, when people were getting cured
left and right. Instead of battles and prisons
and iron cages, Joan could have cruised
the Mediterranean, wherever the floodwaters took that ark.

And Noah would have felt more like Dr. Doolittle,
a supportive Joan saying, "Let's not waste any time!
Hand over those boat blueprints, honey!"
All that sawing and hammering would have helped

calm her nightmares of mean kings and crowns,
a nasty futuristic place called England.
She'd convince Noah to become vegetarian.
She'd live to be much older than nineteen, those parakeets
and antelope leaping about her like children.

Feminism

All over the world, Little Bees, Star Scouts,
and Blue Birds play Telephone, whispering messages
in a chain link of ears—no repeating (that's cheating),
only relaying what they hear their first shot.
Sometimes "Molly loves Billy" becomes "A Holiday in Fiji,"
or "Do the Right Thing" becomes "The Man Who Would Be King."
Still, there is trust. Girls taking the Blind Walk,
a bandana around one's eyes (Pin the Tail on the Donkey-style)
as another leads her through the woods
or a back yard or entire city blocks. Girls helping
where they are needed or inventing ways to aid
where they seemingly are not. Memorizing remedies
for cuts and stings, frostbite, nosebleeds.
Their motto: Be prepared at all times.
Full of anxiety, they watch for home hazards,
check for frayed toaster or hair dryer cords.
Outside they watch for color changes in cloud formations,
the darkening of the sky. They're safest in cars
during electrical storms.
There's so much to remember and learn.
So many impending disasters, yet so many well-wishes
for their world. These girls shut the tap
as they brush their teeth, secure glow-in-the-dark reflectors
on their bikes, and do at least one good turn daily.
They are taught that alone they are small,
but if they can empathize with each other, they can gain power.
Just to see what it feels like, a walking girl
may spend an afternoon in a wheelchair. Another
may stuff cotton in her ears. And to be readied
for what lies ahead when they grow up
and they're no longer Girl Scouts, they make collages
cutting images from magazines showing what they might be:
mothers or lawyers, reporters or nurses.
Or they play Rabbit Without a House, a Brazilian form
of London Bridge, or American Musical Chairs.
There will always be an odd number of girls, always
one left out. The earth and her scarce resources.
Survival in Sudan begins with Sheep And Hyena.

And though the girls may try to protect the one
who is the Sheep in the middle of their circle, most often
the outside Hyena does not give up
and breaks through sore forearms and weakened wrists
to eat her. Red Rover, Red Rover,
it is better when Girl Scouts stay together.
So they bond tightly in their Human Knot,
a female version of the football team's huddle.
And all holding hands, they squeeze their Friendship Squeeze,
knowing each small one-at-a-time grip
is like a Christmas tree light, each a twinkle
the rest of the strand cannot do without.
Each missing face on the missing child poster
like the fairest of all looking into her mirror.

Ego

I just didn't get it—
even with the teacher holding an orange (the earth) in one hand
and a lemon (the moon) in the other,
her favorite student (the sun) standing behind her with a flashlight.
I just couldn't grasp it—
this whole citrus universe, these bumpy planets revolving so slowly
no one could even see themselves moving.
I used to think if I could only concentrate hard enough
I could be the one person to feel what no one else could,
sense a small tug from the ground, a sky shift, the earth changing gears.
Even though I was only one minispeck on a speck,
even though I was merely a pinprick in one goosebump on the orange,
I was sure then I was the most specially perceptive, perceptively sensitive.
I was sure then my mother was the only mother to snap—
"The world doesn't revolve around you!"
The earth was fragile and mostly water
just the way the orange was mostly water if you peeled it
just the way I was mostly water if you peeled me.
Looking back on that third-grade science demonstration,
I can understand why some people gave up on fame or religion or cures—
especially people who have an understanding
of the excruciating crawl of the world,
who have a well-developed sense of spatial reasoning
and the tininess that it is to be one of us.
But not me—even now I wouldn't mind being god, the force
who spins the planets the way I spin a globe, a basketball, a yo-yo.
I wouldn't mind being that teacher who chooses the fruit,
or that favorite kid who gives the moon its glow.

From the Shore

Michele and I pull out our feet from the mud, and begin
to scream from a new spot. We think you are going to drown.
You won't look back as you swim to the middle of the ocean.

"But Ma!" we call. Chills through our arms, down
through our legs as though we've been struck still by lightning
and no one will touch us. We're afraid to touch each other.

If only we could jump out past our bodies, the small ones
you had to lift up when the waves came. Michele and I clung
to your sides and still got mouthfuls of salt water.

Had we dragged mud from the sand castle to the blanket
or sung too loud or fought with each other? The foam
like thrown toys breaking at our feet, unsteadying us.

At sunset, the family beach mostly cleared,
a lady with red veins on her legs and a bathing suit with a skirt
stops to help us. We point you out, the only mother

in the lineup. Your face, a small craft at the point where water
meets choppy sky. The lady says it's about to rain
and starts yelling with us, demanding you get back on shore

to take care of your daughters. I know we've made a mistake
as you turn around and see Michele and me with this other adult.
All the ocean goes silent—the sea sounds, the gulls.

It's like watching TV with the sound turned off.
You rise from the water like a wet monster and the lady,
in a rage, begins to yell and I guess you yell back:

my ears are murmuring a quiet that's louder.
I vow never to tell on anyone again—if ever I see a kid hitting
another kid, if ever I see someone robbing a bank.

My whole body shakes, the sound inside a seashell.
You yank Michele's arm and mine, saying,
"Can't I have one Goddamn minute alone?"

Ray Black

Camille T. Dungy

Born December 30, 1972, in Denver, Colorado. Author of *What to Eat, What to Drink, What to Leave for Poison* (Red Hen Press, 2006), a finalist for the 2007 PEN Center USA Award, Camille T. Dungy won fellowships from the National Endowment for the Arts and The Virginia Commission for the Arts. Assistant Editor of Cave Canem's *Gathering Ground* (University of Michigan, 2006), Dungy is editor of *Black Nature: A Poetry Anthology* (University of Georgia Press, 2009) and co-editor of *Have You Heard: Poems From the Fishouse* (Persea Books, 2009). Associate Professor of Creative Writing at San Francisco State University, Dungy uses frequent flyer miles to spend time in domestic and international airports.

Language

Silence is one part of speech, the war cry
of wind down a mountain pass another.
A stranger's voice echoing through lonely
valleys, a lover's voice rising so close
it's your own tongue: these are keys to cipher,
the way the high hawk's key unlocks the throat
of the sky and the coyote's yip knocks
it shut, the way the aspens' bells conform
to the breeze while the rapids' drums define
resistance. Sage speaks with one voice, pinyon
with another. Rock, wind her hand, water
her brush, spells and then scatters her demands.
Some notes tear and pebble our paths. Some notes
gather: the bank we map our lives around.

Depression

What little he brought home wouldn't buy much
happiness—a chicken to hem trousers
and some eggs to take them in four inches
at the waist. Hell, it wouldn't even buy
milk. He had time enough to stitch his wife
the only tailored dish towels in town,
so he knew only she could keep the house
around them. A nurse will always find work.

What had he provided since their wedding?
The dream of a trip to the Falls; passports
for Canada; a suitcase; a marriage
certificate; all that useless paper—
five hundred dollars, traveler's checks (all
his money) drawn on a Friday-failed bank.

Vo-Tech

Everything we wore that needed rescue,
pants we'd torn and shirts with ripped-off buttons,
went to our Grandpa when we visited.
We modeled while he adjusted our hems.
Because he loved us, he tried to save us,
my sister and me, by restoring clothes
we'd lately damaged. *You should teach the girls*
how this is done, Mother once suggested,
her arms delivering mending, her eyes
collecting Grandpa's hands, the snapped-tight box
that housed his machine, his needles. He ripped
her words as he told us never to do
to a hanging thread. *Let them save their time.*
He took the clothes. *Let them do useful things.*

Before My History Class

I had religion on my mind and knew
questions would stall my mother when she came
to tuck the starched, white sheet under my chin.

I wanted to be older, to be free
like my sister who wore black leather pumps
and stayed awake as late as grown-ups did.
I wasn't a little kid anymore.

I tricked Mom into talking about Christ,
the Bible, and what Heaven held in store.
Why should I sleep? I told her, *When I die*
I want to meet all the dead. They'll be dressed
and acting just like they did when they lived.

She snapped the sheet, a warning, kissed my head.
Someday you'll be more careful what you wish.

From Someplace

Dreams are sometimes livable, provided
there is property enough, and each house
in Buxton had a little plot of land.
All the town's employees had a garden,

and black folks grew theirs right among the whites'.
A Negro could make a life in Buxton,
and Great-grandfather, the village's best
blacksmith, did. His daughter was free to pass
any old place. This is the youth you knew,
and why you knew, years, miles later, you'd leave
the blackening mill town of your marriage.
You found a town with promise, moved your sons
to its white district, wouldn't let them swim
in the mud hole they called the colored pool.

In His Library

Grandpa's wife lived in Springfield. I suppose
that's why he collected those books I read
about the *Great Emancipator's* life,
but hope meant little to me in those days.

The best book proved *villains* could be *vanquished,*
and photos lent support. Conspirators,
friends of John Wilkes Booth, hung. Their hooded heads
all the evidence I needed. My folks
bored me, so I read while they asked Grandpa
if he planned to join his wife in Springfield.

It's not but a few years since lynch mobs ran
that town. What good's Springfield ever done me?

At eight, what did I know of frustration?
I read the book. That's what we call learning.

Jason Blair

Lynn Emanuel

Born March 14, 1949, in Mount Kisco, New York. Lynn Emanuel's third book of poetry, *Then, Suddenly*, won the Eric Matthieu King Award from The Academy of American Poets. Her work has often appeared in the *Pushcart Prize* and *Best American Poetry* anthologies. She has been a member of the Literature Panel for the National Endowment for the Arts, and a judge for the National Book Awards and for the James Laughlin Award from the Academy of American Poets. She has taught at the Bread Loaf Writers' Conference, the Bennington Writers' Conference, the Warren Wilson Program in Creative Writing, and the Vermont College Creative Writing Program. Currently she is a Professor of English at the University of Pittsburgh.

Soliloquy of the Depressed Book

Since I have come to hate Nature & its Poetry,
I hate every landscape pinned down by Scenery—
The Mountain Package, The Garden, The Vista
always flapping in my face;
I can't pour my broken heart into those rented rooms
with their tired aquatinted distances.
Don't be viewy, I think,
& soap shut the blue window of the sky.
I want machinery
to grind the mountains down to Mountain,
to drive the trees, like stakes, through the heart of The Glade.
I want images to inherit the earth
like kudzu spreading its ooze,
its mean replications, its malignant increase
over the landscape,
erasing the boundaries between itself & us,
between show & tell, master & slave,
until The World vanishes,
& we are left with an Image of The World.
Now every pane of glass in every window
is stenciled with images, even the doorknob,
like a tiny goldfish bowl,
is aswarm with them.
Every avenue of escape is closed.
Stop, say the red stop signs
that once were cardinals.
The wet & bloody pulp that once was Sunset seethes.
Night drags its glassy, abstract fingers
against the bottom of the page,
that blank horizon, that palmy nothingness,
they are merely

the lowest stair in the stairway of Being
that we go down and down and down.

The Sleeping

I have imagined all this:
In 1940 my parents were in love
And living in the loft on West 10th
Above Mark Rothko who painted cabbage roses
On their bedroom walls the night they got married.

I can guess why he did it.
My mother's hair was the color of yellow apples
And she wore a velvet hat with her pajamas.

I was not born yet. I was remote as starlight.
It is hard for me to imagine that
My parents made love in a roomful of roses
And I wasn't there.

But now I am. My mother is blushing.
This is the wonderful thing about art.
It can bring back the dead. It can wake the sleeping
As it might have late that night
When my father and mother made love above Rothko
Who lay in the dark thinking *Roses, Roses, Roses*.

Frying Trout While Drunk

Mother is drinking to forget a man
Who could fill the woods with invitations:
Come with me he whispered and she went
In his Nash Rambler, its dash
Where her knees turned green
In the radium dials of the '50s.
When I drink it is always 1953,
Bacon wilting in the pan on Cook Street
And mother, wrist deep in red water,
Laying a trail from the sink
To a glass of gin and back.
She is a beautiful, unlucky woman
In love with a man of lechery so solid
You could build a table on it
And when you did the blues would come to visit.
I remember all of us awkwardly at dinner,
The dark slung across the porch,
And then mother's dress falling to the floor,
Buttons ticking like seeds spit on a plate.

When I drink I am too much like her—
The knife in one hand and in the other
The trout with a belly white as my wrist.
I have loved you all my life
She told him and it was true
In the same way that all her life
She drank, dedicated to the act itself,
She stood at this stove
And with the care of the very drunk
Handed him the plate.

After Your Letter of Elegant Goodbye

This is a road where I could die for love
Nosing the car toward the black falls

The noise of an axe working
Its own way through woods that stand between me

And a view so suicidally inviting
A man has decided to build a house.

This is where I kill the lights,
Coast out toward the cutting of two-by-fours.

Beyond the skeletal bedroom, nothing but down:
The forest is fine and dry as loose handfuls

Pulled from a hen.
Even in this heat he has built a fire,

The mouth of a barrel crammed with burning lath
A blossom of sour smoke growing from charred strata.

I envy him the pines that lavish
His roof with soft touches, the bell of millet

He tied on a low branch swings silently
Above a town tipped with steeples.

I am so tired I could lie down among these trees
Until I was nothing

And let the earth take one slow liberty
After another.

Ordinary Objects

"Hic et ubique?"
Hamlet to the Ghost

I am letting them stand
For everything I love.

The light's unsteady scale
Across the glass, the hard

Brown grit of ants among the roses,
The bittersweet

Everywhere I look I will see
Italy. The flowers will be full

Of prisons and churches,
Of women in black dresses, full

Of motorcycles and genuflecting.
The nightshade's dark, crooked stem

Is your street
And the water in the vase the sea's

Horizon tilting with the tilt
Of your ship. I am going to let

The daffodil be your mistress.
She is tired of you and stands

Looking at her feet.
In the fan's slow wind

The curtains reach for you.
I am full of grief. I am going

To lie down and die and be reborn
To come back as these roses

And wind myself thorn by
Thorn around your house

To fit into the nutshell
And the flat seed, the scar,

The door, the road, the web,
The moon's bald envious eye

Staring at you through the drapes.

Barry Fitzgerald

Claudia Emerson

Born January 13, 1957, in Danville, Virginia. Claudia Emerson's poetry collections are *Pharaoh, Pharaoh* (1997), *Pinion, An Elegy* (2002), and *Late Wife* (2005), which won the 2006 Pulitzer Prize for poetry—all from Louisiana State University Press, which will bring out her *Figure Studies* in 2009. Emerson has been awarded fellowships from the National Endowment for the Arts, the Virginia Commission for the Arts, and the Witter Bynner Foundation. She is the Poet Laureate of Virginia and Professor of English and Arrington Distinguished Chair in Poetry at University of Mary Washington. Emerson is married to musician Kent Ippolito.

After Hours: A Glimpse of My Radiologist

Behind the seamless window that is the cafe's
outer wall, he faces his wife over
a small, candlelit table, a white-aproned
waiter moving—intent, unnoticed—around them.

The sidewalk and streetlights frame their late supper,
begun for him with a squat glass of merlot,
I'd guess by the stouter stem, the dark wine
thick, legs heavy. The flute slender and tall,
hers is more certainly champagne—the bead
I can see streaming clearly from here, despite
the light fall of mist forming on the glass
between us.
All day, he has been reading
films and ultrasounds, x-rays, scans—looking
inside our bodies—the gray-marbled breasts
sequenced by shadowy lungs and hearts,
the rarer brain, the hand's delicate bones
rendered into translucence.
In this moment,
though, he pauses to offer a toast—to her,
I imagine, and to the most ordinary
survival of a long week, or, perhaps,
to the routine *nothing here of any interest*
he has had the unusual pleasure
to say all day, becoming beautiful
and absolute, the *nothing here at all.*

Animal Funerals, 1964

That summer, we did not simply walk through
the valley of the shadow of death; we set up camp there,

orchestrating funerals for the anonymous,
        found dead: a drowned mole—its small, naked palms
still pink—a crushed box turtle, green snake, even
        a lowly toad. The last and most elaborate
of the burials was for a common jay, identifiable
        but light, dry, its eyes vacant orbits.

We built a delicate lichgate of willow fronds,
        supple and green, laced through with chains of clover.
Roles were cast: preacher, undertaker—
        the rest of us a straggling congregation
reciting what we could of the psalm
        about green pastures as we lowered the shoebox
and its wilted pall of dandelions into the shallow
        grave one of us had dug with a serving spoon.

That afternoon, just before September
        and school, when we would again become children,
and blind to all but the blackboard's chalky lessons,
        the back of someone's head, and what was,
for a while longer, the rarer, human death—
        there, in the heat-shimmered trees, in the matted
grasses where we stood, even in the slant
        of humid shade—we heard wingbeat, slither,
buzz, and birdsong—a green racket rising
        to fall as though in a joyous dirge that was real,
and not part of our many, necessary rehearsals.

Zenith

Younger sister he suffers, I am three years old,
        eating supper with my brother: in the photograph
he wears his cowboy boots, dungarees, pajama top—
        his head shaved close to bald, six-shooter holstered
at the small table we share every night. I am also
        in boots, hand-me-down rifle at the ready
by my plate. My helmet from another war,
        its netting I will weave with leaves, broomsedge,
pine fronds, anything to camouflage me,
        confuse the enemy the way he has taught me,
whispering *listen, there, listen—Japanese,*
        Germans, Apaches, Yankees unseen, everywhere.

We don't know how little we have to fear
        in our small country town, for years its only

traffic light a mere caution, the steady
yellow pulse benign as a lightning bug's.
The enemies of this place—drought, hail, an early
or late frost—refuse our aim, the smallest
human industry defined by the health
of tobacco flaming in the fields that surround us.

I can't tell what's on our plates, but if it's Monday,
meatloaf and mashed potatoes, Tuesday,
pork chops and fried apples. But our attentions
are not on the meal, not on the camera—
our mother—but on something just beyond
the picture's border captioned with the date,
January 1960: the black and white
Zenith, tuned to the Rifleman, Daniel Boone,
Andy Griffith—easy heroes.
We can't know
what we're armed against or training for—
another war Walter Cronkite will narrate,
cataloguing the dead nightly in a country
we've not yet heard of, or suspicious rustlings,
wind in the thicket of our bodies, my brother's
illness and too-early death still fifty
years away—with unnumbered other
captures between, like this small, humorous one,
the flash from my mother's camera caught
bouncing off the wall and door behind us,
still-sudden backlight to all we cannot see.

Aftermath

I think by now it is time for the second cutting.
I imagine the field, the one above the last

house we rented, has lain in convalescence
long enough. The hawk has taken back the air

above new grass, and the doe again can hide
her young. I can tell you now I crossed

that field, weeks before the first pass of the blade,
through grass and briars, fog—the night itself

to my thighs, my skirt pulled up that high.
I came to what had been our house and stood outside.

I saw her in it. She reminded me of me—
        with her hair black and long as mine had been—

as she moved in and then away from the sharp
        frame the window made of the darkness.

I confess that last house was the coldest
        I kept. In it, I became formless as fog, crossing

the walls, formless as your breath as it rose
        from your mouth to disappear in the air above you.

You see, aftermath is easier, opening
        again the wound along its numb scar; it is the sentence

spoken the second time—truer, perhaps,
        with the blunt edge of a practiced tongue.

The Spanish Lover

There were warnings: he had, at forty, never
married; he was too close to his mother,
calling her by her given name, *Manuela,*
ah, Manuela—like a lover; even her face

had bled, even the walls, giving birth to him;
she still had saved all of his baby teeth
except the one he had yet to lose, a small
eyetooth embedded, stubborn in the gum.

I would eat an artichoke down to its heart,
then feed the heart to him. It was enough
that he was not you—and utterly foreign,
related to no one. So it was not love.

So it ended badly, but to some relief.
I was again alone in my bed, but not
invisible as I had been to you—
and I had learned that when I drank sherry

I was drinking a chalk-white landscape, a distant
poor soil; that such vines have to suffer; and that
champagne can be kept effervescent by putting
a knife in the open mouth of the bottle.

Maude Clay

Beth Ann Fennelly

Born May 22, 1971, in Rahway, New Jersey. Beth Ann Fennelly received a 2003 National Endowment for the Arts Award and a 2006 United States Artist grant. Her most recent collections are *Tender Hooks* (W. W. Norton, 2004), *Unmentionables* (W. W. Norton, 2008), both poetry, as well as a book of essays, *Great With Child* (W. W. Norton, 2006). Her awards include the *Kenyon Review* Prize, the Pushcart Prize, and inclusion in the *Best American Poetry* series. She is an Associate Professor at the University of Mississippi. In 2009 Fennelly will work and write in Brazil on a Fulbright grant, accompanied by her husband, novelist Tom Franklin, and their children, Claire and Thomas.

Interpreting the Foreign Queen

I rush home after class to slurp her thigh,
to pounce on baby belly, press my lips deep
to spray wet-raspberry kisses. They make her writhe.
I'm spilling giggles, nibbling ticklish feet.
My husband, the anti-tickler, disapproves.
He says she'd just been resting in his lap,
she'd just had food (she's always just had food)—
now, overstimulated, she won't nap.
He swears I shouldn't toss her, not so high.
She gives a shriek—pure terror, pure delight?
We read our own emotions in her eyes.
If only she could speak to say who's right—
to say *I* am. For him, I put her down.
Just two more days till he goes out of town.

People Ask What My Daughter Will Think of My Poems When She's 16

Daughter, the light of
the future is apricot,
and in it you are not
the thigh-child pointing
her earnest index finger
to the yellow balloon clearing
 the willows and drifting
higher, you're the balloon. I'm
the grasping hand. Or I'm
the *oo* in *balloon*. I'll meet you
there. I'm the brown
strings, formerly violets, you
didn't water. I'm the hole
in the photo, you're the un-
safety scissors. I'm the lint

in the corners of my purse
after you steal the coins,
brown-bag lunch you pitch
after leaving my house, buttons
you undo after I've okayed
your blouse. Poems
you burn in the sink. Poems
that had to go and use
your name, never mind
that soon you'll be 16, hate
your name. I'm the resemblance
you deny, fat ass
you hope your boyfriends
never see. I'll meet you
there, that is my promise
and my threat, with this
yellow balloon as my
witness, even if I'm
dead, I'll meet you there.

Cow Tipping

I think I did it three, four times, at least—sneak out, ride
with boys in a truck to a farm, hop the fence with our flashlights
and Coors while small frogs fled the machetes of our feet,
crash through grass to where the Holsteins clustered, slumbered,
grass-breathed, milk-eyed, high as my shoulder, weighing a ton
and worth a grand: they'd topple with a single, bracing shove.

The yoke of their shoulders thundered the ground
and we'd feel it through our feet as we ran, whooping,
me nearly wetting my pants with adrenaline and fear—
those cows could toss me like a sack of trash, snap my bones
like balsa, though mostly what they did was roll to their stomachs,
shake their stupid heads, unfold their forelegs, heave-ho to their feet.

By then we'd be racing home, taking curves so fast
we'd slam against the doorframe, turn up the Springsteen,
me on some guy's knees, dew-slick, grass-etched—
another pair of white Keds ruined—check me out, puffing Kurt's
menthol Marlboro although I didn't smoke. Cough cough.
I could end this by saying how I ran with the boys and the bulls

and no one ever harmed me. I was a virgin then, stayed that way
for years, though I wore Victoria's Secret beneath my uniform skirt.

And no one ever harmed me. But I'm lifting off in a half-empty plane
which clears a field of cows, the meek, long-suffering cows,
and from this heightened window I can't understand
why I can't understand why whole countries hate our country.

Because of our bemused affection for our youthful cruelties.
Because the smug postprandial of nostalgia coats the tongue.
Somehow, despite the planes clearing fields of cows and flying
into buildings full of red-blooded Americans, it's still so hard
to accept that people who've never seen me would like to see me
dead, and you as well. Our fat babies. Our spoiled dogs.

And I, a girl at thirty-two, who likes to think she was a rebel, who lifts
like a crystal this tender recollection every few years to the bright window
of her consciousness, or lobs it into a party for a laugh—*Cow tipping?*
I've done that—who brags (isn't it a brag?) that no harm
ever came to her—what would they make of me, the terrorists
and terrified? Wouldn't they agree I've got it coming?

First Warm Day in a College Town

Today is the day the first bare-chested
        runners appear, coursing down College Hill
                as I drive to campus to teach, hard

not to stare because it's only February 15,
        and though I now live in the South,
                I spent my girlhood in frigid Illinois

hunting Easter eggs in snow,
        or trick-or-treating in the snow,
                an umbrella protecting my cardboard wings,

so now it's hard not to see these taut colts
        as my reward, these yearlings testing the pasture,
                hard as they come toward my Nissan

not to turn my head as they pound past,
        hard not to angle the mirror
                to watch them cruise down my shoulder,

too hard, really, when I await them like crocuses,
        search for their shadows
                as others do the groundhog's, and suddenly

here they are, the boys without shirts,
        how fleet of foot, how cute their buns, I have made it
                again, it is spring.

Hard to recall just now
        that these are the torsos of my students,
                or my past or future students, who every year

grow one year younger, get one year fewer
        of my funny jokes and hip references
                to Fletch and Nirvana, which means

some year if they catch me admiring
        the hair downing their chests, centering
                between their goalposts of hipbones,

then going undercover beneath their shorts,
        the thin red or blue nylon shorts, the fabric
                of flapping American flags or the rigid sails of boats—

some year, if they catch me admiring, they won't
        grin grins that make me, busted,
                grin back—hard to know a spring will come

when I'll have to train my eyes
        on the dash, the fuel gauge nearing empty,
                hard to think of that spring, that

distant spring, that very very very
        (please God) distant
                spring.

Mother Sends My Poem to Her Sister with Post-its

This man is an abstract
painter gives his women
one eye, three breasts
a very famous man

                                She doesn't smoke
                                anymore

                                                a kind of cheese?

This woman is not me
she says even though
I used to ice skate
with Bill in a red
scarf in winter

That's how the French
girls got the silk
from the worms, they
dipped the cocoons
in scalding tubs of water
(13th c.)

this apple is a symbol

She got this wrong
it was me, not her father
who sang her "Irish Rosie"
she was so sick with the measles

When she writes "far gone
train" it means she plans
to come back home

University of Mississippi Printing Services

Ann Fisher-Wirth

Born January 25, 1947, in Washington, DC. Ann Fisher-Wirth is the author of two books of poems, *Blue Window* (Archer Books, 2003) and *Five Terraces* (Wind Publications, 2005) and two chapbooks, *The Trinket Poems* (Wind, 2003) and *Walking Wu Wei's Scroll* (online, *Drunken Boat*, 2005). She has won the *Malahat Review* Long Poem Prize, the Rita Dove Poetry Award, a Poetry Award from the Mississippi Institute of Arts and Letters, and two Poetry Fellowships from the Mississippi Arts Commission. Her work has received a Pushcart Prize Special Mention. She teaches at the University of Mississippi, and has held Fulbright fellowships in Switzerland and Sweden. Fisher-Wirth also teaches yoga. She and her husband Peter Wirth have five grown children.

Ice Storm

In the ice storm Thursday half our trees came down.
Behind the house the forest exploded like popcorn.
We stood by the window watching branches burst and shatter,
tortured by the ice that hurtled down like daggers
from the goddess whose fingers are talons,
whose skirt is knives.
At three a.m. the big one—the hundred-year-old magnolia tree.
The meterbox ripped away, line down, a terrific shudder
of glass and wood, the whole house shook.
Now branches hang crazy, by threads—
willow oaks and pecan trees,
shards of heartwood broken radii and ulnas
jutting into the leadwhite sky
like beggars in a badly acted stageplay
who thrust up stumps, beseeching heaven,
hurling imprecations. But no, the trees submit;
it's only we who cower. The cats are more like us,
they streaked out of the forest to the house
and spent the next day spraying—hats, gloves, doorjambs—
stinky gusts of Here I am, don't mess with my place.
We're like that. Anxious. Fretful. Squabbling.
Anything but silent.
Yet hardest to tell, the knowledge
that we had been given a gift. Not just that we came through
safe, but that, for a few moments
at dawn the second day,
the storm still raging, the forest shining,
branches flying like bullets, like angels,
ourselves beyond fear into rapt calm,
we touched the hem of a final morning.
Now debris, downed lines, no water.
Snarl and tangle of branches interflung, wall-to-wall

disaster. Start here little ants, sort your peas and lentils,
twigs and branches by the curb, chop, saw the big ones,
somewhere under there's
the world as you once knew it: the rosebush, the crocuses.

Rain Stick

I have watched you,
first in the sunny room in Charlottesville
as you were learning Yeats's "Long-Legged Fly,"

and I have lain beside you as you stilled
to remember just how a line turned, the actual adjective.
I've touched your hip as you said me "Tintern Abbey"

or Hardy's "Afterwards," in the dark I've felt that joy,
seen that hedgehog, those white moths.
When I sprained my knee, trying to learn to ski,

I tossed in the bottom bunk of our hut
as your voice at 3 a.m. floated down above me,
murmuring "Fern Hill," the horses "walking warm

out of the whinnying green stable,"
because I begged you, "Tell me something beautiful."
I slept on our wedding night

as you drove for hours through the Blue Ridge Mountains,
waked and slept again, hypnotized by your tenderness
as you said me the whole Rubáiyyát—

And sometimes I have seen you gaze across a room
to recite one of the thousand poems
you know by heart,

have listened to your classes
and heard your husky voice
for more than twenty years, reciting poetry.

*

We were talking on the phone, I in California,
you teaching summer school back home in Mississippi.
You said, "The poems we love are vanishing."

I had nothing to reply. Then after some moments
you brought the rain stick to the phone,
the gourd we bought at a concert long ago,

when Robin Williams played thirty-five instruments—
"the lute, the rebeck, the psaltery, and the harp"—
and sang and chanted Bardic tales and mysteries.

You tipped the gourd so I could hear
the hidden seeds running down its length,
still making the sound of rain.

Blue Window

In that shadowy time before sorrow—
that twilight, October in Berkeley, the early 60's,

when I walked home along Euclid from Mrs. Runkle's
where I'd played Schumann's "Träumerei"

so beautifully, for once, I'd made her cry—
Before the missile crisis, when I sat on the bed in fear and exaltation

and thought of Anne Frank—while on the TV downstairs,
Soviet ships inched closer to Cuba—and wondered,

when they come to get me, when I hide beneath my desk,
my head in my hands, and the walls shake,

will I have told the world
how I love this life I am forced to lose?

Before Christian, my neighbor, drank developing fluid
and his death at Alta Bates took 48 hours, the poison dissolving his stomach,

and his father the beautiful philanderer told my mother,
"The divorce caused it," just failing to add, wringing

his elegant crooked fingers, "He did it for grief of me"—
before Ronnie, my neighbor, took acid and flew out a window,

and Jackie, my neighbor, drove 90 miles an hour into a stone wall
at prep school in Massachusetts, and Kwaasi, my neighbor,

talked to God and carved his arms and died at Napa,
the boys who lived around me lost, all dead by nineteen—

and before I had ever bled yet, ever got high, or
loved a boy, or played at kisses through Kleenex with Mary Lou—

In that time before my father lay in bed
all one year's end, the vast flower of his death blossoming,

and wrote, in a tiny crabbed hand, in the datebook I found years later,
"Had to increase the dosage today. Ann and Jink allowance"—

in that Christian Science household no one spoke,
to this day no one has ever said to me, "It was brain cancer,"

but last winter my husband got drunk in his rare blind fury,
ran weeping into the room and pounded the bed over and over,

shouting, "Don't you understand yet?
In the war they treated men for lice with lindane,

poured it over their heads,
they did it to your father, and now the fuckers tell us

lindane eats your brain." —In that time, that twilight,
when I walked slowly home along Euclid,

how I wanted to belong to the family I saw
through the blue, wisteria-covered window, to be their girl,

enter their garlicky dinnertime kitchen,
later, to sit on a high attic bed, legs crossed tailor-fashion,

and pick dreamily at white chenille—
I wondered, why not be anyone, go anywhere?

when light dies around the oak leaves
and white, ragged moths come out to beat against the streetlight,

why not knock at the door and say "I am yours. I am here"?

Lillian Elaine Wilson

Alice Friman

Born October 20, 1933, in New York, New York. Alice Friman's new collection is *Vinculum* (Louisiana State University Press, 2011). Previous books include *The Book of the Rotten Daughter* (BkMk, 2006) and *Zoo* (University of Arkansas Press, 1999), winner of the Pound Poetry Award from Truman State and the Motton Prize from New England Poetry Club. Her poems appear regularly in *Poetry, Boulevard, Gettysburg Review*, and *Shenandoah*, which awarded her the Boatwright Prize. She was named Writer-in-Residence at Bernheim Forest, Kentucky, and was a *Georgia Review*/Bowers House Literary Center Fellow. Professor Emerita at the University of Indianapolis, Friman is now Poet-in-Residence at Georgia College & State University. She's still ironing. And cooking. But she dances.

Autobiography: The Short Version

I was born under the sign of Libra: up
down, teetering for balance: a spider,
all scurry and retreat, or the brass lamp
lighting up a room.

What I wanted was fulcrum—
the point of the knife: danger and no sleep.
What I got was desire, hard-edged,
gleaming and perfect.

For that I was never forgiven.

I shouted huge, terrorized each day
with a violent fondle to make it give,
imitated the anteater tonguing sweetness up—
or the bear, honeycomb for the taking.

Learning to lie like that . . . that came later.

How to count your days as more
than cracks in a sidewalk. How to say
No, not for a moment to crackers and milk
or the hand-me-down life. How to not
see yourself taped up in the lobster tank—claws
and clappers scraping a slow motion against glass.

How else are we supposed to live,
seeing the boulders in the field sporting
their blue brooches of lichen or the cold night sky
tipsy in sequins and runaway fire?

Diapers for My Father

Pads or pull-ons—*that*
is the question. Whether to buy
pads dangled from straps
fastened with buttons or Velcro—
pads rising like a bully's cup
stiff as pommel with stickum backs
to stick in briefs. Or, dear God,
the whole thing rubberized,
size 38 in apple green, with
or without elastic leg. Or the kind,
I swear, with an inside pocket
to tuck a penis in—little resume
in a folder. Old mole, weeping
his one eye out at the tunnel's end.

The clerk is nothing but patience
practiced with sympathy.
Her eyes soak up everything.
In ten minutes she's my cotton batting,
my triple panel, triple shield—my Depends
against the hour of the mop: skeleton
with a sponge mouth dry as a grinning brick
waiting in the closet.

She carries my choices to the register,
sighing the floor with each step.
I follow, absorbed away to nothing.

How could Hamlet know what flesh is heir to?
Ask Claudius, panicky in his theft,
hiding in the garden where it all began
or behind the arras, stuffing furbelows
from Gertrude's old court dress into his codpiece.
Or better, ask Ophelia, daughter too
of a foolish, mean-mouthed father,
who launched herself like a boat of blotters
only to be pulled babbling under the runaway stream.

Silent Movie

Bernheim Forest

One afternoon of rain and suddenly
creeks rise, babbling in the forest—
backup singers for the silence.

A missed cue. It's November now,
the trees, bare. A light piano of chirp
and scurry is more than enough. Trees
make eloquent speech just by how
they stand or lean in graceful habit.
Or in the case of the sycamore, gleam
like polished marble in the sun.

The towering beech, the naked poplar
speak the language of lips and the moss
that covers them. If the trees sleep now
in this storage locker of the cold,
if they seem aloof and alien strange,
it doesn't mean that beneath the bark,
or underground where roots tangle
and hold, they've forgotten their promise
of smolder and juice. Look at them.
Valentino looked like that—waiting, still.

Snow

Let us speak of love and weather
subtracting nothing.
Let us put your mother and mine
away for a while. Your dying father,
my dead one.
                                        Let us watch
from our bedroom window how a slow
falling snow crowns all nakedness in ermine.
Do not look at me yet. Your face is flushed,
your eyes too love-soaked, too blue.
Outside is white on black
and still. The sky, deaf with stillness.

Don't let it frighten you.
Hush. There's time enough for that.
Be content for now to watch the maples
fill with snow, how they spread themselves,
each naked limb making itself accessible.

Vinculum

for Richard

Do not look at me again like that: between us
is too stripped down to the bare wire of what we were.

The look, umbilical—that cord I thought discarded
in some hospital bin fifty years ago come November.

How strange to find it once more between us,
still beating and so palpable we could

cross over and enter into each other again,
seeing our old selves through new, first eyes.

Plucked from a drumroll of autumns, that one
was ours—autumn of my twenty-third year, autumn

of your final fattening, taking up all the room,
worrying the thinning walls. The rope that seethed

from me to you and back again—our two-
way street—and you, little fish, hanging on

past your lease in a time of narrowing dark,
which you can't possibly remember, but do.

And it comes to me: that look must be what *love* is,
which is why we'll not speak of it nor hunt it down

in each other's eyes again, for you're too worldly
to admit, without wincing, what happened happened.

And I, too conscious of my failed attempts
to fire into language what's beyond words, could not

bear it. Which leaves me holding the bag once more
of foolish thoughts. I know, I know, the universe

has neither edge nor center nor crown, but I want
to think that past Andromeda and out beyond

a million swirling disks of unnamed stars, that cord
we knew, that ghost of an eye-beam floating between us,

arcs in space, lit up like the George Washington Bridge
pulsing with traffic, even after both stanchions are gone.

Michael Paul Thomas

Carol Frost

Born February 28, 1948, in Lowell, Massachusetts. The Queen's Desertion, I Will Say Beauty, Love and Scorn: New and Selected Poems, all from Northwestern University Press, are Carol Frost's recent volumes. Her poems have appeared in four Pushcart Prize anthologies. NEH Distinguished Professor at SUNY Potsdam in 2008, she teaches at Rollins College, where she holds the Theodore Bruce and Barbara Lawrence Alfond Chair in Creative Writing, and for the MFA Program in Poetry at New England College. Frost spends time each spring on Florida's "nature coast" and a few weeks each summer in Elizabeth Bishop's childhood home in Great Village, Nova Scotia, which she owns in partnership with a group of American and Nova Scotian scholars and writers.

Sin

The tree bore the efflorescence of October apples
like the bush that burned with fire and was not consumed.

The wind blew in cold sweet gusts
and the burning taste of fresh snow came with the gradual dark

down through the goldenrod. The blue and scarlet sky
was gently losing its color,

as if from use.
The towers and telephone poles rose in the distance.

And a decline
of spirit, hearing, all senses—where the mind no longer rests,

dwells, intrigues—and Satan's quick perspective of what lies ahead
were foretold by the springing back of a bough.

—We'll never know the all of it: nature's manifesto,
the sleight-of-hand in god's light, the invisible,

visible, sinned against, absolved, no matter the enormity
of trying, and Eve's help.

But come just before sunrise and see and taste again
the apple tree coming into fire

—shadow-glyphs on the crystallized grasses,
geese surging above the loblolly pine, the smell of sap—,

as if willingly through its long life
it held on to one unclarified passion and grew and regretted nothing.

Apiary II

Abandoned bee boxes piled on each other at meadow end . . .
Like clothing taken off,
the bees who had alighted on hat,
gloves, shirt, have flown off somewhere.
Is it so terrible to outlive the mind?
Forget this, forget that—keys, glasses,
what it was you just said, what you meant to say.
Pseudonyms. Silences:
oddball or golden and grave, a dance of signs,
sorrows passing by like shadows,
time running by like a small girl running by like a madwoman.

Apiary VIII (For the ones

who line the corridors and sit
silent in wheelchairs
before the television with the volume off,
whose cares
are small and gray and infinite,
time as ever to be faced . . .
Methuselahs the nurses wash
and dress without haste—
none needed . . .
this one has drunk from the poppy-cup
and drowses in her world of dream . . .
Heliotrope,
carnations, wakeful violets, and lilies in vases—
masses of flowers—wrap
the urine-and-antiseptic air in lace . . .
Please wake up; it is morning;
robins whistle; the bees dance.
Isn't this other one listening
from her shell of silence,
and shouldn't she smile at the green return
and dappled light through windows?
As earth orbits the corridor
clocks are wound . . .
The last hour is a song or wound . . .
Except in this corridor—mother's—
where finity's brainless wind
blows ash, and ash again
blows through their cells:
So much silence, so little to say in the end.)

Egret

Violent leaner: fallen earthward: unconscious
of body left by soul: I am moved by its marble pose
above winter water brown and frothed:
the tiny fish like stars on a cloudy night:
stars stars stars in water at its feet:
it makes its bleak adjustments and waits:
yellow bill held en garde: wind swirling
lashing: if only it could tell: how tides
must move through it: one fish never enough.

Man of War

After there were no women, men, and children,
from the somber deeps horseshoe crabs crawled up on somber shores:
Man-of-Wars' blue sails drifted downwind
and blue filaments of some biblical cloak
floated below: the stinging filaments.
The cored of bone and rock-headed came near:
clouds made wandering shadows:
sea and grasses mingled::
There was no hell after all
but a lull before it began over::

flesh lying alone: then mating: a little spray of soul:

and the grace of waves, of stars, and remotest isles.

Wild Rose

Shall I perfect myself or ramble? The arbor's crumbled
and no one comes to brush the spiders from my petals.
I dislike their pursed and little mouths,
but they can bear themselves aloft.
Umbrels and sconces are vanities,
and if I fold myself in quarters
and anchor to the barn's foundation,
I can stick my face into darkness
and be all the wiser, the spiders say
in all but words. I know winter's dark,
a faded tint of apricot and purple letting go
in surface layers of softest snow
above; and that becomes the greenery I waken to.
For such darkness I must only wait,
but I'll freely search wherever a little loam and water
lie—the southern slopes, a sheltered hollow, this barn
corner—for the other. Only if the dark conceives it
must I think of beauty—my interiors, silks
there, and the looping quiet in the morning of the spiders.

Stacey Lynn Brown

Allison Funk

Born February 27, 1951, in Princeton, New Jersey. Allison Funk has published three books of poems: *The Knot Garden* (Sheep Meadow Press, 2002), *Living at the Epicenter* (Northeastern University Press, 1995), winner of the Morse Prize, and *Forms of Conversion* (Alice James Books, 1986). She won a National Endowment for the Arts fellowship and prizes from *Poetry* and the Poetry Society of America. Her work appears in *The Best American Poetry, The Paris Review, Poetry,* and *Shenandoah.* She is Professor of English at Southern Illinois University Edwardsville, where she edits *Sou'wester.* Since moving to the Midwest, she has developed a love for prairies, but still misses the little coastal state of Delaware, where she grew up.

The Escape Artist in the Prairie

See how the wildflowers open,
as if nothing restrains them. No sign
of a lock that's been picked, handcuffs

sprung. Coneflower, bee balm,
sweet clover. Who can tell
how far they tunneled,

if they fumbled like the blind
for a key. Dirt clings to none,
none of them reeks

of the grave. Not that feathery pink
showoff, queen-of-the-prairie,
or the towering cow parsnip

ready to accept whatever lands
in its nets. Even the loosestrife,
whose name

betrays a second self,
the double life
the blooms in the prairie conceal,

puts purple on
as leisurely as a woman
might draw a dark stocking

up over her ankle and knee,
feeling the silkiness,
every inch of it, going on.

The woman I'm thinking of
doesn't rush. With the same ease,
when it's time, she'll take it off.

Forms of Conversion

Measured in miles or kilometers,
the distance we travel is the same.
A man is so many stone;
pounds do not increase him,

and the beggar who trades rubles
for dollars is still a poor soul.
Yet there are forms of conversion
we regard as miracles: coal, water and air

by some process she does not understand
become the nylons a woman removes
as carefully as a fisherman
loosens a fish from his hook.

And a man who trades one wife
for another sincerely believes
he increases his chances
for love. True—

a stereoscope can synthesize two images
of a London street, giving a viewer the illusion
of entering a foreign place. But bread
remembers its ancestors: wheat and yeast.

Copernicus did not invent our poles
of joy and grief when he found the world
was a guest in the galaxy
circulating shyly around an impressive host.

What does it take to change a person's blood
from say *A* to *O*; banish one's parents
to the last seats in a theater; separate
for all time milk from the meat?

The rabbis were rightly suspicious
when I entered the mikvah. They knew
the last breath I took before immersion
would be the air I would choke on again when I surfaced.

After Ovid

I kneeled, I lay down
next to it, and still no fish,
no frog or insect surfaced.

No mayfly, stonefly,
dragon or damsel
beginning in water

as nymph. In the heart
of a prairie, in a pool
barely the depth of my hand

the sand at the bottom
spun round and around
drawing me down

as if toward the source of churning
in a world of trembling aspen,
hawkweed and stargrass,

each on the edge of becoming
something else—
like the voice

I heard then from the water
weeping as a mother does for her child,
one in grief so long I'd swear

her limbs had thinned to splinters,
the bow of one arm and the other's arrow
whittled so, she could no longer aim.

Fortress-back, the hills of her shoulders, pelvic sling,
all relented. Even what had been soft
to begin with, belly and breasts,

gave in. Kin of wind,
what she'd been goddess of
she became.

The Lake

Around the lake the rhododendron bloomed.
Each bud unclenched, revealing a baby's palm.
As I awoke mornings in my cousin's room
I heard the water licking its live fur calm
Beside the creaking house. It was the summer
The hair began like webs beneath our arms
And we saw in mirrors not ourselves, but strangers
Remote and older, ones with foreign charms.
Later that year we discovered the waterfall
With its silver neck broken on the rocks. They found
My cousin down among the fish, so small,
Looking up through the lake's dark layers, drowned.
It was then the lake became as still as one
Asleep, translucent palms upturned, and stunned.

Women

Women are mostly metamorphic,
  gneiss, marble, schist, slate,
recrystalized only under great heat
  or pressure.
    Or, compare us

to a levee
  keeping the river from the fields.
In flood time, I've heard,
  the wall takes a deep breath
    before going under.

Once, on a train,
  I met a singer who told me
that forced to her third-story window by fire
  she was carried faster
    than any scale she had sung

to the sidewalk she hit
  headfirst,
shattering her instrument.
  After the accident of birth,
    people speak of what befalls us

as if from the compound
  of *being* and *falling*
we are made.
  Queen Anne's Lace.
    Black-eyed Susan,

all the wildflowers along the roads
  I love have women's names.
Mid-summer,
  the cicadas singing their praises,
    I am far

from those stations we passed,
  New London, Old Saybrook,
outside our window, snow
  filling a sky
    the tincture of smoke.

Trying her new voice,
  she got this close—saying, *look,*
you can hardly see the scars.
  White water. Fire. Whatever vise
    bears down upon us.

Long afterwards,
  I see her jump,
dark head, arms, legs:
  an eighth, sixteenth note
    quickening as she falls.

Richard Goldberg

Beckian Fritz Goldberg

Born May 9, 1954, in Hartford, Wisconsin. Beckian Fritz Goldberg's most recent poetry collections are *The Book of Accident* (University of Akron Press, 2006) and *Lie Awake Lake*, winner of the 2004 *FIELD* Poetry Prize (Oberlin College Press, 2005). Other awards include the Theodore Roethke Poetry Prize, the University of Akron Poetry Prize, and two Arizona Arts Commission Poetry Fellowships. Her work appears in anthologies and journals including *Best American Poetry, American Poetry Review, The Gettysburg Review*, and *Harper's*. She teaches at Arizona State University and lives with her husband and two cats in Carefree, Arizona, where the post office is on Easy Street, near the intersection of Ho and Hum Roads—no kidding!

List

It was all new.
One day I bought birds-of-paradise.
One day I cleaned the oven.
One day I made a list.
The next

I did the list.
One day I sat out and watched
yellow burrs fall from
the sweet acacias.
I did

all the being you
I could, father,

all the rest
of this life.

Mimesis as Part of the Body

We are what we repeat
like the breath itself an ocean
the eye itself a fish,
the belly—soup
brought to its first bubble,
the clear omphalos.
Mine repeating you over
and over, the heart
beating up through the sex,

each step, each bump,
each fall like the last,
body of leaves, body of no mercy,
the breast repeating itself
and the sternum a pond
where shadow repeats its lips, oh,
love is everywhere, isn't it?
The guitar is everywhere, isn't it,
the moon and the wrinkled purse
the fig drops once in childhood,
seven times in memory,
a sickly droning of the blood
when a child puts her finger
in her ears at night
and vows to stay
the way she is forever . . .

Prologue as Part of the Body

It begins with something backward—
gardenia tucked behind
the ear as if scent could hear
its undoing

the fantastic bodice of a space
no larger than this plump
of sweetness, yeastlike, tropic

it begins with a turning, a trope,
that fragrance spiraling the cochlea
and the body confused by the enchantment
of the wrong orifice wrong passage—it was

after all where music should be unwinding,
cry shedding its epithelial layers, the tac-tac
of someone entreating, far away, some door . . .

But it was summer trying to enter, swoon its way
into the skull, the Parfum Fatale collapsing
on the organ of Corti

a secret island discovered by the Italian anatomist
of the last century though it was always there
in the body, the locus of quivering
like the letter M

deep in its alphabet, the humming
on either side. Beginning is

the flower to the ear
the flute to the palm, the glittering mirror to
the back of the head, the steaming rice and the plums
in honey

to the feet, to the vertebrae, to the pineal gland:

oblivion, oblivion, oblivion.

Wren

Once I fished a wren
from the pool
held it

little volt
in my hand

This I won't forget:

my mother's shoulders

I'm in the backseat
holding my brother's hand

my sister is driving

I don't have to see
anyone's face

the box of ashes
queerly heavy
like metal

like
the soaked sleeve of your sweater

long ago

the way something would rather drown
than trust

the hand that would lift it

Open

In the city of it
how soon grief
becomes exhaustion—

buildings pain-high
sheening like lead in the March sun,
here

and there, a crust of snow.
Sometimes in the middle of dinner
I want to go to sleep.
Sometimes

in the middle of this
white, white, separating rose
I have to
shut my eyes—
unearthly civilization—

the fumes, the radios, the nervous
buses, the man at the pay phone
shouting, So you're leaving me—

hates me for hearing—
but once

the wound is open, it all
must go that way . . .

Hal Lum

Linda Gregg

Born September 9, 1942, in Suffern, New York. Linda Gregg's seven collections of poetry include, most recently, *In the Middle Distance* (Graywolf Press, 2006), *Things and Flesh* (1999), and *Chosen by the Lion* (1994). Her honors include fellowships from the Guggenheim Foundation, the Lannan Literary Foundation, and the National Endowment for the Arts, and a Whiting Writer's Award. She was the 2003 winner of the Sara Teasdale Award and the 2006 PEN/Voelcker Award winner for Poetry. She has taught at the University of Iowa, Columbia University, and the University of California at Berkeley. She currently lives in New York and teaches at Princeton University.

Elegance

All that is uncared for.
Left alone in the stillness
in that pure silence married
to the stillness of nature.
A door off its hinges,
shade and shadows in an empty room.
Leaks for light. Raw where
the tin roof rusted through.
The rustle of weeds in their
different kinds of air in the mornings,
year after year.
A pecan tree, and the house
made out of mud bricks. Accurate
and unexpected beauty, rattling
and singing. If not to the sun,
then to nothing and to no one.

The Precision

There is a modesty in nature. In the small
of it and in the strongest. The leaf moves
just the amount the breeze indicates
and nothing more. In the power of lust, too,
there can be a quiet and clarity, a fusion
of exact moments. There is a silence of it
inside the thundering. And when the body swoons,
it is because the heart knows its truth.
There is directness and equipoise in the fervor,
just as the greatest turmoil has precision.
Like the discretion a tornado has when it tears
down building after building, house by house.
It is enough, Kafka said, that the arrow fit

exactly into the wound that it makes. I think
about my body in love as I look down on these
lavish apple trees and the workers moving
with skill from one to the next, singing.

She Writes to the Man Who Writes of Her in His Poems

You tried to hide me in darkness,
tried to live half of your time with me
in the dark. You invented me.
Finally went back to your people.
Were obedient. Were received
with praise. But in the supermarket
you suddenly needed to know
where I was. Turned to face
each direction of the universe
there in the aisle. But nowhere
did anything return to you.
I am here in this morning
with your picture on the table,
leaning against a vase of flowers.
(One of them has fallen in my sleep.)
A bird is singing, repeating
itself over and over. And over.

Like Lot's Wife

The Italian town is empty.
It was built well
but nobody moved in.
She is there maybe
looking for someone.
She won't find him.
She stands in the middle
of the day, blasted
by brightness. In silence.
The stillness meeting
the stillness inside her.

Asking for Directions

We could have been mistaken for a married couple
riding on the train from Manhattan to Chicago

that last time we were together. I remember
looking out the window and praising the beauty
of the ordinary: the in-between places, the world
with its back turned to us, the small neglected
stations of our history. I slept across your
chest and stomach without asking permission
because they were the last hours. There was
a smell to the sheepskin lining of your new
Chinese vest that I didn't recognize. I felt
it deliberately. I woke early and asked you
to come with me for coffee. You said, sleep more,
and I said we only had one hour and you came.
We didn't say much after that. In the station,
you took your things and handed me the vest,
then left as we had planned. So you would have
ten minutes to meet your family and leave.
I stood by the seat dazed by exhaustion
and the absoluteness of the end, so still I was
aware of myself breathing. I put on the vest
and my coat, got my bag and, turning, saw you
through the dirty window standing outside looking
up at me. We looked at each other without any
expression at all. Invisible, unnoticed, still.
That moment is what I will tell of as proof
that you loved me permanently. After that I was
a woman alone carrying her bag, asking a worker
which direction to walk to find a taxi.

I Wage My Life Against This Your Body

I cannot keep you with me. You must live apart,
live far off and die in order to trespass,
as the moon is filled with its own story. As music
dignifies and represents what we are and want to be.
As thistles stand with their blue translations
of the sun after the hillside poppies outside
Mithymna, windblown over the sea, have gone, have
died impossibly of their own blood-red tenderness,
and disappeared. The song, the human song of you,
is seed impregnating the cypress by the grave.
The day focuses the light for a moment just before
it ends, just before the sun goes down and evening
as always tries to make everything seem all right.

Margaretta Mitchell

Marilyn Hacker

Born November 27, 1942, in Bronx, New York. Marilyn Hacker is the author of eleven books of poems, including *Desesperanto* and *Essays on Departure*, and of seven collections of translations from the French of poems by Claire Malroux and by Vénus Khoury-Ghata. She received an Award in Literature of the American Academy of Arts and Letters in 2004. Her translation of Marie Étienne's *King of a Hundred Horsemen* received the first Robert Fagles Translation Award of the National Poetry Series and will be published in 2008. She lives in New York and Paris, where she serves on the editorial board of the literary magazine *Siècle 21*, and has begun studying Arabic.

Glose

Blood's risks, its hollows, its flames
Exchanged for the pull of that song
Bone-colored road, bone-colored sky
Through the white days of the storm
Claire Malroux, "Storm"
Translated by Marilyn Hacker

Once out of the grip of desire,
or, if you prefer, its embrace,
free to do nothing more than admire
the sculptural planes of a face
(are you gay, straight or bi, are you *queer*?)
you still tell your old chaplet of names
which were numinous once, you replace
them with adjectives: witty, severe,
trilingual; abstracting blood's claims,
blood's risks, its hollows, its flames.

No craving, no yearning, no doubt,
no repulsion that follows release,
no presence you can't do without,
no absence an hour can't erase:
the conviction no reason could rout
of being essentially wrong
is dispelled. What feels oddly like peace
now fills space you had blathered about
where the nights were too short or too long,
exchanged for the pull of that song.

But peace requires more than one creature
released from the habit of craving
on a planet that's mortgaged its future
to the lot who are plotting and raving.

There are rifts which no surgeon can suture
overhead, in the street, undersea.
The bleak plain from which you are waving,
mapped by no wise, benevolent teacher
is not a delight to the eye:
bone-colored road, bone-colored sky.

You know that the weather has changed,
yet do not know what to expect,
with relevant figures expunged
and predictions at best incorrect.
Who knows on what line you'll be ranged
and who, in what cause, you will harm?
What cabal or junta or sect
has doctored the headlines, arranged
for perpetual cries of alarm
through the white days of the storm?

Ghazal: *min al-hobbi ma khatal*

for Deema Shehabi

You, old friend, leave, but who releases me from the love that kills?
Can you tell the love that sets you free from the love that kills?

No mail again today. The retired diplomat
stifles in the day's complacency from the love that kills.

What once was home is across what once was a border
which exiles gaze at longingly from the love that kills.

The all-night dancer, the mother of four, the tired young doctor
all contracted HIV from the love that kills.

There is pleasure, too, in writing easy, dishonest verses.
Nothing protects your poetry from the love that kills.

The coloratura keens a triumphant swan song
as if she sipped an elixir of glee from the love that kills.

We learn the maxim: "So fine the thread,
so sharp the necessity" from the love that kills.

The calligrapher went blind from his precision
and yet he claims he learned to see from the love that kills.

Spare me, she prays, from dreams of the town I grew up in,
from involuntary memory, from the love that kills.

Homesick soldier, do you sweat in the glare of this checkpoint
to guard the homesick refugee from the love that kills?

Ghazal: Myself

They say the rules are: be forgotten, or proclaim myself.
I'm reasonably tired of that game, myself.

I watched some friends rush off, called by the wild,
and stayed home to make coffee for the tame myself.

There are actions I was pressured or seduced to,
but for omissions, I can only blame myself.

Do I think that my averted glance
nullifies suffering? First of all, I maim myself.

Did sex ever seem like work to *you*?
Sometimes, five minutes after I came myself.

Although I'm manifestly "not my type"
the one in my bed this morning was, all the same, myself.

Not Elektra, Clytemnestra, nor Iphigenia,
I'll remain an unsung keeper of the flame myself.

Burnished oak surrounds a rectangle of glass
at the top of the stairs, in which I frame myself.

A signature hangs, unwritten, below the last
line on the page, where I'm obliged to name myself.

Glose

> *A child, I knew how sweet departure was*
> *from having never left the skiff*
> *of hills, split open any horizon*
> *but the rain's when it closed off the morning*
> Guy Goffette, "O Caravels"
> Translated by Marilyn Hacker

Staying put provides the solidest
comfort as daylight diminishes at four:

the street becomes, again, a palimpsest
of hours, days, months and years that came before
and what is better was, and what is best
will be its distillation. In the pause
when blinds are drawn, when tea is brewed, when fast-
falling evening makes lamplight seem more
private and privileged, I can be still because
a child, I knew how sweet departure was

and planned, extravagantly, voyages,
encounters, divagations, chronicles
of travel, unpronounced truths, bright lies.
Imagined stonework of facades, and smells
not of tinned soup or ink. Gratuitous
enormities could be enacted, if . . . .
Without constructing model caravels
of balsa-wood or plastic, I saw skies
between the masts, inferred a different life
from never having left the skiff

moored at a dock of dark mahogany
claw feet of overstuffed postwar club chairs
whose own piled or brocade upholstery
recalled cities that were not anywhere
inscribed in that apartment's memory.
There was only one window, opening on
an alley, garbage cans, one tree, a square
of sky on which the day's calligraphy
scribbled in slate-gray rain, anticipation
of hills, split open any horizon.

Now, even tawdry dreams turn polyglot,
suggestion of the wished-for western wind.
Two syntaxes, more tenses, alternate
merging reflections that are less than kind
(and more than kin) into a better plot
that has to do with transformation. Waking
was easy. The street outside was wet: it rained
all night. The sky's washed clean, and I am not
anticipating any leave-taking
but the rain's when it closed off the morning.

1953: The Bus to Menton

Her own displacement seemed easy in comparison.
She had been a reporter. She would be a novelist
and her country (she'd write about it) seemed provincial.
The war was over. Near the roadside, sheaves
were tied. Gossip behind her, a new dialect. She listened.
Beyond sprawled olive terraces, unlike the farms

of home, whose outbuildings circled like a garrison.
Her notebook's lined page waited to be kissed.
The noon heat condensed into a mortal chill
up her spine. A blondish man with rolled-up sleeves
had pushed the bus window open. Sunlight glistened
on the long number tattooed on one of his sunburned arms.

Roy Groething

Rachel Hadas

Born November 8, 1948, in New York, New York. Rachel Hadas is Board of Governors Professor of English at the Newark campus of Rutgers University, where she has taught for many years. She lives in New York City. Her most recent book of poems is *The River of Forgetfulness* (David Robert Books, 2006) and of prose is *Classics, Selected Prose* (Textos Books, 2007). She has a new poetry manuscript, *The Ache of Appetite*, and is currently co-editing an anthology, due out from Norton in 2009/10, of Greek poetry in translation from Homer to the present. She is also at work on a series of prose pieces about her husband's neurodegenerative condition.

The Red Hat

It started before Christmas. Now our son
officially walks to school alone.
Semi-alone, it's accurate to say;
I or his father track him on the way.
He walks up on the east side of West End,
we on the west side. Glances can extend
(and do) across the street; not eye contact.
Already ties are feeling and not fact.
Straus Park is where these parallel paths part;
he goes alone from there. The watcher's heart
stretches, elastic in its love and fear,
toward him as we see him disappear,
striding briskly. Where two weeks ago,
holding a hand, he'd dawdle, dreamy, slow,
he now is hustled forward by the pull
of something far more powerful than school.

The mornings we turn back to are no more
than forty minutes longer than before,
but they feel vastly different—flimsy, strange,
wavering in the eddies of this change,
empty, unanchored, perilously light
since the red hat vanished from our sight.

Conklin 455, 3:55 PM, Wednesday, March 3, 2004

Hardy's kneeling oxen; Merrill's sword
dangling death over the youth in bed;
Frost's lover hankering for a counter-word;
Ransom's white geese that cried in goose Alas—

you poems we read my brother in those last
phone calls, so that instead of silences
the valedictory music of each phrase
filled his weeks and days,

help me today, please. Come with me to class.
Up two flights to Conklin Hall, fourth floor.
Pause; door is closed. Regroup. It's five to four.
Remember who is waiting for me there.

David, who died twelve hours ago,
is part of me, and I am part of you,
Serene, Muhammad, Gladies, Osner, Chad.
I offer you no more than what I've had

lavished on me. Love what you give away:
aha! you get to keep it till you die.
The keeping is synonymous with giving.
My brother gave as long as he was living,

and longer, after, more.
I open the door.

Riverside Park

I've always loved the autumn. Trees bleed amber,
the sun moves south to sink into the river.
For several of these seasons you were here—
if not precisely this noon, bench, or air,
still in New York, October, and inside
my heart. Our timing's trick
was elegantly simple: although sick,
you had not yet died.

How could I resist the chance to share
(shyly at first; more freely the last year)
fusses, ideas, encounters, daily weather?
So for a space we took life in together
reciprocally, since what came your way
you passed along to me.
Experience doubled and then halved kept giving
itself to both as long as both were living.

I pause to watch the afternoon's red ray
advance another notch. Across the way

a mother tends her toddler, and a pair
of strolling lovers vanish in the glare
flung from the river by the westering sun.
I can hardly claim to be alone.
Nevertheless, of all whom autumn's new
russet brocades are draping, none is you.

Crystal Lake

To live life and to comment on it at the same time—
to meta-live—is the preserve of women,
our province and our presence,
women waist-deep in water,
quietly chatting, not missing a narrative beat.

Look back! What's gaining on you?
A seagull struts over to the towel in search of food
but finds only fishing rods, a book of poems,
a bottle a quarter full of tepid Coke,
and a Santa Fe magazine entitled *THE*

which features an interview with the art critic Dave Hickey.
Everybody knows that your parents are assholes
and your grandparents are really great people.
This is just a given. No more to build on there;
the gull stalks off with its cohorts.

At the far end of the beach,
my son and his best friend and his girlfriend are fishing.
Her narrative is nestling under his;
he will not really speak to me, so neither will she in his presence.
Oh lives of males, untalked-of,

untalking; engaged in the act with no
need to construe it beforehand and no soft
voice-over as it is played out.
Oh symmetries of lake, shore, sky; wide bowl
of—you supply the word. I'm running out of names.

Skirts

Deep-girdled, deep-bosomed, floating-gowned—
generic or Homeric terms for what
sways even today above the ground

somewhere between the ankle and the knee.
If I had to concoct an epithet
for women facing fifty, I'd say *vast—*
skirted—longish, full, and swinging free,
and gathered (not too tightly) at the waist,
whose well-worn cottons—calico, batik,
faded denim—furnish a good gauge
(a single downward glance, no need to speak)
less of chronology or build than how
we carry it, this soft, this post-maternal age
enfolding half our bodies, old and new.

The Bond

The tact, the decorum, the gradual distancing
of parents and growing children
in their delicate dance of disengagement

tugs, repels both sides. By twelve or so
I could see clearly that my mother
preferred her best friend's company to mine,

but I moved past this pothole on the long
road of adolescent self-absorption,
so that by the time my mother died

and this same friend of hers could not conceal
her grief, but even more, her disappointment
that I, the daughter, should be such a dog

in the manger of the living, while her dear
friend was nowhere to be found—I think
I understood. I even sympathized.

This double memory helps me now I see
my son turn to his friends first, not to me,
as for that matter I turn first to mine,

not that the bond between
mother and daughter, mother and son
fails to pull taut every now and then,

and twang, and hum.

Bayard Stern

Barbara Hamby

Born July 29, 1952, in New Orleans, Louisiana. Barbara Hamby's third book of poems, *Babel*, was chosen by Stephen Dunn to win the 2003 AWP Prize and was published by the University of Pittsburgh Press. Other awards include a Pushcart Prize and inclusion in the *Best American Poetry* series. She and her husband, David Kirby, guest edited Issue 128 of *TriQuarterly*. Hamby teaches at Florida State University and is an inveterate packrat. Her many collections include kimonos, Bakelite bracelets, milagros, 45-rpm records, pre-1965 Barbie dolls, plumeria trees, and nurse novels.

I Beseech Thee, O Yellow Pages

I beseech thee, O Yellow Pages, help me find a number
for Barbara Stanwyck, because I need a tough broad
in my corner right now. She'll pour me a tumbler
of scotch or gin and tell me to buck up, show me the rod
she has hidden in her lingerie drawer. She has a temper,
yeah, but her laugh could take the wax off a cherry-red
Chevy. "Shoot him," she'll say merrily, then scamper
off to screw an insurance company out of another wad
of dough. I'll be left holding the phone or worse, patsy
in another scheme, arrested by Edward G. Robinson
and sent to Sing Sing, while Barbara lives like Gatsby
in Thailand or Tahiti, gambling the night away until the sun
rises in the east, because there are some things a girl can be sure
of, like morning coming after night's inconsolable lure.

The Language of Bees

The language of bees contains 76 distinct words for stinging,
        distinguishes between a prick, puncture,
and mortal wound, elaborates on cause and effect as in a sting
        made to retaliate, irritate, insinuate, infuriate,
incite, rebuke, annoy, nudge, anger, poison, harangue.
        The language of bees has 39 words for queen—
regina apiana, empress of the hive, czarina of nectar,
        maharani of the ovum, sultana of stupor,
principessa of dark desire. The language of bees
        includes 22 words for sunshine, two for rain—
big water and small water, so that a man urinating
        on an azalea bush in the full fuchsia of April
has the linguistic effect of a light shower in September.
        For man, two words—roughly translated—
"hands" and "feet," the first with the imperialistic connotation
        of beekeeper, the second with the delicious

resonance of bareness. All colors are variations on yellow,
        from the exquisite sixteen-syllable word meaning
"diaphanous golden fall," to the dirty ochre of the bitter pollen
        stored in the honeycomb and used by bees for food.

The language of bees is a language of war. For what is peace
        without strife but the boredom of enervating
day-after-day, obese with sweetness, truculent with ennui?
        Attack is delightful to bees, who have hundreds of verbs
embracing strategy, aim, location, velocity: swift, downward swoop
        to stun an antagonist, brazen, kamikaze strike
for no gain but momentum. Yet stealth is essential to bees,
        for they live to consternate their enemies, flying up pant legs,
hovering in grass. No insect is more secretive than the bee,
        for they have two thousand words describing the penetralia
of the hive: octagonal golden chamber of unbearable moistness,
        opaque tabernacle of nectar, sugarplum of polygonal waxy walls.

The language of bees is a language of aeronautics,
        for they have wings—transparent, insubstantial,
black-veined like the fall of an exotic iris.
        For they are tiny dirigibles, aviators
of orchard and field. For they have ambition, cunning,
        and are able to take direct aim.
For they know how to leave the ground, to drift, hover,
        swarm, sail over the tops of trees.

The language of bees is a musical dialect, a full, humming
        congregation of hallelujahs and amens,
at night blue and disconsolate, in the morning bright and bedewed.
        The language of bees contains lavish adjectives
praising the lilting fertility of their queen: fat, red-bottomed
        progenitor of millions, luscious organizer of coitus,
gelatinous distributor of love. The language of bees
        is in the jumble of leaves before rain,
in the quiet night rustle of small animals, for it is eloquent
        and vulgar in the same mouth,
and though its wound is sweet it can be distressing,
        as if words could not hurt or be meant to sting.

Betrothal in B Minor

All women bewail the betrothal of any woman,
beamy-eyed, bedazzled, throwing a fourth finger

about like a marionette. Worse than marriage
in many ways, an engagement, be it moments or millennia,

is a morbid exercise in hope, a mirage, a romance
befuddled by magazine photographs of lips, eyebrows,

brassieres, B-cups, bromides, bimbos bedaubed
with kohl, rouged, bespangled, beaded, beheaded,

really, because a woman loses the brain
she was born with if she believes for a moment

she of all women will escape enslavement of mind,
milk, mooring, the machinations of centuries,

to arrive in a blissful, benign, borderless
Brook Farm where men are uxorious, mooning,

bewitched, besotted, bereft of all beastly,
beer-guzzling qualities. Oh, no, my dear

mademoiselle, marriage is no *déjeuner sur l'herbe*,
no bebop with Little Richard for eternity,

no bedazzled buying spree at Bergdorf or Bendel,
no clinch on the beach with Burt Lancaster.

Although it is sometimes all these things, it is
more often, to quote la Marquise de Merteuil, "War,"

but war against the beastliness within that makes
us want to behave, eat beets, buy beef at the market,

wash with Fab, betray our beautiful minds
tending to the personal hygiene of midgets.

My God, Beelzebub himself could not have manufactured
a more Machiavellian maneuver to bedevil an entire

species than this benighted impulse to replicate
ourselves ad nauseam in the confines of a prison

so perfect, bars are redundant. Even in the Bible
all that begetting and begatting only led to misery,

morbidity, Moses, and murder. I beseech you,
my sisters, let's cease, desist, refrain,

take a breather, but no one can because we are
driven by tiny electrical sparks that bewilder,

befog, beguile, becloud our angelic intellect.
Besieged by hormones, we are stalked by a disease

unnamed, a romantic glaucoma. We are doomed to die,
bespattered and besmirched beneath the dirt,

under the pinks and pansies of domestic domination.
Oh, how I loathe you—perfect curtains, exquisite chairs,

crème brulée of my dreams. Great gods of pyromania,
begrudge not your handmaiden, your fool, the flames

that fall from your fiery sky, for my dress is tattered
and my shoes are different colors, blue and red.

Ode to My 1977 Toyota

Engine like a Singer sewing machine, where have you
        not carried me—to dance class, grocery shopping,
into the heart of darkness and back again? O the fruit
        you've transported—cherries, peaches, blueberries,
watermelons, thousands of Fuji apples—books,
        and all my dark thoughts, the giddy ones, too,
like bottles of champagne popped at the wedding of two people
        who will pass each other on the street as strangers
in twenty years. Ronald Reagan was president when I walked
        into Big Chief Motors and saw you glimmering
on the lot like a slice of broiled mahi mahi or sushi
        without its topknot of tuna. Remember the months
I drove you to work singing "Some Enchanted Evening"?
        Those were scary times. All I thought about
was getting on I-10 with you and not stopping. Would you
        have made it to New Orleans? What would our life
have been like there? I'd forgotten about poetry. Thank God,
        I remembered her. She saved us both. We were young
together. Now we're not. College boys stop us at traffic lights
        and tell me how cool you are. Like an ice cube, I say,
though you've never had air conditioning. Who needed it?
        I would have missed so many smells without you—
confederate jasmine, magnolia blossoms, the briny sigh
        of the Gulf of Mexico, rotting possums scattered

along 319 between Sopchoppy and Panacea. How many holes
 are there in the ballet shoes in your back seat?
How did that pair of men's white loafers end up in your trunk?
 Why do I have so many questions, and why
are the answers like the animals that dart in front of your headlights
 as we drive home from the coast, the Milky Way
strung across the black velvet bowl of the sky like the tiara
 of some impossibly fat empress who rules the universe
but doesn't know if tomorrow is December or Tuesday or June first.

Andrea Hollander Budy

Lola Haskins

Born November 13, 1943, in New York, New York. Desire Lines: New and Selected Poems (BOA, 2004) and *The Rim Benders* (Anhinga, 2001) are the most recent poetry collections by Lola Haskins. Two prose books appeared in 2007: *Not Feathers Yet: A Beginner's Guide to the Poetic Life* (Backwaters Press) and *Solutions Beginning with A*, fables about women, with images by Maggie Taylor (Modernbook). Retired from teaching Computer Science at the University of Florida, Haskins now teaches in the Rainier Writers Workshop, a low-residency MFA program in Washington. Haskins is a passionate lover of swamp, river, salt marsh, and mountains. She has begun to study north Indian classical singing.

To Play Pianissimo

Does not mean silence,
the absence of moon in the day sky
for example.

Does not mean barely to speak,
the way a child's whisper
makes only warm air
on his mother's right ear.

To play pianissimo
is to carry sweet words
to the old woman in the last dark row
who cannot hear anything else,
and to lay them across her lap like a shawl.

Fortissimo

To play fortissimo
hold something back.

It is what the father does not say
that turns the son.

The fact that the summit cannot be seen
that drives the climber on.

Consider the graceless ones:
the painter who adds one more brush stroke.

the poet of least resistance
who writes past the end of his poem.

For Someone Considering Death

I told you.
Life is one big Hanon
up and down the piano,
ten fingers skipping over each other
in every conceivable way,
two hands getting stronger.

And sure,
the notes are the same for everyone,
but you can choose to whisper or shout,
to fade or grow.
And haven't you noticed that some people's hands sing,
but others are Midwestern on the keys,
each crescendo a secretarial swell.

Think about this.
How can you dream to play the *Pathétique*,
how can the moment come to truly look
into someone's eyes
and say, *The hell with everything, I love you*,
when you haven't done your time,
hour after hour, year after year
in that small closed room.

For Mother, After the Vision Fire

Point Reyes, California

It is what you secretly thought, lying in bed at night.
That when you die, your particulars will disappear.
The kitchen where you held the coffeepot under
the faucet every morning at seven-ten exactly,
the frayed arms of the couches you had not replaced
because you were nearing your own death.
Instead, it all went first.
                    The nutmeg wreath, the crèche,
the Christmas bells. The tall shelves of books you'd
have read if you had not run out of time. The painting
of the boy lying on his dreamy back that Daddy gave
you with such ceremony one birthday, having hidden
it for weeks in the garage. A list of losses to dry up
your pen. You were not there as witness. That was
no surprise.

But how obscene it is, you here now,
poking at the warm ground, disturbing only ash that
puffs in soft grey clouds around the tennis shoes you
always wear. Like some human part, projecting hard
from the detritus of your burnt life, that you see
and do not want to name.

Dogwood, December

for Peter Behr, 1915–1997

We notice not going but absence.
And therefore, looking through
the window at the framed tree,
for the first time we see its bones

and understand that the night
brought flurries, which lie
now on busy ground, out of
our line of view. And we think

how gray it is, how even the air
in the house seems gray. But
then we sense vibrations not quite
flutters, and a bunting, dazzling

as lazuli, appears, and another;
and then a canary in shy gold,
three cardinals, and a tiny
woodpecker, black and white,

with a crest bright as the tip
of a child's nose, who pecks
at the berries from underneath.
William Henry Hudson wrote

that the sky is always full of wings
but we do not see them unless
there is a storm. I used to think this
poetic, but untrue. I believe it now.

Words

Some hang in the air like diesel fumes.
Some spread with the scent of
flowering vines, so a child, playing in
a cross-town park lifts her head,
and wonders what is about to happen.
Some arrive in flocks, to chitter side
by side on wires which vibrate
with their weight, like plucked strings.
Others camp wherever they can find
on the hard white winter of the page.
Growing cold and colder, they dig
into the snow. They hold each other,
say out loud what would have been
too large, too foolish. Night falls.
In the morning the page is blank again.

Nick Rosza

Jane Hirshfield

Born February 24, 1953, in New York, New York. Jane Hirshfield's six books of poetry include *After* (HarperCollins, 2006), shortlisted for England's T.S. Eliot Award, and *Given Sugar, Given Salt* (HarperCollins, 2001), a finalist for the National Book Critics Circle Award. Also the author of *Nine Gates: Entering the Mind of Poetry* (HarperCollins, 1997), she has edited and co-translated three books collecting the work of women poets from the past. She received fellowships from the National Endowment for the Arts, the Guggenheim and Rockefeller Foundations, and The Academy of American Poets, among other honors. Her books have been on bestseller lists in San Francisco, Detroit, Krakow, and Canberra, and she has been featured in two Bill Moyers PBS specials.

A Hand Is Shaped for What It Holds or Makes

A hand is shaped for what it holds or makes.
Time takes what's handed to it then—warm bread, a stone,
a child whose fingers touch the page to keep her place.

Beloved, grown old separately, your face
shows me the changes on my own.
I see the histories it holds, the argument it makes

against the thresh of trees, the racing clouds, the race
of birds and sky birds always lose:
          the lines have ranged, but not the cheek's strong bone.
My fingers touching there recall that place.

Once we were one. Then what time did, and hands, erased
us from the future we had owned.
For some, the future holds what hands release, not make.

We made a bridge. We walked it. Laced
night's sounds with passion.
Owls' pennywhistles, after, took our place.

Wasps leave their nest. Wind takes the papery case.
Our wooden house, less easily undone,
now houses others. A life is shaped by what it holds or makes.
I make these words for what they can't replace.

The Heat of Autumn

The heat of autumn
is different from the heat of summer.
One ripens apples, the other turns them to cider.

One is a dock you walk out on,
the other the spine of a thin swimming horse
and the river each day a full measure colder.
A man with cancer leaves his wife for his lover.
Before he goes she straightens his belts in the closet,
rearranges the socks and sweaters inside the dresser
by color. That's autumn heat:
her hand placing silver buckles with silver,
gold buckles with gold, setting each
on the hook it belongs on in a closet soon to be empty,
and calling it pleasure.

All Day the Difficult Waiting

All day the difficult waiting.
"Continuance" repeating itself inside the ears,
as if a verb, or choice.

As if Levin during his long spring in *Anna Karenina*—
reading and suffering
because he could not understand what he read or suffered.

Planting and mowing what was outside him.

The heart's actions
are neither sentence nor its reprieve.

Salt hay and thistles, above the cold granite.
One bird singing back to another because it cannot not.

Shadow: An Assay

Mostly we do not think of, even see you,
shadow,
for your powers at first seem few.

Why command "Heel," ask "Sit,"
when before the thought is conceived,
you are already there?

True that sometimes you run ahead, sometimes behind,
that *early* and *late*,
to you, must be words of the deepest poignance:
while inside them, you are larger than you were.

Midday drives you to reticence, sulking,
a silence
I've felt many times inside me as well.

You came with me to Krakow, Glasgow, Corfu.
Did you enjoy them?
                                        I never asked.
Though however close my hand came to the table,
you were closer, touching before my tongue
the herring and cheeses, the turpentine-scented retsina.

Many times I have seen you sacrifice yourself
without hesitation,
disentangling yourself like Anna Karenina from her purse
before passing under the train wheels of her own thoughts.
Like art, though, you are resilient: you rose again.

Are you then afterlife, clutterless premonition?
You shake your head as soon as I do—
no, we think not.
Whatever earth I will vanish silently into, you also will join.

You carry, I have read,
my rages, fears, and self-regard.
You carry, I have read, my unrevealed longings,
and the monster dreamed as a child, tongueless and armless.
Your ordinary loneliness I recognize too as my own.

When you do not exist,
I have gone with you into darkness,

as the self of a former life
goes into the self that was tortured and beaten
and does not emerge again as it was,
though given a clean shirt to leave in, given pants and new shoes.

For this too is shadow, and mine,
however unspoken:
though you are tongueless, and armless, you harm.
Your inaction my own deepest failure, close by my side.

You who take nothing, give nothing, instruct me,
that my fate may weigh more than yours—

The hour is furious, late.
Your reach, horizontal, distant, leans almost forgiving,
almost indistinguishable from what it crosses.

Rainstorm Visibly Shining in the Left-out Spoon of a Leaf

Like grief
in certain people's lives:
as if something
still depended on the straightness of the spine.

Critique of Pure Reason

"Like one man milking a billy-goat,
another holding a sieve beneath it,"
Kant wrote, quoting an unnamed ancient.
It takes a moment to notice the sieve doesn't matter.
In her nineties, a woman begins to sleepwalk.
One morning finding pudding and a washed pot,
another the opened drawers of her late husband's dresser.
After a while, anything becomes familiar,
though the Yiddish jokes of Auschwitz
stumbled and failed outside the barbed wire.
Perimeter is not meaning, but it changes meaning,
as wit increases distance and compassion erodes it.
Let reason flow like water around a stone, the stone remains.
A dog catching a tennis ball lobbed into darkness
holds her breath silent, to keep the descent in her ears.
The goat stands patient for two millennia,
watching without judgment from behind his strange eyes.

The Lost Love Poems of Sappho

The poems we haven't read
must be her fiercest:
imperfect, extreme.
As it is with love, its nights, its days.
It stands on the top of the mountain
and looks for more mountain, steeper pitches.
Descent a thought impossible to imagine.

The Woodpecker Keeps Returning

The woodpecker keeps returning
to drill the house wall.
Put a pie plate over one place, he chooses another.

There is nothing good to eat there:
he has found in the house
a resonant billboard to post his intentions,
his voluble strength as provider.

But where is the female he drums for? Where?

I ask this, who am myself the ruined siding,
the handsome red-capped bird, the missing mate.

Brad Fowler

Marie Howe

Born October 17, 1950, in Rochester, New York. Marie Howe is the author of three volumes of poetry, *Kingdom of Ordinary Time* (2008), *The Good Thief* (1998), and *What the Living Do* (1997), and the co-editor of a book of essays, *In the Company of My Solitude: American Writing from the AIDS Pandemic* (1994). Stanley Kunitz selected Howe for a Lavan Younger Poets Prize from The American Academy of Poets. She has also been a fellow at the Bunting Institute at Radcliffe College and a recipient of fellowships from the Guggenheim Foundation and The National Endowment for the Arts. Currently, Howe teaches creative writing at Sarah Lawrence College, Columbia, and New York University.

Non-violence 2

My daughter doesn't like the fly that keeps bugging her
as she eats her Cheerios this morning

but we had a talk about the ants yesterday, so she says,
The fly is alive, and I am alive, and covers her bowl

with a dish towel which she lifts a little every minute or so
so she can slip in her spoon.

But six hours later I want to murder that fly—landing on my arm
on my knee—want to find a book and flatten it.

This morning's newspaper says the British policeman checking
through the rubble of the bombed subway car thought,

because she was moaning, that the woman was alive. I don't want
to think about Donny who hung flies from his open desktop

and plucked off their wings,
or his gentle younger brother Bobby who killed himself when

he lost a lot of other people's money in the market.
My mother made a point, as she told the story, of mentioning he was

so considerate he pulled a plastic bag over his head before he did it.
A full summer day outside—hot, humid,

the fly that was bothering me, gone who knows where.
Now some detritus falling through the tree branches and air:

blossoms and seeds.

What the Woman Said

I don't want to offend anybody but I never did like
fucking all that much. Like I always say

the saw enjoys the wood more than the wood enjoys
the saw—know what I mean?
                                                  I used to think

I could be like the girl in the movies—
then I watched myself—when it was happening—

my eyes closed, my head tilted back as if I were
him seeing me—and I couldn't feel anything.

I was watching me, and I was someone else who
looked like she was having a good time. Seems like

I spent years like that, watching him (whoever he was)
watching me—I have to admit

it was easier when he left. I'd watch myself watch him
leave and hear the strain of music swell up like a story,

watch myself walk back into the house and close the door
and lean against it.

I want to tell you everything I know about being alive but I
missed a lot of living that way—

My life was a story, dry as pages. Seems like he should have known
enough to lick them even lightly with his thumb

But he didn't. And I have to admit I didn't much like the idea
of telling him how.

Hurry

We stop at the dry cleaners and the grocery store
and the gas station and the green market and
Hurry up honey, I say, hurry hurry,
as she runs along two or three steps behind me
her blue jacket unzipped and her socks rolled down.

Where do I want her to hurry to? To her grave?
To mine? Where one day she might stand all grown?

Today, when all the errands are finally done, I say to her,
Honey I'm sorry I keep saying Hurry—
you walk ahead of me. You be the mother.

And, Hurry up, she says, over her shoulder, looking
back at me, laughing. Hurry up now darling, she says,
hurry, hurry, taking the house keys from my hands.

What the Living Do

Johnny, the kitchen sink has been clogged for days, some utensil probably fell down there.
And the Drano won't work but smells dangerous, and the crusty dishes have piled up

waiting for the plumber I still haven't called. This is the everyday we spoke of.
It's winter again: the sky's a deep headstrong blue, and the sunlight pours through

the open living room windows because the heat's on too high in here, and I can't turn it off.
For weeks now, driving, or dropping a bag of groceries in the street, the bag breaking,

I've been thinking: This is what the living do. And yesterday, hurrying along those
wobbly bricks in the Cambridge sidewalk, spilling my coffee down my wrist and sleeve,

I thought it again, and again later, when buying a hairbrush: This is it.
Parking. Slamming the car door shut in the cold. What you called *that yearning*.

What you finally gave up. We want the spring to come and the winter to pass. We want
whoever to call or not call, a letter, a kiss—we want more and more and then more of it.

But there are moments, walking, when I catch a glimpse of myself in the window glass,
say, the window of the corner video store, and I'm gripped by a cherishing so deep

for my own blowing hair, chapped face, and unbuttoned coat that I'm speechless:
I am living, I remember you.

Michael Trombley

Lynda Hull

Born December 5, 1954, in Newark, New Jersey. Lynda Hull is the author of *Collected Poems* (Graywolf Press, 2006); *The Only World: Poems* (1995); *Star Ledger: Poems* (1991), which won the 1991 Carl Sandburg Award and the 1990 Edwin Ford Piper Award; and *Ghost Money* (1986), which won the Juniper Prize. Recipient of fellowships from the National Endowment for the Arts and the Illinois Arts Council, Hull also received four Pushcart Prizes. She taught English at Indiana University, De Paul University, and in the MFA writing program at Vermont College. She also served as a Poetry Editor for the journal *Crazyhorse*. Hull died in an automobile accident in Plymouth, Massachusetts, on March 29, 1994.

At Thirty

Whole years I knew only nights: automats
& damp streets, the Lower East Side steep

with narrow rooms where sleepers turn beneath
alien skies. I ran when doorways spoke

rife with smoke & zippers. But it was only the heart's
racketing flywheel stuttering *I want, I want*

until exhaustion, until I was a guest in the yoke
of my body by the last margin of land where the river

mingles with the sea & far off daylight whitens,
a rending & yielding I must kneel before, as

barges loose glittering mineral freight
& behind me façades gleam with pigeons

folding iridescent wings. Their voices echo
in my voice naming what is lost, what remains.

Adagio

Across Majestic Boulevard, *Steam Bath*
neons the snow to blue, and on her table
a blue cup steams, a rime of stale cream
circling its rim. Before finding the chipped case

behind the mirror, she waits for morning
the way an addict must wait, a little longer,
and studies the torn print on the wall—
lilies blurred to water stains, a woman

floating in a boat trailing fingers
in its wake. Someone rich. Someone gone.
Maybe a countess. She lets herself drift in the boat
warming thin translucent hands in coffee steam.

She's not a countess, only another girl
from the outer boroughs with a heroin habit as long
as the sea routes that run up and down the coast.
She's read all winter a life of Hart Crane, losing

her place, beginning again with Crane in a room
by the bridge, the East River, spending himself
lavishly. She's spent her night
circulating between piano bars and cabarets

where Greek sailors drink and buy her
cheap hotel champagne at 10 bucks a shot
before evaporating to another port on the map
of terra incognita the waterlilies chart

along her wall. The mantel is greened with
a chemical patina of sweat and time, and she can't
call any of this back. Hart Crane sways,
a bottle of scotch in one hand, his face plunged

inside the gramophone's tin trumpet, jazzed
to graceless oblivion. She rinses her face
in the basin, cold water, then turns to glance
across the boulevard where life's arranged

in all its grainy splendor. The steam bath sign
switches off with dawn, a few departing men
swathed in pea coats. The bath attendant climbs
as always to the roof, then opens the dovecote

to let his pigeons fly before descending to his berth.
They bank and curve toward the harbor that surrenders
to the sea. She knows Crane will leap
from the *Orizaba*'s stern to black fathoms

of water, that one day she'll lock this room
and lose the key. The gas flame's yellow coronet
stutters and she rolls her stocking down at last
to hit the vein above her ankle, until carried forward

she thinks it's nothing but the velocity of the world
plunging through space, the tarnished mirror
slanted on the mantel showing a dove-gray sky
beginning to lighten, strangely, from within.

The Charmed Hour

for my mother

On the radio, gypsy jazz. Django Reinhardt
  puts a slow fire to Ellington's *Solitude*
    while ice cubes pop in your martini. The sting
of lime on my palm. By the sink you lean,
  twisting your rings. Turn to the window.

In shadow you could be sixteen
  again, in your mother's kitchen
    above Cleveland, the cafés of Warsaw still
smoky in your mind with talk and cigarettes,
  English still a raw mystery of verbs.

Windows brighten across the city at the hour
  when voices steam from the street
    like some sadness—the charmed hour
when, smooth as brilliantine, Phil Verona
  with his Magic Violin slides from the radio.

Ice-blue in silk, his All-Girl Orchestra sways
  through the parlor. You let yourself
    step with them, let a gardenia release
its vanilla scent in your hair.
  Over terraces, you dance above vapor-lights,

Gold Coast streets where club doors swing
  like the doors of banks that never fail.
    In back rooms men and women spend themselves
over green baize tables, the ivory poker chips.
  In their chests wings beat, steady

as the longing wakened to from every dream
  of flying. We could shut the door
    on this vertigo, but Mother when we
come to ourselves our feet skim the tiles.
  Spoons shine on the table, and Mother,

we're dancing. I'm mouthing the words
  to a song I never knew, singing when
    evening arrives and flattens the sky
to a last yellow crease of light,
  thin as a knife, as a wish.

Midnight Reports

That's how billboards give up their promises—
they look right into your window, then whisper
sex, success. The Salem girl's smoke plume
marries the gulf between the high-rise projects,
the usual knife's edge ballet enacted nightly there
for the benefit of no one. It's just that
around midnight every love I've known flicks open
like a switchblade and I have to start talking,
talking to drown out the man in the radio
who instructs me I'm on the edge of a new day
in this city of Newark which is not a city

of roses, just one big hockshop. I can't tell you
how it labors with its grilled storefronts, air
rushing over the facts of diamonds, appliances,
the trick carnations. But you already know that.
The M-16 Vinnie sent—piece by piece—from Vietnam
is right where you left it the day you skipped town
with the usherette of the Paradise Triple-X Theater.
You liked the way she played her flashlight down
those rows of men, plaster angels flanked around
that screen. Sometimes you'd go fire rounds over
the landfill, said it felt better than crystal meth,
a hit that leaves a trail of neon, ether.

I keep it clean, oiled, and some nights it seems
like a good idea to simply pick up that rifle
and hold it, because nothing's safe. You know
how it is: one minute you're dancing, the next you're flying
through plate glass and the whole damn town is burning
again with riots and looters, the bogus politicians.
We'd graduated that year, called the city ours,
a real bed of Garden State roses. I've drawn x's
over our eyes in the snapshot Vinnie took commencement
night, a line of x's over our linked hands. The quartet
onstage behind us sang a cappella—four brothers
from Springfield Ave. spinning in sequined tuxedos,

palms outstretched to the crowd, the Latin girls
from Ironbound shimmering in the brief conflagration
of their beauty, before the kids, before
the welfare motels, corridors of cries and exhalations.
I wore the heels you called my blue suede shoes,
and you'd given yourself a new tattoo, my name across
your bicep, in honor of finishing, in honor of the future
we were arrogant enough to think would turn out right.
I was laughing in that picture, laughing when the rain
caught us later and washed the blue dye from my shoes—
blue, the color of bruises, of minor regrets.

Allison Joseph

Allison Joseph

Born January 18, 1967, in London, England. Allison Joseph is the author of five books of poems, most recently *Imitation of Life* (Carnegie-Mellon University Press, 2003) and *Worldly Pleasures* (Word Press, 2004). In 2007, she received an Individual Artists Fellowship in Poetry from the Illinois Arts Council and a $5,000 prize in the Dorothy Sargent Rosenberg Annual Poetry Competition. She lives and works in Carbondale, Illinois, where she's on the faculty at Southern Illinois University. She serves as editor and poetry editor of *Crab Orchard Review*, a national journal of creative works, and directs the Young Writers Workshop, an annual summer conference for teenaged writers.

Falling Out of History

> *The rage of the disesteemed is personally fruitless, but it is also inevitable: this rage, so generally discounted, so little understood among the people whose daily bread it is, is one of the things that makes history.*
>
> James Baldwin

On TV the friendly pickaninny
wags his head, dances a buck and wing,
so black the whites of his eyes
bulge as he rolls them back.
Damn cartoon, I think, as my cousin,
age four, does not move, watching
this prancing boy loll his head.
I thought this was behind us, past tense,
like separate fountains, lunch counters.
Still, in the language, it's *black magic,*
black widow, black-and-blue.
At twelve, I wanted to control it,
lured to Woolworth's messy aisles
by cheap perfume, eye shadow, rouge.
With effort, I could be pretty,
fade myself into one polished certainty
of skin, until I didn't offend, not black
but something I couldn't recognize.
My mother would close a wet thumb and forefinger
over my nose, hoping to narrow it.
Nothing changed. Phillis Wheatley,
country of origin unknown, came
to America at seven, by thirteen wrote poems,
at twenty wrote: *Some view that sable race*
with scornful eye: "Their color is a
diabolic dye." I open the paper, read:
Slavery brought blacks here to share
in the country with the greatest opportunity
on earth . . . a man in Michigan calls racism

unfair, asks *Would anyone know Cosby,*
Jackson or Murphy if they were born in Africa?
Phillis wrote: *I, young in life, was snatched*
from Africa's fancied happy seat—her nation's curio,
the foreword to her poems signed by eighteen
famous Massachusetts men. Finally freed,
she died alone at thirty-one, obscure
in a run-down boarding house.
It's all buying and selling, I think,
try to divine what Phillis knew
beyond pious couplets: *Remember, Christians,*
Negroes black as Cain may be refined and join
the angelic strain. I can't guess much,
my language not falling easily into couplets,
breaking down when I examine it, the concept
of race as actual and arbitrary as anger.
My cousin, bored now with the television,
wanders away, content to push
his fire engine across the floor,
slowly, intently, inch-by-inch.

The Valley of the Shadow

Mornings my mother sang no music,
walked worn tile, efficient,
a woman in need of nothing,

not even her wedding ring, now
dulled bald gold. Her fingers
shaped dumplings from flour

and water, pinched them into balls
she'd flatten with one palm, house
redolent with the stove's kiss

of heat, smell of rising dough.
She'd eat standing up, too busy
to sit when our clutter could

take over, our dishes, crumbs.
I thought she would never need
to be healed, and only rarely

did she come to my bed, chanting
unfamiliar words. She prayed
to forgive, to be forgiven,

psalms a luxury only for this dark.
My mother wanted forgiveness
bestowed upon us like benediction,

and I, sullen, sleepy child,
lay shivering at this voice,
its recitation of the valley

of the shadow of death, a place
so far away I thought we'd never
know it. I lay there, her voice

alive in that dark, a power
I couldn't *see*, couldn't touch,
but knew, solicitous, quivering.

The Inner Life

Today I dare to claim the unnamed,
the deep febrile inner life

I slough off each month, loss that's
one less life gravitated to earth,

no matching sets of x and y,
chromosomes not to build their life

in me, not yet. I'm not yet sad
for that loss, feel no remorse

to wash your seed from me, rinsing
away its scent, the heat I've come

to love, your signature inside me
trailing off to disuse. So much

of what we have we don't use,
content to let our bodies go

only so far before we pull back, out,
stopping to watch each other, take

each other in. Yes, I'm muscle, sinew,
cartilage, artery—yes, my body is gaining

and losing, just as yours is gaining
and losing, our potential seemingly

infinite, as we could not wear away,
never leave behind bones becalmed

and drained. This is chemistry:
this mixing and turning, diminution

of cells and waste, a lessening
I know each month as damp, secret.

Not out of shame now, but out of awe,
I carry this secret, feel allegiance

to the jazzy mechanics of birth, its names—
Fallopian tubes, ovum, uterus.

I can hum these names to myself,
steady against the pain, cramps

pulling deep strings within
the belly. I can chant

this inner life, feel its tension
and release, constriction and ease.

And I can give that life to you,
knowing it safe from ridicule,

knowing it can grow one day
into inestimable riches, wealth of birth.

Heidi Lynne Photography

Julia Spicher Kasdorf

Born December 6, 1962, in Lewistown, Pennsylvania. Julia Spicher Kasdorf's books of poetry include *Eve's Striptease* (University of Pittsburgh Press, 1998) and *Sleeping Preacher* (1992), which received the Agnes Lynch Starrett Poetry Prize and the Great Lakes Colleges Award for New Writing. She is also the author of the biography *Fixing Tradition: Joseph W. Yoder, Amish American* (2003) and *The Body and the Book: Writing from a Mennonite Life, 1991–1999* (2001), which won the Book of the Year Award from the Modern Language Association's Conference on Christianity and Literature. Her poems have appeared in *The New Yorker, Paris Review,* and *Poetry,* as well as numerous anthologies. She teaches creative writing at Pennsylvania State University.

The Knowledge of Good and Evil

When beautiful Snow White bit and swooned
on the dwarfs' cottage stoop, pale bosom heaving,
and a chuckling crone scooted off with her basket
of ruby apples, I shrieked, kicking theater seats.
No hushing would stop me, so I was dragged across
strangers' knees, up a dark, inclined aisle, over
the lobby's red carpet, past ushers sharing smirks
with a candy case lady, out onto the sidewalk
which was just there on Clay Avenue in Jeannette,
Pennsylvania. The glassworks was still going
and Gillespie's still sent receipts in pneumatic tubes
when you bought a slip or new pair of shoes. Only then
I stopped screaming and grasped my shuddering breath,
blinking at parking meters, grateful it was still light
outside that story, which was worse than disobedience
or the snake I saw slithering beyond the frame
of my Bible story page. I'd studied Adam's face
and Eve, who tempted him, hair hiding her breasts
as they walked in that exotic garden, already bent
over with guilt, palm fronds at their waists.
Mom coaxed me back to the lobby, and I hovered
in buttery light by the popcorn machine. *The prince*
returns! She comes back to life! Go in and see!
she crooned with the ushers, but I refused. Even when
they pushed me toward a crack in the dark double doors
and I glimpsed a prince and lavish wedding dress,
I could not believe she was alive and happy ever after.
I was a heretic too insulted by the cross
to accept resurrection. I knew that marriage
is just a trick cooked up by the grown-ups
to keep me from screaming my head off.

Eve's Striptease

Lingerie shopping with Mom, I braced myself
for the wedding night advice. Would I seem
curious enough, sufficiently afraid? Yet
when we sat together on their bed, her words
were surprisingly wise:
        Whatever happens, remember this—
        it keeps getting better and better.
She had to be telling the truth. At ten,
I found a jar of Vaseline in her nightstand,
its creamy grease gouged deep, and dusting
their room each week, I marked the decline
of bedside candles. But she didn't say lust
is a bird of prey or tell me the passion
she passed on to me is no protector of borders.
She'd warned me only about the urges men get
and how to save myself from them. Though
she'd flirt with any greenhouse man
for the best cabbage flats, any grease monkey
under the hood, she never kissed anyone but Dad.
How could she guess that with *Jesus Loves Me*
on my tongue, constantly suffering crushes
on uncles, I would come to find that
almost everything gets better and better?
The tiny bird she set loving in me must
keep on, batting the bars of its cage
in a rage only matched by my cravings
for an ample pantry and golden anniversary.
She let me learn for myself all the desires
a body can hold, how they grow stronger
and wilder with age, tugging in every direction
until it feels my sternum might split
like Adam's when Eve stepped out,
sloughing off ribs.

Sinning

When I was seven, Mom asked if I knew
what rabbits in the hutch were up to.
"Fucking," farm cousins told me long before.
"We call it intercourse," she said
and began the cautionary tales right then—
hurry-up weddings generations back, and look
at the children now: moved away, sloppy,

overweight. Her own name, like the state's,
a reminder forever of a virgin queen,
and her mother's name—Vesta, a pagan
goddess, but her servants were virgins.
At thirteen, I took classes to learn how to ease
my behind into couches without looking down,
to cross legs at the ankles, not knees, and keep hands
cupped on my lap. In *Becoming a Woman*, I read
a fast girl is a blighted rose, no man
wants handled merchandise. I watched sad,
young couples lean together to mumble a confession
before God and a titillated congregation,
earning the kind of church wedding where
everyone turns to check if the bride is showing.
What other sin got such attention? No wonder
I grew weary of bearing that cargo
and finally chose a boy with a saint's name
who would moan from deep in his throat,
"Oh, my God," when I finally broke.

A Pass

Forgive us our trespasses
as we forgive, I softly recite

among strangers, remembering
the hand of an older man

gliding up my thin dress.
I twist free of him,

keep speaking as if he is just
a rich family friend chatting,

and I am still safe
in the shape of my skin.

Of course, it sets me back,
as each death resurrects

the memory of all other deaths,
and you must return to mourn

your full store of passings afresh.
A child cannot be accused

of seducing a neighbor man,
but as the girl grows, the bones

of her cheeks and pelvis jut
like blades beneath her skin,

gorgeous weapons of revenge.
At last, the lusts of *those*

who trespass against us bear
some resemblance to our own:

shame and rage, heavy as coins
sewn in the lining of an exile's coat.

When an immigrant ship went down
in Lake Erie, passengers who refused

to shed their heavy garments
drowned, yards from shore.

Norma Marder

Brigit Pegeen Kelly

Born April 21, 1951, in Palo Alto, California. Brigit Pegeen Kelly wrote *The Orchard* (BOA Editions, 2004); *Song* (1995), winner of the Academy of American Poets Lamont Poetry Prize; and *To the Place of Trumpets* (Yale Series of Younger Poets, 1997). Her work has been included in five volumes of the *Pushcart Prize Anthology* and six volumes of *The Best American Poetry.* Other honors include the Cecil Hemley Award from the Poetry Society of America, a Whiting Writers Award, and fellowships from the Illinois State Council on the Arts, the National Endowment for the Arts, the Guggenheim Foundation, and the New Jersey Council on the Arts. Kelly is a professor of English at the University of Illinois.

Harmony Stoneworks, Late Winter

Sunday is silence in the pit, the gate locked,
the trucks gone, the road all mine, mine the stone wall

I sit upon that borders the field, tree-locked
and locked within a larger field. This is where

the spaniel comes, where the alleys of stubble fill
with darkness and wash him toward me—one-eyed spaniel,

filthy, wearing his patched body like a madman's coat
as he runs up one side of the wall and down the other.

Why does he cross this field of stones and cold, of
sodden cobs the reaper dropped, where the hackberries

wrestle to bring forth new leaves? Why does he run
this ring around me? O spaniel, mad spaniel,

are you lost to the whistle, wet in your master's mouth,
too high-pitched or too remote for my ears, calling you

North, calling you South? Or lost to your small heart
telling you cross, cross space and you will own it?

The swallows build the bank. Are you my fear?
Blind as the wind that works to pull their nests down?

After Your Nap

for Maria

I carry you outside
and we sit on the porch,

before us the vast expanse of bee-studded lawn
and the blank pastel shingle of the housing opposite.

In an upstairs window the dim t-shirt of a man moves,
is swallowed, returns again from shadow—a buoy

indolently bobbing on a gray and mild sea.
You roll away from me and lie on your back,

the small sack of your body filling slowly with itself,
while children careen and call

and I cradle my marriage gently in my lap—
a quiet thing, small, a thing barely breathing,

like those curtains rising so faintly opposite
that could at any moment become taut, full-bellied

or fall to utter stillness.
The sky is ash colored, purple to the North—

they are burning grass from the fields.
The light is growing loose, the way clothes do

after having been worn for a long time.
In wide banded circles the birds rise and fall.

I run my hand over the neat purse of your small belly
the hard knot of your pubis

and think how surely we are contained,
how well our small boundaries love us.

The Thief's Wife

He took things and that was bad, but it also
made me feel pleasure, as when we lay by the lake
and he did things to me in broad daylight
that should not have been done, people walking

arm in arm below who must have seen, but I,
stunned with heat, keeping my eyes shut, thinking
that the world when my eyes were shut
was a world that would forgive those who could not see;
or when, another time, he told me he had slept
years before with his sister, thieving even then,
and suddenly that which I could not have imagined
was mine, hundreds of blackbirds massing
in the air outside my door, and he afraid
I would walk away, but I drawn even more toward
that body that made another body lie down
in darkness under it and die. When you are weak
those who walk with evil and live look strong
to you. And if that which was to be your strength
fails you, you will take strength where you can.
And then there were the things. They were so beautiful.
The axes he sharpened and hung over the fence,
their blades like ships' flags, the sky sailing
over them as over water, raising waves of light, and
the hammers and nails with their fine biting sounds,
and rolls of chicken wire stretched in sagging rows
that the honeysuckle spiraled over
in summer, and the bellies of the pigs, soft
as butter, and the eraser blue spots
beneath the rabbits' ears, and baskets of fruit
which grew pungent as it spoiled, and candy
in gold papers and Scotch in swollen-necked bottles,
and needles and pins, and the silk he brought
me once for my birthday, yards of gray silk,
yards of it, lovely as the herons dropping
on wide wings over the lake. I used those things,
saying This is bad, but using them nonetheless.
I never took anything myself, but what is
the difference? Your hand passes over something
that is stolen and settles on it—the way
chicken feathers settled this morning in the honey
I spilled on the table—and then forever
your hand is one with that thing, forever that thing
is in your room. That is why people steal, I think.
To make things last.

A woman with bibles comes to visit me.
Each time she brings a different man in a shiny
brown suit, and each time I let them in, though at night
I dream that they all become beetles
in my yard, swarming in their slick shells, and no way

to put them out. Still, when a poor woman comes
I give her soup, even if my son
strikes me—we will have more where that came from—
and I feed the dogs in the alley since
my own son is a dog, and sometimes I laugh
when I look up at the clock face of the moon
and think that at least my husband wasn't able
to steal that, for if he had, I would have put my hands
all over it—and never let it go.

Song

Listen: there was a goat's head hanging by ropes in a tree.
All night it hung there and sang. And those who heard it
Felt a hurt in their hearts and thought they were hearing
The song of a night bird. They sat up in their beds, and then
They lay back down again. In the night wind, the goat's head
Swayed back and forth, and from far off it shone faintly
The way the moonlight shone on the train track miles away
Beside which the goat's headless body lay. Some boys
Had hacked its head off. It was harder work than they had imagined.
The goat cried like a man and struggled hard. But they
Finished the job. They hung the bleeding head by the school
And then ran off into the darkness that seems to hide everything.
The head hung in the tree. The body lay by the tracks.
The head called to the body. The body to the head.
They missed each other. The missing grew large between them,
Until it pulled the heart right out of the body, until
The drawn heart flew toward the head, flew as a bird flies
Back to its cage and the familiar perch from which it trills.
Then the heart sang in the head, softly at first and then louder,
Sang long and low until the morning light came up over
The school and over the tree, and then the singing stopped . . . .
The goat had belonged to a small girl. She named
The goat Broken Thorn Sweet Blackberry, named it after
The night's bush of stars, because the goat's silky hair
Was dark as well water, because it had eyes like wild fruit.
The girl lived near a high railroad track. At night
She heard the trains passing, the sweet sound of the train's horn
Pouring softly over her bed, and each morning she woke
To give the bleating goat his pail of warm milk. She sang
Him songs about girls with ropes and cooks in boats.
She brushed him with a stiff brush. She dreamed daily
That he grew bigger, and he did. She thought her dreaming
Made it so. But one night the girl didn't hear the train's horn,

And the next morning she woke to an empty yard. The goat
Was gone. Everything looked strange. It was as if a storm
Had passed through while she slept, wind and stones, rain
Stripping the branches of fruit. She knew that someone
Had stolen the goat and that he had come to harm. She called
To him. All morning and into the afternoon, she called
And called. She walked and walked. In her chest a bad feeling
Like the feeling of the stones gouging the soft undersides
Of her bare feet. Then somebody found the goat's body
By the high tracks, the flies already filling their soft bottles
At the goat's torn neck. Then somebody found the head
Hanging in a tree by the school. They hurried to take
These things away so that the girl would not see them.
They hurried to raise money to buy the girl another goat.
They hurried to find the boys who had done this, to hear
Them say it was a joke, a joke, it was nothing but a joke . . . .
But listen: here is the point. The boys thought to have
their fun and be done with it. It was harder work than they
Had imagined, this silly sacrifice, but they finished the job,
Whistling as they washed their large hands in the dark.
What they didn't know was that the goat's head was already
Singing behind them in the tree. What they didn't know
Was that the goat's head would go on singing, just for them,
Long after the ropes were down, and that they would learn to listen,
Pail after pail, stroke after patient stroke. They would
Wake in the night thinking they heard the wind in the trees
Or a night bird, but their hearts beating harder. There
Would be a whistle, a hum, a high murmur, and, at last, a song,
The low song a lost boy sings remembering his mother's call.
Not a cruel song, no, no, not cruel at all. This song
Is sweet. It is sweet. The heart dies of this sweetness.

Michael Kelly-DeWitt

Susan Kelly-DeWitt

Born December 8, 1947, in San Francisco, California. Susan Kelly-DeWitt is the author of *The Fortunate Islands* (Marick Press, 2008) as well as a number of chapbooks—most recently, *Cassiopeia Above the Banyan Tree, Poems About Hawaii* (Rattlesnake Press, 2007). She has won a number of awards for her work, including a Wallace Stegner Fellowship, and her poetry has also been featured on "Writer's Almanac" and "Verse Daily." Currently an instructor for the University of California Davis Extension, she lives in Sacramento, California, where she is also an exhibiting visual artist and a resurrected book reviewer.

Egrets at Bolinas Lagoon

They looked like callas or tulips
you could gather with a fist

or white amaryllis
you could snip from their shimmering
place in the world

you could slip from their stems
with sharp scissors

but they were toiling
the salt under-veins, tunneling
the weedy caverns

with yellow pickaxes
hunting up
a shining nugget
of flesh.

I thought of Van Gogh again:
"Making progress is like miner's work."

The birds that glowed like headlamps
were transformed by those alchemical
words, into painters and poets.

That same night
I woke nauseous, in a sweat,
with all the old worries.

Pomegranates

My mother, gray bird
beside a white bowl
of pomegranates.

They flare
against her face,
creating an odd
balance.

She is retelling the family
myths. In this one, her mouth
is cut and bleeding, her teeth
pop out like seeds.

It is winter.
My father is King
of the Underworld.

"My whole mouth,"
she explains, drawing open
her lower lip, exposing the hidden
scars, "was pulp."

I memorize exactly, word
for word:

He was quick
and strong, his punch
like a boxer's.

We'd been married
only six months, still newlyweds . . .

as I pluck a pomegranate
from the bowl, hack it

open, place

a single blood
red seed on my tongue.

Crossing the Mojave at Night

This is how we outran
the word *Fugitive*:

The needle climbed
the glowing dial of digits,

the tires lifted off
to become night air

as my father topped
ninety.

The warrant
at his back scratched

its head, flashed
its bloody reds

and began the slow
wail that followed us

across three states.
The swollen vein

at his temple grew
tough as pipeweed.

Why I Don't Like to Travel

They loaded us
into the car—a blue
Pontiac. Father
hid the shotgun, shells
in the trunk; mother
brought along a few
pictures, our clothes.

I have forgotten
what I carried, except
for the small hand
of my brother.

We locked the door
to the tract house.
We said goodbye
to the sweet alyssum
mother had planted.

We left before daylight
and drove through the desert
across the state line.

My father must have thought:
Now I'm safe.
My mother must have worried:
What happens next?

I looked out the window
as the sun came up,
gentle then harsh
in the east.

Roller Derby, 1958

The sound of the rollers, grunts
and gasps; cartilage squinched
under padded knees. An elbow
to ribs, a shoulder to mid-torso
and Weston glided free of the pack

—hands to hips, wrists bent, ankles
flexed, as the referee blew the whistle.
Behind her the others collided, groaned
and toppled in a sorry pile of muscled
pectorals, satin shorts, bone and gristle.

I had never seen such unabashed
toughness in women. Buttressed
against pain, my women were docile,
genteel—their voices like silk
bandages over the wound of talk.

for Joan Weston, in memory

Ken Williams

Jane Kenyon

Born May 23, 1947, in Ann Arbor, Michigan. During her lifetime Jane Kenyon published four books of poetry—*Constance* (1993), *Let Evening Come* (1990), *The Boat of Quiet Hours* (1986), and *From Room to Room* (1978)—and a book of translation, *Twenty Poems of Anna Akhmatova* (1985). In December 1993 she and her husband Donald Hall, whom she married in 1972 when she was a student at the University of Michigan, were the subject of an Emmy Award-winning Bill Moyers documentary, *A Life Together.* At the time of her death from leukemia, in April 1995, Kenyon was New Hampshire's poet laureate. *Otherwise: New and Selected Poems,* was released in 1996 by Graywolf Press.

Coats

I saw him leaving the hospital
with a woman's coat over his arm.
Clearly she would not need it.
The sunglasses he wore could not
conceal his wet face, his bafflement.

As if in mockery the day was fair,
and the air mild for December. All the same
he had zipped his own coat and tied
the hood under his chin, preparing
for irremediable cold.

Prognosis

I walked alone in the chill of dawn
while my mind leapt, as the teachers

of detachment say, like a drunken
monkey. Then a gray shape, an owl,

passed overhead. An owl is not
like a crow. A crow makes convivial

chuckings as it flies,
but the owl flew well beyond me

before I heard it coming, and when it
settled, the bough did not sway.

Happiness

There's just no accounting for happiness,
or the way it turns up like a prodigal
who comes back to the dust at your feet
having squandered a fortune far away.

And how can you not forgive?
You make a feast in honor of what
was lost, and take from its place the finest
garment, which you saved for an occasion
you could not imagine, and you weep night and day
to know that you were not abandoned,
that happiness saved its most extreme form
for you alone.

No, happiness is the uncle you never
knew about, who flies a single-engine plane
onto the grassy landing strip, hitchhikes
into town, and inquires at every door
until he finds you asleep midafternoon
as you so often are during the unmerciful
hours of your despair.

It comes to the monk in his cell.
It comes to the woman sweeping the street
with a birch broom, to the child
whose mother has passed out from drink.
It comes to the lover, to the dog chewing
a sock, to the pusher, to the basket maker,
and to the clerk stacking cans of carrots
in the night.
                                   It even comes to the boulder
in the perpetual shade of pine barrens,
to rain falling on the open sea,
to the wineglass, weary of holding wine.

After an Illness, Walking the Dog

Wet things smell stronger,
and I suppose his main regret is that
he can sniff just one at a time.
In a frenzy of delight
he runs way up the sandy road—
scored by freshets after five days
of rain. Every pebble gleams, every leaf.

When I whistle he halts abruptly
and steps in a circle,
swings his extravagant tail.
Then he rolls and rubs his muzzle
in a particular place, while the drizzle
falls without cease, and Queen Anne's lace
and goldenrod bend low.

The top of the logging road stands open
and bright. Another day, before
hunting starts, we'll see how far it goes,
leaving word first at home.
The footing is ambiguous.

Soaked and muddy, the dog drops,
panting, and looks up with what amounts
to a grin. It's so good to be uphill with him,
nicely winded, and looking down on the pond.

A sound commences in my left ear
like the sound of the sea in a shell;
a downward vertiginous drag comes with it.

Time to head home. I wait
until we're nearly out to the main road
to put him back on the leash, and he
—the designated optimist—
imagines to the end that he is free.

Otherwise

I got out of bed
on two strong legs.
It might have been
otherwise. I ate
cereal, sweet
milk, ripe, flawless
peach. It might
have been otherwise.
I took the dog uphill
to the birch wood.
All morning I did
the work I love.

At noon I lay down
with my mate. It might
have been otherwise.
We ate dinner together
at a table with silver
candlesticks. It might
have been otherwise.
I slept in a bed
in a room with paintings
on the walls, and
planned another day
just like this day.
But one day, I know,
it will be otherwise.

Lynne Knight

Matt Phillips

Born May 27, 1943, in Philadelphia, Pennsylvania. Lynne Knight is the author of four full-length collections and four chapbooks, including most recently *Then Time* (Sixteen Rivers Press, 2009) and *Night in the Shape of a Mirror* (David Roberts Books, 2006). She teaches writing at two San Francisco Bay Area community colleges and lives in the Berkeley hills. Other than poetry, her main obsession is mastering French.

Eighteen

My father was driving over Storm King,
the old highway, carved into the side
of the mountain, sudden curves,
so he had to stare straight ahead
but would have anyway because he was talking
about passion, by which he meant
sex, sex being a word he couldn't say
in reference to me and my boyfriend, to whom
he objected because I'd had sex with him
and written home about it, a long rhapsodic
letter on the loss of my virginity, a shorter
version of which I'd typed out for my grandmother
who wrote back saying my grandfather, two years
dead, would probably have recommended waiting.
My father was telling me passion wouldn't last,
even when passion was good it only lasted
a couple of years, I shouldn't be confusing it
with love and deciding to drop out of school,
run off to Mexico, write novels and screw,
a word he could say, to make me hear
his despair, and all this time I was thinking
What does he know, what does he know,
looking down at my hands
that had been everywhere on my lover,
looking over at my father's hands
that once had held the whole of me,
had moved all over my mother,
What does he know, his hands and mine
both freckled, tensed—
so much tenderness lost
in fear of loss.

Her Story

Who ends up telling it
matters as much as what's told:
Imagine Leda controlling her trembling

as the swan thrust deeper,
losing all sense of time
until she picked at a feather stuck to her thigh,

whispering *It was more*
like death than life. Dissolve to real
time, annihilated by the white sun, the white

man coming into the hut
while the woman lay in shadow, knowing
her screams would only mix in with the cicadas,

the crows, the words he would
deny like the coldness he could feel
trembling through her though she lay still, lay

still enough for death. I
have my own version, woke to it
one morning years ago, someone's hands

at my throat, my voice
through the cloth of the pillowcase
already hollow with what I was about to lose,

had already lost because
sleep had become a place violence
could invade with the dream's ease, the dream's

silence. I tried to tell
the story until it became someone
else's, until the hands at my throat

dissolved, dream image
offering no clear portent,
like the feather from the pillow

stuck to my brow afterwards
when I looked into the mirror and saw
another woman trembling to seize control.

Now There Were More of Them

They were fleeing through the forest
like the children in the story
only now there were more of them,
children, women, even men
too old or maimed to be of use.
The capable men already taken.
Nothing for those remaining but to flee
the takers, who would take her if she
slipped or lost her breath though she was
strong, at twenty, strong enough to make it.
The deeper they fled everything blurring
together like the shadows in her terrors or
words to the story her mother once read to her
over and over. The trees closer together
and in the green blind overhead,
birds singing . . . . She ran. She could hear
her breath like the child at the story:
Go on. Go on. Then images rushing from
the dark mesh of tree trunks:
Blood. Men's faces, grimacing
with lust. Legs forced open—women's, girls'.
In the green overhead, the birds never
stopped, their cries so loud and various
she could not tell her mother's cries . . . .
And now she did slip, her foot
catching in a dirt pocket, the tree
she stumbled against so calm, so still
she embraced it. Then bent to massage
her ankle. How easy to make the noose—
a child could do it, and the tree so adequate . . .

Pure chance, that the photographer found her body hanging
in the trackless forest. The shot taken
of her back, to spare us. And the next day
all of us staring at her picture in the paper
with the same terror we felt at the story
we were too young to read
though we had the rhythms by heart,
knew every word like our blood.

Living Apart

My mother is not a woman I can ask about sex.
Her body is like a building she has driven past
on the way to somewhere else, not paying
much heed. She knows the major stories,
but that's about it. Until she fractured it last year,
she had no idea where her pelvis was.
She speaks of her insides, her plumbing.
But she is not a stupid woman,

so I can talk to her about need.
She knows about the spirit, having lived apart
from the body for so long. She says I mustn't be
too greedy. She loves me, but then there is the world.
The cold place, she calls it. If I could talk to her
about sex, I could ask her if she thinks I crave
the spirit like a lover who just uses you,
takes and takes and then leaves—

if that's what she means by my greed.
We all need something, she said the other day
when I visited. She was looking out at the woman
who walks up and down the street all day long
like someone who's lost her door.
The poor soul, my mother says, and waves,
though the woman can't see her.
I want to know if the hollow my mother feels then

is the same as I feel after sex, like watching
someone lose the body altogether in the distance.
But when I talk about my lover, simple things
like how he fixes salmon, a little lime and butter,
cilantro, my mother looks away, as if I'm talking
of sex in disguise. So instead I sit quiet, like spirit,
thinking if I practice living apart from the body,
my greed for hers won't break me when she's gone.

Andrea Hollander Budy

Maxine Kumin

Born June 6, 1925, in Philadelphia, Pennsylvania. Maxine Kumin's most recent collections are *Jack and Other New Poems* (2005) and *Still to Mow* (2007), both from W. W. Norton. In 2005 she received the Harvard University Arts Medal and in 2006 the Robert Frost Medal from the Poetry Society of America. Kumin is Distinguished Poet-in-Residence in the low-residency MFA program of New England College. She also teaches a June workshop in the Fine Arts Work Center in Provincetown, Massachusetts. She and her husband live on a farm in Warner, New Hampshire, with their first foal, now thirty-three years old, two other retired horses, and two rescued dogs.

A Brief History of English Romanticism

How chaste was it? Does it matter?
Did ever a poet have such a sister?

It's true that he gave her the ring
to wear all day the day before his wedding

which she didn't attend for fear
of drenching the ceremony with tears.

For seven years she'd had him
to herself, her only William,

without a murmur she'd gone with him
to settle his finances on "Mme Williams"

who'd been his mistress, and the child he'd never seen,
nine-year-old adorable Caroline.

I love that they all bathed together that day,
a make-believe family on the beach at Calais.

And later, the rift with Coleridge, by then a goner—
to think two men who'd been closer than blood brothers

could break up over poetry
and years go by in icy formalities . . . .

Well, two of my brothers died unreconciled
though neither was addicted, merely livid

with rage at the other. At least Will and Sam
closed lovingly despite the wrack of laudanum

and even though *Christobel, Part Two*
never got written and William's few

late poems didn't add much to his oeuvre
nothing could detract from that first creative surge

side by side those months in the Quantock hills
and I'll never forget how Coleridge walked 40 miles

to meet Wordsworth, the very beginning of this story
that leads us back into the title: A Brief History . . . .

Coleridge's Laundry

I wanted to talk about Coleridge
who was anything but handsome
and was always leaving his wife

to walk amazing distances
for conversations with his pals:
Poole, Lamb, Wordsworth et al.

I said, so what if the Pantisocratic
ideal was just another hippie
utopia where everyone labored by hand

in the morning and studied or wrote
in the afternoon? So what if the project
conceived in poverty went down

in unexpected endowments,
the Lannans and MacArthurs of their day?
I wanted to read about laudanum:

how many drops at bedtime and
did he add them to water or tea
or something stronger.

When I closed my book I fell
asleep as instantly as if I'd downed
50 drops in two fingers of Scotch straight up.

In my dream this poem was given
a communion wafer
and a blood transfusion.

I woke with baked cotton on my tongue.
My pulse was vigorous, my heart
was with Sara, the mountain

of laundry, her always absent Coleridge.
Domesticity and migraines,
miles and miles on foot.

Nurture

From a documentary on marsupials I learn
that a pillowcase makes a fine
substitute pouch for an orphaned kangaroo.

I am drawn to such dramas of animal rescue.
They are warm in the throat. I suffer, the critic proclaims,
from an overabundance of maternal genes.

Bring me your fallen fledgling, your bummer lamb,
lead the abused, the starvelings, into my barn.
Advise the hunted deer to leap into my corn.

And had there been a wild child—
filthy and fierce as a ferret, he is called
in one nineteenth-century account—

a wild child to love, it is safe to assume,
given my fireside inked with paw prints,
there would have been room.

Think of the language we two, same and not-same,
might have constructed from sign,
scratch, grimace, grunt, vowel:

Laughter our first noun, and our long verb, howl.

Watering Trough

Let the end of all bathtubs
be this putting out to pasture
of four Victorian bowlegs
anchored in grasses.

Let all longnecked browsers
come drink from the shallows
while faucets grow rusty
and porcelain yellows.

Where once our nude forebears
soaped up in this vessel
come, cows, and come, horses.
Bring burdock and thistle,

come slaver the scum of
timothy and clover
on the cast-iron lip that
our grandsires climbed over

and let there be always
green water for sipping
that muzzles may enter thoughtful
and rise dripping.

Waiting to Be Rescued

There are two kinds of looting,
the police chief explained.
When they break into convenience stores
for milk, juice, sanitary products,
we look the other way.

When they hijack liquor, guns,
ammunition, we have to go in
and get them even though
we've got no place to put them.

Hoard what you've got,
huddle in the shade by day,
pull anything that's loose
over you at night, and wait
to be plucked by helicopter,

saved by pleasure craft,
coast guard skiff,
air mattress, kiddie pool,
upside down cardboard box
that once held grapefruit juice

or toilet paper, and remember
what Neruda said: poetry should be useful
and usable like metal and cereal.
Five days without shelter,
take whatever's useful.

Death, Etc.

I have lived my whole life with death, said William Maxwell,
aetat ninety-one, and haven't we all. Amen to that.
It's all right to gutter out like a candle but the odds are better

for succumbing to a stroke or pancreatic cancer.
I'm not being gloomy, this bright September
when everything around me shines with being:

hummingbirds still raptured in the jewelweed,
puffballs humping up out of the forest duff
and the whole voluptuous garden still putting forth

bright yellow pole beans, deep-pleated purple cauliflowers,
to say nothing of regal white corn that feeds us
night after gluttonous night, with a slobber of butter.

Still, Maxwell's pronouncement speaks to my body's core,
this old body I trouble to keep up the way
I keep up my two old horses, wiping insect deterrent

on their ears, cleaning the corners of their eyes,
spraying their legs to defeat the gnats, currying burrs
out of their thickening coats. They go on grazing thoughtlessly

while winter is gathering in the wings. But it is not given
to us to travel blindly, all the pasture bars down,
to seek out the juiciest grasses, nor to predict

which of these two will predecease the other or to anticipate
the desperate whinnies for the missing that will ensue.
Which of us will go down first is also not given,

a subject that hangs unspoken between us
as with Jocasta, who begs Oedipus not to inquire further.
Meanwhile, it is pleasant to share opinions and mealtimes,

to swim together daily, I with my long slow back and forths,
he with his hundred freestyle strokes that wind him alarmingly.
A sinker, he would drown if he did not flail like this.

We have put behind us the State Department tour
of Egypt, Israel, Thailand, Japan that ended badly
as we leapt down the yellow chutes to safety after a botched takeoff.

We have been made at home in Belgium, Holland, and Switzerland,
narrow, xenophobic Switzerland of clean bathrooms and much butter.
We have travelled by Tube and Metro *in the realms of gold*

paid obeisance to the Wingèd Victory and the dreaded Tower,
but now it is time to settle as the earth itself settles
in season, exhaling, dozing a little before the fall rains come.

Every August when the family gathers, we pose
under the ancient willow for a series of snapshots,
the same willow, its lumpish trunk sheathed in winking aluminum

that so perplexed us forty years ago, before we understood
the voracity of porcupines. Now hollowed by age and marauders,
its aluminum girdle painted dull brown, it is still leafing

out at the top, still housing a tumult of goldfinches. We try to hold still
and smile, squinting into the brilliance, the middle-aged children,
the grown grandsons, the dogs of each era, always a pair

of grinning shelter dogs whose long lives are but as grasshoppers
compared to our own. We try to live gracefully
and at peace with our imagined deaths but in truth we go forward

stumbling, afraid of the dark,
of the cold, and of the great overwhelming
loneliness of being last.

Laurie Kutchins

Born May 30, 1956, in Casper, Wyoming. Laurie Kutchins has three books of poems: *Slope of the Child Everlasting* (BOA Editions), *The Night Path* (BOA Editions) and *Between Towns* (Texas Tech University Press). Her poems and lyric nonfiction have appeared widely, including in *The New Yorker, The Kenyon Review, Poetry, Ploughshares, Orion, The Georgia Review,* and *The Southern Review.* She teaches creative writing at James Madison University in Virginia and at the Taos Summer Writers' Conference.

Daughter

I hear her
splintering like the seed inside
the pinecone, the furious grease
inside the smoke and speed of the fire
of our bodies. The hard red seed of her,
her pink nipple, her penis-husk,
her odors and hairs,
her molecular dust,
her dream file, her first and last word,
her undiscussed déjà vus,
her lovers and scorners,
the ones her unformed fingers navigate or swiftly shun,
her gravity gathered from the moon,
shivering across our backs and buttocks:
whoever she is
I hear her
in a moment's galactic after-stretch,
in the flatness of exile when your body recedes
like the mollusk oozing back
into its own space upon touch.
She is imprinted with our silence,
the scent of our tongues,
she comes home to our breath's cradle,
sifts through our pores
bringing only her memory
which she will lose
as she grows into my body,
bringing only the smoke of her name.
Having come from the sperm of you,
not you,
and from the black infinite ash of my egg,
she is more egg than sperm,
more than lips or the sound sex makes,

though it will be a long time before she whispers
her name through my skin.
I listen longer than you,
long after you and she are sleeping,
I listen to my fear,
and smell it,
and it is the forest
I was born in
burning like an eyelash.

Heartbeat

My pants pushed down around my knees
as the nurse instructed, I regress to schoolgirl twitches.
My still-slim ankles clank the base of the padded
examination table, my fingers twist an unconscious fringe
in the sanitary paper sheet until the doorknob rolls
and the no-eye-contact ob/gyn enters this pink room.
Like a fan across the whole span of my stomach, he opens
his cold manly hand that smells of antiseptic and metal.
Did the boy-skin of his hands understand they could grow
this gnarled and large, did they fathom they would be touching
the bodies of women all day in such sexless ways?
At this stage, my skin cannot fathom stretching past a holiday feast,
rounding to the jump-ball shapes of expectant girls
I saw leave the clinic with cigarettes already in hand.
Where he first spread his palm, the doctor places the ear
of a stethoscope attached to a transistor box. He turns the dial
until the sound of an ocean comes to me, the water of my breath.
And faintly—inside the inside—I have to stop breathing to hear it—
ticticticticticticticticticticticticictic . . .
It's the end of the eighth week, the indifferent period I've read about,
when the labiascrota splits into two words, two worlds,
and I hear it pushing time like a dark clock,
this speck of abstract sex in the fluids,
this sound with its own plan.

Joy

The day you left
the sky wept
six days the mountain hid
bobcat bear deer coyote rabbit
bloated from the sudden upland puddles

part of you stayed behind
to love the mud back
your palm prints
softened with
hoof tongue paw

with old thirst and red earth
earth made clay by rain
you were not done
banks of the filled arroyos
felt your feet

patter the washed-out path
handfuls of snails fell
into the empty garden
rain fattened the apricots
a flat roof dripped

you pulled from the owl
apologies for the lost cats
the river pushed and gushed
the mesas slicked past all darks
the desert shivered

would not shine whole
no thing
nothing
not changed
by your going.

River Keeper

How clear the river is
only moments after loss.

Gurgle of a sandhill crane.
Orange flash of a western tanager.

Sagebrush that needs the rain.
I found a simple bench carved from an evergreen.

A plaque in stone with a boy's name,
two dates that subtract

to nineteen years.
River, do you know him?

Someone is building a new bridge across
without handrails.

When I walk on it I get dizzy
from wanting to hold on.

Under there's the long young spine.
Always the swift current,

never the same. And the river,
more stones than stars.

Skin

Everything has a voice, even the skin
the black snake left beside the house
the day the golden tulips bloomed
and overpowered the sun. Never seen,
that snake leaves its skin behind
each spring like a secret gift
no longer dark or urgent without
its body. *Oh*
look at me, I've grown
and grown more beautiful, its voice
thralls from the grass, all
its language new and moving
in the skin like thunder
gathering into a noon
yet to form:
Have you heard me
down in the ductwork
of your house
living on mice?
Have you lived yet
a day without fear?
If not skin, what
will you come to shed?

The Placenta

After he has fallen asleep, after the last nursing
at the end of the undulant dusk when Venus has grown into a solitary
glitter in the western sky and his lips still tug at my nipple,
dreaming it into the smooth cave of his mouth as I carry him

sprawled out and limp from so much milk, as I move and stop
on each step to keep the sleep intact, toward the loft
where the shadows of dusk still shine on the cabin logs;
after I bend to lay him down, careful not to break the deep
and rhythmical breath, careful to transfer the feel of my arms into
the flannel I pack around him, cloth that smells of my milk and
high summer and him; after I watch the eyelids quiver, the lips smack,
the small limbs flinch and stretch as if to awaken but this is
his body settling into the arms of night; then I am free
to go back down and step outside,
and in the first full gasp of nightfall I find I am still thinking
about the placenta,
how strong and sinewy it was, how fast the doctor pulled it out
with rubber gloves and forceps made to fit a baby's head before it was
ready to leave, how he treated it like something worthless
and foul, medical rubbish to be quickly analyzed, disposed of,
when, in fact, I know it should have been paused over, admired, touched
and blessed; I look at the stars forming their nests overhead
and wonder, are you up there somewhere, sure of us
like an angel, like another child I made and lost?

John Campbell

Dorianne Laux

Born January 10, 1952, in Augusta, Maine. Dorianne Laux's fourth book of poems, *Facts about the Moon* (W.W. Norton), won the Oregon Book Award and was a finalist for the National Book Critics Circle Award. Co-author of *The Poet's Companion*, she received two Best American Poetry Prizes, a Best American Erotic Poems Prize, a Pushcart Prize, a fellowship from the Guggenheim foundation, and two from The National Endowment for the Arts. Before her many years teaching at the University of Oregon and, more recently, at Pacific University's low-residency MFA Program, she waited tables. She and her husband, poet Joseph Millar, now live in Raleigh where she is a Poet-in-Residence at North Carolina State University.

Family Stories

I had a boyfriend who told me stories about his family,
how an argument once ended when his father
seized a lit birthday cake in both hands
and hurled it out a second-story window. That,
I thought, was what a normal family was like: anger
sent out across the sill, landing like a gift
to decorate the sidewalk below. In mine
it was fists and direct hits to the solar plexus,
and nobody ever forgave anyone. But I believed
the people in his stories really loved one another,
even when they yelled and shoved their feet
through cabinet doors or held a chair like a bottle
of cheap champagne, christening the wall,
rungs exploding from their holes.
I said it sounded harmless, the pomp and fury
of the passionate. He said it was a curse
being born Italian and Catholic and when he
looked from that window what he saw was the moment
rudely crushed. But all I could see was a gorgeous
three-layer cake gliding like a battered ship
down the sidewalk, the smoking candles broken, sunk
deep in the icing, a few still burning.

Fast Gas

for Richard

Before the days of self service,
when you never had to pump your own gas,
I was the one who did it for you, the girl
who stepped out at the sound of a bell

with a blue rag in my hand, my hair pulled back
in a straight, unlovely ponytail.
This was before automatic shut-offs
and vapor seals, and once, while filling a tank,
I hit a bubble of trapped air and the gas
backed up, came arcing out of the hole
in a bright gold wave and soaked me—face, breasts,
belly and legs. And I had to hurry
back to the booth, the small employee bathroom
with the broken lock, to change my uniform,
peel the gas-soaked cloth from my skin
and wash myself in the sink.
Light-headed, scrubbed raw, I felt
pure and amazed—the way the amber gas
glazed my flesh, the searing,
subterranean pain of it, how my skin
shimmered and ached, glowed
like rainbowed oil on the pavement.
I was twenty. In a few weeks I would fall,
for the first time, in love, that man waiting
patiently in my future like a red leaf
on the sidewalk, the kind of beauty
that asks to be noticed. How was I to know
it would begin this way: every cell of my body
burning with a dangerous beauty, the air around me
a nimbus of light that would carry me
through the days, how when he found me,
weeks later, he would find me like that,
an ordinary woman who could rise
in flame, all he would have to do
is come close and touch me.

What My Father Told Me

Always I have done what was asked.
Melmac dishes stacked on rag towels.
The slack of a vacuum cleaner cord
wound around my hand. Laundry
hung on a line.
There is always much to do and I do it.
The iron resting in its frame, hot
in the shallow pan of summer
as the basins of his hands push
aside the book I am reading.
I do as I am told, hold his penis

like the garden hose, in this bedroom,
in that bathroom, over the toilet
or my bare stomach.
I do the chores, pull weeds out back,
finger stink-bug husks, snail carcasses,
pile dead grass in black bags. At night
his feet are safe on their pads, light
on the wall-to-wall as he takes
the hallway to my room.
His voice, the hiss of lawn sprinklers,
the wet hush of sweat in his hollows,
the mucus still damp
in the corners of my eyes as I wake.
Summer ends. Schoolwork doesn't suit me.
My fingers unaccustomed to the slimness
of a pen, the delicate touch it takes
to uncoil the mind.
History. A dateline pinned to the wall.
Beneath each president's face, a quotation.
Pictures of buffalo and wheatfields,
a wagon train circled for the night,
my hand raised to ask a question,
Where did the children sleep?

Return

My daughter, ten and brown—another summer
in Arizona with her father—steps
nonchalantly down the ramp as planes
unfurl their ghostly plumes of smoke.
I had forgotten how his legs, dark
and lean as hers, once strode toward me
across a stretch of hammered sand.
And her shoulders, sloped like his, a cotton
blouse scooped so low I can see
her collar bones arched gracefully
as wings, the cruel dip
in the hollow of her throat. And my throat
closes when she smiles, her bangs
blown into a fan around her face, hair
blond as the pampas grass that once waved
wild behind our fence. Whatever held us
together then is broken, dishes
in pieces on the floor, his dead

cigarettes crushed one after another
into the rail of the porch.
Now she opens her arms as he
used to, against a backdrop of blue sky,
so wide I worry she'll float up on these
gusts of clutching wind and disappear,
like a half-remembered dream, into
the perilous future, into the white
heart of the sun.

Bird

For days now a red-breasted bird
has been trying to break in.
She tests a low branch, violet blossoms
swaying beside her, leaps into the air and flies
straight at my window, beak and breast
held back, claws raking the pane.
Maybe she lunges for the tree she sees
reflected in the glass, but I'm only guessing.
I watch until she gives up and swoops off.
I wait for her return, the familiar
click, swoosh, thump of her. I sip cold coffee
and scan the room, trying to see it new,
through the eyes of a bird. Nothing has changed.
Books piled in a corner, coats hooked
over chair backs, paper plates, a cup
half-filled with sour milk.
The children are in school. The man is at work.
I'm alone with dead roses in a jam jar.
What do I have that she could want enough
to risk such failure, again and again?

Dust

Someone spoke to me last night,
told me the truth. Just a few words,
but I recognized it.
I knew I should make myself get up,
write it down, but it was late,
and I was exhausted from working
all day in the garden, moving rocks.

Now, I remember only the flavor—
not like food, sweet or sharp.
More like a fine powder, like dust.
And I wasn't elated or frightened,
but simply rapt, aware.
That's how it is sometimes—
God comes to your window,
all bright light and black wings,
and you're just too tired to open it.

Ada Limón

Born March 28, 1976, in Sonoma, California. Ada Limón's first book, *lucky wreck*, was the winner of the Autumn House Press Poetry Prize and her second book, *This Big Fake World*, was the winner of the Pearl Poetry Prize. With an MFA from New York University in creative writing, she's won the Chicago Literary Award and fellowships from the Provincetown Fine Arts Work Center and the New York Foundation for the Arts. She is the Copy Director for *GQ Magazine* and teaches a master class for Columbia University's MFA program. She is particularly fond of rivers and is at work on a third book of poems and a novel.

Miles Per Hour

The painted tiles are riddled with blue
cornflowers and unnaturally green stems,
as unnatural as trying to concentrate
on the blossoms covering the bathroom walls,
the way when we were driving 66 miles per hour,
and each lupine had become not one,
but rather one massive stain of purple and blue,
like one large bruise covering the right side
of Highway Twelve and the more I tried
to find one leaf, one petal, the more dizzy
I became until the search for something
simple had ruined its way into nausea, into
that throbbing in the middle of my eyes
when we knew it was over, all of it and yet
we were still in the car, still going to meet
the family and when we pulled over on
Old Sonoma Road under the tree to make
love once more before the parental hand
shake made love more difficult, more
permanent, my head swelled not knowing
whether or not to hold onto the handle
or the stick shift or to shove my foot
on the dashboard or just to remain pinned
like that, pummeled in the car seat, what we called
screwing, the hard stuff, the times when we were more
angry than anything else, the turn-on being the
pain. And through the car window I could
see everything in summer heat, the oak leaves
the tires had crushed in their masculine heaviness,
the fungus that grew on the side of the tree making
a shape like a face or a birthmark and each single
thing made me grab you harder, want to be connected
to something larger, as if we could swell into the
universe itself, the movement of hips propelling
us up into some, I don't want to say celestial, body,

but something as big as that, where we could watch
over everything, the towns growing smaller like
little painted toys, those giant oaks and cedars,
turning into a brushstroke of blue and green, small and
unrecognizable as these flowers now, painted
haphazardly and scattered, like the memory
itself, the car driving farther and farther down
the highway, my face pressed up against the window
unable to discern whether or not I was as much
of a blur as the things I passed.

The Firemen Are Dancing

I am running my finger through the rough knotted hole
on the edge of the stained, oak, bar table.

It looks like it could be an eyehole and I think it
would be the scariest thing in the world if I were an ant,

a hole where the bottom drops out, just like that, on to the floor.

I don't want to drink tonight, or if I do, I want to drink a lot, enough
to lie down on the ash blackened floor and watch everything through
the eyehole.

Everyone is talking about parties, the vice cop keeps looking
at the guy we call Red and that's fine by me
because I don't like him, never have.

O and the firemen are dancing. My favorite part is how
they are dancing so close.

One is pulling the other to his hip and one with the hat is laughing
and tossing his head back as if they were seventeen or, even, as if they
were alone.

And it's okay that I don't have a specific *you* right now and it's okay
that I'm not sure who this *you* I am speaking to is anymore.

The firemen are dancing and one of them has leaned his head on the
other's blue shoulder and the ones at the window are singing
and watching with big, lovely, fireman smiles.

And it's okay that you weren't here to see it, I'm going to tell you
all about it. Even if you never ask, I will.

Centerfold

Crouched in the corner of the barn,
we sat with the cedar chest splayed,
and the magazines laid out in perfect
piles. I was the first to reach the
centerfold and together we stared.
These women, these giantesses,
folded over couches, on bear rugs,
or steel bars, their bodies so slick
they could slip through the pages
and then through your fingers.
One, in particular, was my favorite,
with her left leg perched on a ballet bar and her
hair piled around her shoulders,
I thought she must be famous.
I thought how lovely it would be to
be her, to be naked all the time,
and dancing.

The Different Ways of Going

I keep calling that bird in the window a *flight risk*
while watching you get dressed from the bed.

And it's remarkable how a mood can change everything,
like a car accident.

Your footsteps have a color, if you could call it that,
                    the color of wool uniforms.

This weather makes me wonder how many hands I've held.

I'll never see you again, but that's a note I tear up in my mind.

Two days from now I'll be in a field, picking peaches
and feeding the retired police horses, with names like Bullet, and Justice.

On the field, we call it the long one, I will come close
to a hawk in the oaks, I will say, *That bird looks like a flight risk*
and no one will hear me except the hawk and the blue into which it goes.

Selecting Things for Vagueness

I want to know some things
for certain, and other things
for vague. Have some vague idea
of where you are, not an address,
no train stop, no telephone,
no relative, no neighbor, no local,
no highway blah blah blah, no turnpike,
no regional, no county, no watershed,
no school district, no supermarket,
no tributary, no mailbox, no corner,
no state bird, no "as the crow flies,"
'cause what I'd do when I find you,
well mister, this I know for certain.

Mark Olencki

Susan Ludvigson

Born February 13, 1942, in Rice Lake, Wisconsin. Susan Ludvigson's most recent collection is *Escaping the House of Certainty* from Louisiana State University Press (2006). Her awards include fellowships from the Guggenheim, Rockefeller, Fulbright, and Witter Bynner Foundations, and the National Endowment for the Arts. She recently retired from many years of teaching at Winthrop University in South Carolina. She and her husband, fiction writer Scott Ely, spend most summers in Puivert, France. They are members of a pack that includes four dogs who, alas, do not get to join Susan and Scott in France.

What I Think It Is

The suddenness of old.
Under the influence
of hormones, the pink flush
of the cheeks says youth. The mind's
what it once was, reasonably stable, emotions
paddling their several canoes carefully,
upstream and down, knowing
where the currents change, how to avoid
the falls. Until

age drapes itself over
your thin shoulders, a loose-knit shawl,
the boat rolls over, and you're propelled
into a sinkhole, where you nearly drown.

Even as gravity keeps pulling
you down, you start drifting backward, where
every adolescent fear becomes
your flailing twin. Old sins return,
specters mocking the you
you thought you'd left behind.

The House

Praise for the daily miracles. Praise for the luck of the past.
Praise for what happens and doesn't. Praise for what happens last.

Ramshackle, patched, too small, leaning into the street—
he buys it. Oh well, a man can live like that. But the man,
how could I forget, is unlike others. Soon,

he opens the door to friends. The house no longer grips the curb,
is set back in a grove. Its wide walk lined with pecan trees
leads to a shady porch.

In the foyer—boards piled against the wall, plaster
dust, a smell of sawdust and beer.
The things one might expect. But then
the hall widens. Branches. The house has grown wings.

He follows me into the kitchen, whispers something intimate,
the life we might have known. I want him

to say more, instead he takes my hand. Whisks me
into a turret room, walls hung with streamers,
candle-lit, the shadows grand.

A ceremony has begun, to honor him. He leads me
through applauding crowds to a podium. A wreath is placed on his head.

We glide back through a flow of men. One pulls me aside, insists,
"You should marry him."

"I'm already married," I say, remembering my husband,
who's strolling ahead and humming. We're practically
at the door. "Come out and sit on the porch with me,"
my husband calls back, "there's softness in the air."

Hush, for the Night Is Stealthy

Hush, for the night is stealthy—hear it breathe
your name, you who lose yourself on waking.
Tender to someone the darkness of your dreams,

for dreams, we know, are seldom what they seem.
Asleep, you say *bougainvillea,* your voice breaking.
Hush, for the night is stealthy—hear it breathe?

Close your eyes once more and try to see
a volcanic mountain—beyond, a white-misted lake.
Then tender to someone the darkness of your dreams.

Think of the voice you can't forget, keening,
the violin played as if music itself could ache.
Hush, for the night is stealthy—hear it breathe?

In any language this is what it means:
We're not who they think, we all believe we're faking.
Time to tender the darkness of our dreams.

How, you ask, can blossoms be born of leaves?
How can trust come of the body's quaking?
Hush, for the night is stealthy—hear it breathe?
Tender to someone the darkness of your dreams.

Always Paris

late late suitcases not packed no
tickets haven't written home
or called in in months in years
meet Mary at La Closerie de Lilas
pink clouds follow the falling sun
dusty air glowing mid-beer maybe
it's today I should have left call
Drusilla Linda Carol stroll
Blvd. St. Germain stopping to buy
lilies on the way to Mimi's where
across the river a symphony someone
singing a voice so pure and light it drifts
across like yes like silk think
home again the ones who worry there
and back in my tiny flat look
at shelves two stories high filled
with clothes and pots and pans
and canned tomatoes cassoulet
and peas decide to leave the food still
the suitcase will not close look across
the courtyard building under
renovation new apartments
being sold listen through the window
hammering whistling still not
dressed close the window now
in shadow in the glass who is
she red hair fallen from her crown
where it was pinned dreaming lilacs
a small garden walled by blooming
lilacs mother gone Mary gone where who
does she think she is

Dear Sharon,

I think I need a break from words
strung endlessly
down left margins. It's the middle
of the night and I'm awake, my eyes
so tired I push my manuscript
off to the side. The poems look like
EKGs, their jagged lines,
spikes and drops, a record of the dangers
a patient passed through,
heart battering its stubborn way
through love toward the inevitable.
Is everything a story of the body's
relentless drives, the spirit's quaking?

Now lightning, an expected storm. It too
registers the irregular paths of things. I picture
shorelines, rivers on a map.

I start thinking of a man I knew who'd charted
his life, each stage undertaken at the planned
and proper moment—education, marriage,
children, academic career.
"I think it's the right time now,"
he said to me once, "for an affair." I took it not
as invitation, but the disposition some of us have
toward managing fate.

Do you ever feel the need for a break
from lines pushed down the page,
from too many pages?

Now it's 4:00 a.m. and I find myself in
a kitchen meditation.

I'll make a tarte for my husband, I decide,
and maybe another to take to a friend.
I rummage through the pantry. Of course
I don't have everything I need. No applesauce for a base.
I find cream of coconut—that might work—
or maybe pumpkin. The crusts take a little time,
but soon tartes are steaming on the counter,
scenting the kitchen with cinnamon, which, it occurs to me,
I've heard is an aphrodisiac.

And I'm back in bed, husband stirring beside me.
Everything, we know, connects.

I sleep half an hour, wake again to the poems I'd left
spread over the bed, some of the pages
on the floor,

surprised how, in the space of a few dark hours,
the lines cascading down the page
have turned to waterfalls in spring surrounded
by rhododendron, how similes slip like fish over stones
at the bottom of that whispering fall's quick stream.
I tilt the pages on their sides again,
meaning to stack them,
and see they're no longer medical
but musical notation, major and minor chords
echoing through my mind, just as the birds outside
begin to sing.

Angela Pratt

Kathleen Lynch

Born October 29, 1943, in Sampson, New York. Kathleen Lynch's *Hinge* won the Black Zinnias Press National Poetry Competition. Her chapbooks are *How to Build an Owl* (Select Poet Series Award, Small Poetry Press), *No Spring Chicken* (White Eagle Coffee Store Press Award), *Alterations of Rising* (Small Poetry Press Select Poet Series) and *Kathleen Lynch: Greatest Hits* (Pudding House Publications). Other awards include the *Spoon River Poetry Review* Editor's Choice Award, *Salt Hill* Poetry Award, *Two Rivers Review* Prize, and a 2007 Ucross Foundation Fellowship. Lynch is married to Eddie (a completely obsessed bird watcher) and is called "Maga" by grandsons Joe and Elliot.

Yard Work

My mother prowled the yard, winding wires around bare
stems of rose bushes, attaching Woolworth's plastic roses—
her flowered house dress puffed out full,
hair lifting like flames. I watched, embarrassed

by how tacky, how pathetic
but it had been a bad spring all around
what with Dad's drinking and with nothing
blooming, and from where I stood

I had to admit they looked pretty. The distance
between shame and pride is so mutable we use
both words for the same thing:
She has no shame. She has no pride.

Can this be true? By my calculation over forty
thousand hours have passed since that moment
and still I see her and the bell of that dress,
not a scrim in sight, just sheets snapping

on the line behind her, weeds shivering at her ankles.
And the way she moved, the way she went at it
—a driven thing—another of the countless gestures
she would subsume in silence, a look

in the eye we all knew meant: Say nothing.
And when she sank away into the heap of mystery
books on the couch, a theater of colors in the window
behind her—the strange brilliance and juxtaposition

of fake and real—I began to believe in hope
as something that could be invented
even under dire skies, even when wind
sliced around thorns and we waited

for the phone to ring, and for spring
to become spring.

Soaps Fan

I love the evil twin the best,
especially the one no one knew existed.
Especially when it shows up with an axe
to grind. Or the dead ringer paid to pretend
to be brother, sister, old lover
risen from the grave. I love the way
anyone can come back from the dead
even after the whole cabin burns down
and they find the ring in the ashes.
Even after the lake is dragged and every
stone turned. How great
that you can be buried alive for months
and still make it to the New Year's Eve bash
in something with sequins.

I admit I'm a sucker for wardrobe: women
in their slit and plunged business suits; natty
men who only don jeans for the Fourth of July
picnic in a park with shaky fake shrubs.
Even the token lower class family
wears Sears' Best until they marry up,
or get arrested, or give themselves to God.
There is, by the way, proof God exists: Look
at their hair: how it flows like a river
of light, how it defies gravity
and even after calamity looks good,
and so perfectly frames the face
of the bitch who slips arsenic
into her mother's teatime brandy.

I love the way the men sit in the cafeteria
and discuss the latest upturn
or downturn in their *relationships*. I love
all those coffee breaks, all the eating,
everyone meeting for lunch at a place
with cloth napkins, or dropping
in at the checkered local diner, or reserving
the Private Banquet Room
for a special occasion. Oh,

I love those Special Occasions
when they find the rare
organ donor, cure the rare
terminal illness. Or when the loyal
housekeeper ends up in the arms
of the gardener who doesn't even know
he is the son of the master. Lineage
is tricky business. My own father
died not knowing that his father,
who deserted early, died drunk
on a wharf in San Francisco.
But that's another story . . .
Not as good as the one where the father
adopts his own son, not knowing,
of course, but loving him so and so wanting
a son to love him.

When I am in Big Trouble,
such as: the bridge gives out or blows
up just as my car crosses, wipers
slash-slash, slash-slash & me
going so fast & reckless because at last
I know Who Did It, but no one else knows—
please get me to a Soaps Hospital
where my gurney will be wheeled
through the Main entrance.
Doctors who have known me
all my life will gather around,
ply my lids & shout STAT,
& the same physician who delivered
my long lost half sister's miracle baby
will also perform the delicate brain surgery
that will save me from death.

And even if for a few weeks it looks like
I've really become nothing more than a vegetable,
trust me, one day, with the steady
background music of the heart
monitor & visits
from every major character in my life
I will come out of my coma
and, to everyone's surprise and/or horror
I—or someone who looks just like me—
will tell everything I know.

Observation

I saw a life enter a life, yesterday, by the water,
when the peregrine swooped and snagged a plump dowitcher

and rose with the caught bird still alive and struggling.
And the falcon, pumping higher, lifted the writhing feast

with both talons to its bill and snapped the flailing neck,
not putting it out of its misery, just putting it out,

making it quiet, making the ride to the top branch smooth.
All of this took place in air. At last, settled

with its kill, the hunter pulled strand after strand
of flesh from the soft feathery body, and ropes of skin,

sinews and bones, until there was no shape left to it, only
a scrap of spine. I kept my focus while he did his work, the wind

coming up, the sun sliding down, the black arms
of the trees waving, the light on the water bending

and breaking, and I understood that where there were two birds,
there were still two birds: One who carries. One carried away.

How to Build an Owl

1. Decide you must.

2. Develop deep respect
   for feather, bone, claw.

3. Place your trembling thumb
   where the heart will be:
   for one hundred hours watch
   so you will know
   where to put the first feather.

4. Stay awake forever.
   When the bird takes shape
   gently pry open its beak
   and whisper into it: *mouse*.

5. Let it go.

Noah Musher

Anne Marie Macari

Born July 18, 1955, in Queens, New York. Anne Marie Macari has published three books of poetry, most recently *She Heads into the Wilderness* (Autumn House Press, 2008). In 2000 her book *Ivory Cradle* won the *APR*/Honickman first book prize for poetry, chosen by Robert Creeley, and was followed by *Gloryland* (Alice James Books, 2005). Also winner of the James Dickey prize for poetry from *Five Points* magazine, Macari is director of the Drew University Low-Residency Program in Poetry. She lives in the Delaware River town of Lambertville, New Jersey, where her house is the home-base for two sons in college, Noah and Lukas. She lives with her youngest son, Jeremy, and her long-time companion, Gerald Stern.

Sunbathing

Once, when I was twenty-one, a hundred students
naked around a lake,

and in loathing I let myself be free and lay
on my towel, breasts

to the sun, swam that way, and squatted
and dried, and looked

to see whose body was better, whose worse,
whose gathered

like cotton under the skin, who sagged,
strutted, stared down.

For comfort I thought, *they're frightening,*
who love themselves,

diving, splashing, swimming up to the men,
their breasts floating.

What the sun did to my tender skin that day
I don't want to remember.

Even fish have their scales, animals fur,

not just this small arrow-shaped patch of hair
pointing toward the hidden bulb,

hollowed ground of lost Eden, where the tree waits
to respring, and the fruit

to drop at my feet.

In time I understood what I was made for.
Knew how long the bulb

could wait underground before it split
into flower,

how later it would rot and when I'd die
I'd taste the ground-up

mineral of petal and stem, the well
of mucous and blood,

and come to see I had loved this body

without knowing it, and it had loved me—

body and spirit—small, floating—
how we sometimes moved

as one, unclothed in the moist air.

Palace of Longing

How many minute doors
in the body? Valves and
pinched places. Eyelids,
the many drums. And did

the artist think of them when
he painted the corpse, bent
over like a mourner,
his face, color of the strange

sky above? I'm all
mixed up, lost in this
last room of the exhibit
the painting on the wall

so large that the exit door
looks like a mouse hole,
and the shuffling feet seem
to come from inside me.

And painted near an angel's
wing is the artist himself
looking so much like the man
I loved so long who

didn't in return, humbled
above the dead man, yet
larger than he should be,
as if he knew I'd be here

reading the captions, mute
and so close, still not painted
into the scene, remembering
when I wanted to be

the brush in his hand,
the pigment he ground.
In the hollow of my neck,
in the holes behind

my eyes, at all the gates
of being where I once
waited, a ghost haunting
myself, I finally passed

into myself, wanting
to live. In the painting
there's a woman behind
the artist, her weeping face

half-covered. I don't know
how I stopped leaning
into his absence, how I
stepped through the door—

left the palace of longing—
hands unclenched, even
the wild crown
of the head

dilated.

from **Their Eyes Were Opened**

I (We Always Ate from that Tree)

We always ate from that tree. The women
with child craved its fruit, sweetest, most red.

The way she held it that day, and pressed it to
her cheek like a pillow, and slowly slit it with

her teeth, and ate it while rubbing her sore
back against the tree like a horse. Then many

of them rushing her, screaming she was unclean,
pushing her into the dirt like a serpent where

she writhed from them, where they taught her right from
wrong and when they were done they bound and covered

her outlaw breasts, her spirit garden below.
And they threw the fruit of the tree to the animals

and smashed the clay figures. And it went on
like that, beyond memory, on and on.

XII (Paradise Came Over Me Once)

Paradise came over me once. A grove
of tall eucalyptus trees, long red leaves

we picked off the ground, animals following us.
His voice echoing among the trees, naming

everything, filling the silence with brittle
kingdoms: moon-faced owls, finches, a dead mouse,

core of an apple. He couldn't stop himself.
I mocked him: earlobe, nipple, throat. He floated

from me, brooding like the huge trees with their
gigantic solitude. I turned away.

For a long time we had been enough: what I'd
later name happiness. Sweet kernel within

my despair. Don't ask why. Think of your own hunger,
how it gets worse no matter what you feed it.

XXVIII (What I Wake To)

What I wake to in the layered winter bed,
and fall back into in the sling of sleep,

and walk around all day, in and out of.
Beneath the papery skin around my eyes

another life. Snow, gray and brittle, the sky
sagging so low it might be a rag around

my head. Thoughts—cold, sharp—dirty ice crackling
at the edge of the walk. Unrest inside,

the unseen trying to stir the frozen
underworld. I don't say it. The white roots

inside me, winter-glazed. I don't say it.
And even when everything is at risk,

sore with longing, I don't say it, and soon
it carves a space inside me with its absence.

XXXVI (She Heads into the Wilderness)

She heads into the wilderness, weeping
and stunned by shame, her eyes open. Into

another country, bent and becoming,
fibrous and heavy in her body, feeling

that she is the tree, or that she is the fruit
that ripens and falls, that falls and will keep

falling her whole life. As if all that mattered
was plummeting to earth and splitting open.

And who hasn't stumbled out of herself
into the body of suffering? Into

bare flesh, stooped shoulders, and the dark hole
of the mouth. Threats still ringing, and that taste

she never forgot, taste with no end, world with
no end. Gates fading, the wind shushing her on.

Kirsten Lara Getchell

Gail Mazur

Born November 10, 1937, in Cambridge, Massachusetts. Gail Mazur is the author of five books of poems, most recently *They Can't Take That Away from Me*, finalist for the 2001 National Book Award, and *Zeppo's First Wife: New and Selected Poems*, finalist for the 2005 *Los Angeles Times* Book Prize and winner of the Massachusetts Book Award. She is Distinguished Writer-in-Residence in the graduate writing program of Emerson College and in 2009 will be teaching in Boston University's Graduate Program in Writing. She lives in Cambridge, Massachusetts, where she was founder and director of the Blacksmith House Poetry Series, and in Provincetown, where she serves on the Writing Committee of the Fine Arts Work Center.

Desire

It was a kind of torture—waiting
to be kissed. A dark car parked away
from the street lamp, away from our house
where my tall father would wait, his face
visible at a pane high in the front door.
Was my mother always asleep? A boy
reached for me, I leaned eagerly into him,
soon the windshield was steaming.

Midnight. A neighbor's bedroom light
goes on, then off. The street is quiet. . . .

Until I married, I didn't have my own key,
that wasn't how it worked, not at our house.
You had to wake someone with the bell,
or he was there, waiting. Someone let you in.
Those pleasures on the front seat of a boy's
father's car were "guilty," yet my body knew
they were the only right thing to do,

my body hated the cage it had become.

One of those boys died in a car crash;
one is a mechanic; one's a musician.
They were young and soft and, mostly, dumb.
I loved their lips, their eyebrows, the bones
of their cheeks, cheeks that scraped mine raw,
so I'd turn away from the parent who let me
angrily in. And always, the next day,

no one at home could penetrate the fog
around me. I'd relive the precious night

as if it were a bridge to my new state
from the old world I'd been imprisoned by,
and I've been allowed to walk on it, to cross
a border—there's an invisible line
in the middle of the bridge, in the fog,
where I'm released, where I think I'm free.

Bluebonnets

I lay down by the side of the road
in a meadow of bluebonnets, I broke
the unwritten law of Texas. My brother

was visiting, he'd been tired, afraid of
his tiredness as we'd driven toward Bremen,
so we stopped for the blue relatives

of lupine, we left the car on huge feet
we'd inherited from our lost father,
our Polish grandfather. Those flowers

were too beautiful to only look at;
we walked on them, stood in the middle
of them, threw ourselves down,

crushing them in their one opportunity
to thrive and bloom. We lay like angels
forgiven our misdeeds, transported

to azure fields, the only word for
the color eluded me—delft, indigo,
sapphire, some heavenly word you might

speak to a sky. I led my terrestrial brother
there to make him smile and this
is my only record of the event.

We took no pictures, we knew no camera
could fathom that blue. I brushed
the soft spikes, I fingered lightly

the delicate earthly petals, I thought,
This is what my hands do well
isn't it, touch things about to vanish.

They Can't Take That Away from Me

The way the blue car spun tonight
on imperceptible ice—that stop-
time: bare pocked sycamores, the river's
black sheen, the football stadium
empty of Romans, the oblivious sky-
line shining like a festivity—
and, shaken, I could still straighten
the formidable blue invention,
slide the delinquent wheels to a curb;

the way, in South China, the car radio
says, believers crowd closet-like shops
to purchase tiny packets of Bear Bile,
a favorite cure-all, while bears go mad
in their abscessing bodies, in cages
barely their height, hurling themselves,
banging their agonized heads at the bars—
lifetimes of pain only, for the ancient
sake of a fierce "medicinal harvest";

the way a mother stirring sweet batter
in a well-lit kitchen, feels the Pyrex
bowl slip to the floor, and it breaks,
and seeing there'll be no upside-down cake
for dinner, shrieks at her little boy
cowering in the doorway, *Look what*
you made me do! and lunges to smack him,
the way she'd struck yesterday and last week,
though he's still as a stalled truck;

the way I felt last night when she hung up
on me, I knew I had hurt her because her mind
's gone, and I refused for my life
to let mine follow again; the way I held
the dead phone, relieved to be not
listening at last—*the memory of all that,*
no no—relieved, selfish, and empty:
wouldn't I choose if I could not be human or
any other animal programmed for cruelty?
No, they can't take that away from me

Young Apple Tree, December

What you want for it what you'd want
for a child: that she take hold;
that her roots find home in stony

winter soil; that she take seasons
in stride, seasons that shape and
reshape her; that like a dancer's,

her limbs grow pliant, graceful
and surprising; that she know,
in her branchings, to seek balance;

that she know when to flower, when
to wait for the returns; that she turn
to a giving sun; that she know to share

fruit as it ripens, that what's lost
to her will be replaced; that early
summer afternoons, a full blossoming

tree, she cast lacy shadows; that change
not frighten her, rather change
meet her embrace; that remembering

her small history, she find her place
in an orchard; that she be her own
orchard; that she outlast you;

that she prepare for the hungry world,
the fallen world, the loony world,
something shapely, useful, new, delicious.

for Florence Ladd

Donald Devet

Rebecca McClanahan

Born August 24, 1950, in Lafayette, Indiana. Rebecca McClanahan's most recent books are *Deep Light: New and Selected Poems 1987–2007* and *The Riddle Song and Other Rememberings*, winner of the 2005 Glasgow Award for Nonfiction. She has also published four previous volumes of poetry and two writing texts. Her work has appeared in *The Best American Poetry, The Best American Essays*, and in numerous other anthologies. Her awards include the Wood Prize from *Poetry*, a New York Foundation for the Arts Fellowship, a Pushcart Prize and the Carter Prize for the Essay. A resident of New York, she teaches in the MFA program of Queens University and the *Kenyon Review* Writers Workshop. An incurable dancer, she is also a professional aunt to fifteen nieces and nephews and eight (at last count) great nieces and nephews.

Good Fences

Mornings like this I am grateful
for thin blue lines that separate. I know why
the asylum inmate, when handed a sheet of paper, writes
his name as close to the edge as possible. God
himself moved early toward margins. Lost in galaxies
of pure freedom, the first motherless child cried out
to the terrible dark. How good it must have felt
when that first word found its shape. Stopped. Cleared
a space for the next, and next. *Let there be light!*
sweet baby talk of creation. And what a surprise
when chaos obeyed, split in two, the first neighborly
fence between night and day. Now there was something
to lie in, something to wake to, that first watery morning.
Day poured itself around him. His head was swimming,
where to put it? So Heaven was born, first hint of *up*.
Down followed soon, his feet sucked toward Earth
where he rattled the first seeds into being, divided
the hairy clumps: Grasses. Trees. Herbs. Fruits.
Here was work to cut out for himself—sorting
the firmament into lesser and greater lights, the waters
into fish and fowl, into feather and fin, then the teeming
multiplications of beasts and men which are yet
recombining. No wonder he named the seventh day
Rest! and gasped to see what he had done.

Visit with the Newlyweds

She does not know how white her neck,
or how naked. He cannot pass her
without touching. It is summer,

their cotton clothes soft as gauze.
The relatives have given gifts
they will grow into. China teacups.
Glass birds. A clock with a second hand.
I have brought Sweet Williams.
She is amazed something so pink
can bloom every year without planting.
Yes, I answer. *Eleven years for us.*
Eleven? she asks and looks at the clock
as if everything were told in hours.
Upstairs by their bed, the wedding pillow.
Every night they marry again.
I want to tell them how crowded
the bed will become, how soon
he will sleep with her mother.
The bride yawns, her eyes
turning back the sheet.
Back home the sheets are thin,
the roses worn smooth
beneath bodies so familiar
we wear our skin like clothes.
You touch me and I move to lower
the straps I pretend are there.
Some nights I forget we are married.
Some nights it is all I know.

To the Absent Wife of the Beautiful Poet at the Writers' Conference

I want you to know that nothing happened,
and everything that might have is now sewn
into the hoop of Arizona sky
that stretched above our heads that shy
evening of talk when we left our books
and went out to read the papery news
of bougainvillea. Here was vegetation
more animal than plant, the dangerous spine
of cactus, its fleshy stem and thistle,
and those rubbery tongues lolling speechless
in the desert air where even domestic
herbs turn wild, parsley and dill spilling
over their planned containers. When your husband
broke off a piece of rosemary and held it
out to me, I smelled the sharp clean scent
of marriage, the scent that fills my loved world
three time zones away. My garden, the spotted

cat and aged brandy, the bed pillow minted
with the imprint of my husband's head.
Yet I confess that part of me wanted
to take in that moment the man you more
than half-made, knowing that what I love
most in married men is what is given
by wives. The elbow he leans upon
is *your* elbow, his listening quiet,
your quiet, practiced in twenty years
of bedtime conversation. If he loved,
in that instant, anything in me, it was
the shape and smell of one whole woman
made from the better halves of two—
your hard earned past and my present, briefly
flaming. Not long ago I watched a girl
I might have been twenty years ago, sit
literally at my husband's feet and adore him.
There are gifts we can give our husbands,
but adoration is not one. If I could,
I would be one woman diverging, walk
one road toward those things that matter
always, the trail long love requires.
The other, for what burned in the eyes
of your husband as he asked, *What is the secret
to a long marriage?* I gave my grandfather's
bald reply: *You don't leave and you don't die.*
There are no secrets. Together, the four of us—
your husband, mine, you and I,
have lasted. I started to say forty
married years, but no, it is eighty,
each of us living those years sometimes,
by necessity, singly, the whole of love
greater than the sum of its combined hearts.
That's what I mean about the sky. Its blueness
and the way it goes on forever. An old
teacher told me if you break a line in half
again and again, you will never reach an end.
Infinity is measured by the broken spaces
within as well as by the line spooling out
as far as we can see. I love my husband.
Still, there were spaces in that evening
that will go on dividing our lives. And if
the sky had not begun in that moment
to blink messages of light from stars I thought
had died out long ago, I might have answered
your husband's eyes another way.
And there would have been heaven to pay.

Autobiography of the Cab Driver who Picked Me Up at a Phoenix Hotel to Catch a Four A.M. Flight and Began to Speak in (Almost) Rhyming Couplets

I got two problems. One,
I never see the sun
and two, if I did,
I couldn't take it, never could.
Now, my sister? Out one day
and brown the next. That's the way
my father was. We never
took vacations but he used to steer
on Sundays with one arm
out the window. Get dark as a black man.
Something in his blood, I guess.
Once I bought me a mess
of tanning cream, but something
kept me from using it.
He's been dead a whole
year. They say there's not a soul
on the streets this hour,
but the souls are just now rousing.
Yes Ma'am, when I see daylight I slide
into my coffin and close the lid.
Cooler that way. They say if you can survive
a summer in this heat, you're a native.
My brother's child? She claims to be one,
but I tell her she's got Made in Japan
stamped all over her keister.
Hey lady, you still on Eastern
time? You can have it. Yesterday
the TV reporter in Cincinnati
was three feet in snow. I phoned
my old drinking buddy back home
to rub it in. Lied and said I was out
today without a shirt. Barefoot.
He said you can keep those hundred
degrees. I said you don't have to shovel
a heat wave. Young lady, you okay?
Looks like you're fading. The longest day
I ever lived was the night
I left for Vietnam. What a sight,
would you look at that? Damn
jackhammers at three a.m.
They sure like to play in the dirt here.
Yes Ma'am. It's the same everywhere.
The shortest distance between
two points is always under construction.

Jo McDougall

Born December 15, 1935, in Little Rock, Arkansas. Jo McDougall's five books of poetry include, most recently, *Dirt* and *Satisfied with Havoc*, both from Autumn House Press. *Towns Facing Railroads*, a production featuring her work, was staged at the Arkansas Repertory Theatre in 2006. McDougall has received awards from the DeWitt Wallace/Reader's Digest Foundation and fellowships from the MacDowell Colony; recently she was named to the Arkansas Writers Hall of Fame. Associate Professor Emerita at Pittsburg State University, she serves on the board of directors for The Writers Place in Kansas City. She and her husband, Charles, are owned by Starr, a registered Sheltie, and Spike, a found cat.

Parlors

We were the nieces, the daughters.
They were the uncles, the fathers. They
had keys
to houses, wives, offices,
to God.
After supper they jostled into the parlor
to smoke.
They lowered their voices
away from us.
They told us
part of the joke,
some of the story.

Boyfriend

We were both in high school, sixteen,
me headed for college.
They said he was bad.
They said his dad
was the one had bitten off the sheriff's ear
the night the sheriff came looking
for the still.

I'd hang around the gym
after the football team finished its practice,
hoping to see him.
I lied to my mother.

I saw a brightness, saw us dancing,
saw children who had his eyes.
Even now, I can smell the woodsmoke
in his jacket.

He never got out of the twelfth grade.
They said he went to work for the highway.
The girl he got pregnant was thirteen.
She wasn't from around here.

Labor Day

The boy's mother hears it on the radio.
A fishing boat has been found.
She walks through the house,
reassuring the backs of chairs.

Her husband comes from the lake.
Dusk filters through the screen.
Sit down, he says.
He puts his hat on the table.

Dumb

You would think the dog,
lemon-sized brain notwithstanding,
would understand by now
that the truck with the broken muffler
passing down our street each night
is not his master's truck
and will not turn into our driveway;
the familiar key will not undress itself
in our lock.
Still, he bounds to the door
at the muffler's first faint cough.
Thus hope outfoxes reason,
the dog and I growing dumber by the week.

Dirt

Its arrogance will break your heart.
Two weeks ago
we had to coax it
into taking her body.
Today,
after a light rain,
I see it hasn't bothered
to conceal its seams.

Mammogram

"They're benign," the radiologist says,
pointing to specks on the x-ray
that look like dust motes
stopped cold in their dance.
His words take my spine like flame.
I suddenly love
the radiologist, the nurse, my paper gown,
the vapid print on the dressing room wall.
I pull on my radiant clothes.
I step out into the Hanging Gardens, the Taj Mahal,
the Niagara Falls of the parking lot.

Jennifer Chandler

Jane Mead

Born August 13, 1958, in Baltimore, Maryland. Jane Mead is the author of *The Usable Field* (Alice James, 2008), *House of Poured-Out Waters* (Illinois, 2001) and *The Lord and the General Din of the World* (Sarabande, 1996). Her poems appear regularly in literary journals such as *Poetry* and *American Poetry Review* and in many anthologies. She is the recipient of a Guggenheim Fellowship, a Lannan Foundation Completion Grant, and a Whiting Award. For many years Poet-in-Residence at Wake Forest University, Mead now manages a vineyard in Northern California. When time permits, she can be found roaming the hills near her house with her dogs, or retreating to Iowa to write.

The Laden Henceforth Pending

My assignment was *one useful plan,*
to make one useful plan of the surrounding
thirteen hundred acres of chaparral

and oak, manzanita and bunchgrass
in the season of the oak's unfurling,
in the season of the blue-eyed grasses,

wind-washed and rain-swept and moving
toward the scorch of summer,—*make*
an afternoon of it, he said.

Three dogs came with me up the hill
named for its sugar-pines, to what
we call the *little pike*—that farthest

meadow of my childhood,—the red head
of the vulture bent with watching,
the red tail of the hawk spread wide.

Your memory casts a shadow when you
go into the future, and the shadow
wants to know what owns you—-the red

and lichened trunk of the madrona
or the twin dry creeks converging as matter
and lack of matter meeting. You have to be

nothing, take whatever amnesty is offered—
the case for love is not the case
for tragedy revisited, or there is

for certain now—a laden henceforth pending.

Concerning That Prayer I Cannot Make

Jesus, I am cruelly lonely
and I do not know what I have done
nor do I suspect that you will answer me.

And, what is more, I have spent
these bare months bargaining
with my soul as if I could make her
promise to love me when now it seems
that what I meant when I said "soul"
was that the river reflects
the railway bridge just as the sky
says it should—it speaks *that* language.

I do not know who you are.

I come here every day
to be beneath this bridge,
to sit beside this river,
so I *must* have seen the way
the clouds just slide
under the rusty arch—
without snagging on the bolts,
how they are borne along on the dark water—
I must have noticed their fluent speed
and also how that tattered blue T-shirt
remains snagged on the crown
of the mostly sunk dead tree
despite the current's constant pulling.
Yes, somewhere in my mind there must
be the image of a sky blue T-shirt, caught,
and the white islands of ice flying by
and the light clouds flying slowly
under the bridge, though today the river's
fully melted. I must have seen.

But I did not see.

I am not equal to my longing.
Somewhere there should be a place
the exact shape of my emptiness—
there should be a place
responsible for taking one back.
The river, of course, has no mercy—
it just lifts the dead fish
toward the sea.

Of course, of course.

What I *meant* when I said "soul"
was that there should be a place.

On the far bank the warehouse lights
blink red, then green, and all the yellow
machines with their rusted scoops and lifts
sit under a thin layer of sunny frost.

And look—
my own palm—
there, slowly rocking.
It is *my* pale palm—
palm where a black pebble
is turning and turning.

    Listen—
    all you bare trees
    burrs
    brambles
    pile of twigs
    red and green lights flashing
    muddy bottle shards
    shoe half buried—listen

    listen, I am holy.

Passing a Truck Full of Chickens at Night on Highway Eighty

What struck me first was their panic.

Some were pulled by the wind from moving
to the ends of the stacked cages,
some had their heads blown through the bars—

and could not get them in again.
Some hung there like that—dead—
their own feathers blowing, clotting

in their faces. Then
I saw the one that made me slow some—
I lingered there beside her for five miles.

She had pushed her head through the space
between bars—to get a better view.
She had the look of a dog in the back

of a pickup, that eager look of a dog
who knows she's being taken along.
She craned her neck.

She looked around, watched me, then
strained to see over the car—strained
to see what happened beyond.

That is the chicken I want to be.

Blueflower Arts

Marilyn Nelson

Born April 26, 1946, in Cleveland, Ohio. Marilyn Nelson is the author or translator of twelve books. Her work has won many prizes, including the Annisfield-Wolf Award, the Poets' Prize, the *Boston Globe*/Horn Book Award, and the Flora Stieglitz Straus Award; most recently *A Wreath for Emmett Till* was a 2006 Coretta Scott King Honor Book. Other honors include two fellowships from the National Endowment for the Arts, a Fulbright Teaching Fellowship, three honorary doctorates, and a fellowship from the Guggenheim Foundation. Nelson is Professor Emerita of English at the University of Connecticut; founding director of Soul Mountain Retreat, a small writers' colony; and the former (2001–2006) Poet Laureate of the State of Connecticut.

Drifter

Something says find out
why rain falls, what makes corn proud
and squash so humble, the questions
call like a train whistle so at fourteen,
fifteen, eighteen, nineteen still on half-fare,
over the receding landscapes the perceiving self
stares back from the darkening window.

The Perceiving Self

Fort Scott, Kansas, 1879

The first except birds
who spoke to us, his voice high
and lilting as a meadowlark's,
with an undertone of windsong,
many-petaled as the meadow,
the music shaped and colored
by brown lips, white teeth, pink tongue.
Walking slowly, he talked to us,
touched our stamens,
pleasured us with pollen.
Then he squealed, a field mouse taken
without wingbeat,
with no shadow.
His yellow feet crushed past, running,
his bare legs bruised, he trampled, his spew
burned, his scalding urine.

The icedrift of silence.
Smoke from a torched deadman, barking laughter
from the cottonwoods at the creek.

Unmentionables

Miss Pru's father hauls water barrels from his well
to our laundry kitchen, where we soak and scrub
unmentionables, then carry our pails
of wrung-out undies (growing increasingly drab
and dank from being hung to dry upstairs
instead of billowing in sun-bleaching air)
up to the attic and hang them in the dark,
where some of the girls believe a spirit lurks,
waiting, among the ghostly pantaloons
and petticoats, in the distorted light
of the starburst window. After several moons
together day by day and night by night,
most of us hang our linens side by side,
our march to the attic a private parade of pride.

All-Night Melodies

An evening on the piano: ecstasy
could not be sweeter. Even simple scales
promise hymn chords, while six-note harmony
must be a taste of heaven's color wheel.
A fire on the hearth, the dishes put away,
twenty girls sit by oil lamps to read or sew
until Miss Teacher signals time to retire.
We form a blessing circle before the fire
as silence fills us with its constant thrum.
My fingers remember the ebony and ivory keys,
my feet the pedals. All-night melodies
unplayed, unheard, swirl in our shared bedroom,
meet other dreams, converge, become a sound
silent enough to convert every bigot in town.

Fire from the Gods

I didn't know how much I didn't know.
Like Brer Mosquito on Brer Elephant,
now I know my capacity for awe
is infinite: this thirst is permanent,
the well bottomless, my good fortune vast.
An uneducated mind is a clenched fist
that can open, like a bud, into a flower
whose being reaches, every waking hour, .
and who sleeps a fragrant dream of gratitude.

Now it's "illegal," "illegitimate"
to teach brown girls who aren't state residents.
As if Teacher's stealing fire from the gods.
As if the Ancestors aren't tickled to death to see
a child they lived toward find her mind's infinity.

Marion Ettlinger

Aimee Nezhukumatathil

Born December 23, 1974, in Chicago, Illinois. Aimee Nezhukumatathil is the author of *At the Drive-In Volcano* and *Miracle Fruit* (both from Tupelo Press), which was named Poetry Book of the Year by *ForeWord Magazine*, and the winner of the Global Filipino Literary Award. She is Associate Professor of English at SUNY-Fredonia, where she was awarded a Chancellor's Medal of Excellence and the Hagan Young Scholars Award. She lives in berry and wine country in Western New York with her husband, infant son, and their geriatric long-haired dachshund, Villanelle.

Hippopotomonstrosesquipedaliophobia

The fear of long words

On the first day of classes, I secretly beg
my students *Don't be afraid of me*. I know
my last name on your semester schedule

is chopped off or probably misspelled—
or both. I can't help it. I know the panic
of too many consonants rubbed up
against each other, no room for vowels

to fan some air into the room of a box
marked *Instructor.* You want something
to startle you? Try tapping the ball

of roots of a potted tomato plant
into your cupped hand one spring, only
to find a small black toad who kicks
and blinks his cold eye at you,

the sun, a gnat. Be afraid of the X-rays
for your teeth or lung. Pray for no
dark spots. You may have

pneumonoultramicroscopicsilicovolcanokoniosis:
coal lung. Be afraid of money spiders tiptoeing
across your face while you sleep on a sweet, fat couch.
But don't be afraid of me, my last name, what language

I speak or what accent dulls itself on my molars.
I will tell jokes, help you see the gleam
of the beak of a mohawked cockatiel. I will

lecture on luminescent sweeps of ocean, full of tiny
dinoflagellates oozing green light when disturbed.
I promise dark gatherings of toadfish and comical shrimp
just when you think you are alone, hoping to stay somehow afloat.

My Name

At four, I was ready: fat pencil and paper, lined
the way I like it best—two strong sky blue lines
with a dotted line in between the two, a soft ceiling
for the tops of lower case letters to brush up against.

In New Guinea, to identify a person's family, you ask,
What is the name of your canoe? My seventh grade
social studies teacher made up a dance to help him
remember how to pronounce my name—he'd break it

into sharp syllables, shake his corduroyed hips
at roll call, his bulge of keys rattling in time.
I don't remember who first shortened it to Nez,
but I loved the zip of it, the sport and short of it,

until the day I learned Nez means *nose* in French.
Translation: beloved nose. My father tells me part
of our name comes from a flower from the South Indian
coast. I wonder what it smells like, what fragrance

I always have dabbed at my neck. Scientists say some flowers
don't have a scent, but they *do*—even if it's hints of sweat
from blooms too long without drink or the promise
of honey from the scratchings of a thin bee leg, feathered

with loosestrife and sage. I wonder if I've ever smelled
our flower, if the smell ever wafted clear across the ocean.
I would swim out to meet it, brush the salt and bits
of pink shell away, apologize for the messiness of my hair.

Fishbone

At dinner, my mother says if one gets stuck
in your throat, roll some rice into a ball
and swallow it whole. She says things
like this and the next thing out of her mouth

is *did you know Madonna is pregnant?*
But I want to ponder the basket of fried smelt
on the table, lined with paper towels to catch
the grease—want to study their eyes

like flat soda, wonder how I'm supposed
to eat them whole. Wonder why we can't
have normal food for breakfast like at Sara's house—
Cheerios, or sometimes if her mother is home:

buttered toast and soft-boiled eggs
in her grandmother's dainty blue egg cups
and matching blue spoon. Safe. Pretty.
Nothing with eyes. Under the flakes of fried crust,

I see a shimmer of skin as silver as foil,
like the dimes my mother tapes to a board
for each year I'm alive. How she tucked this
into my suitcase before I left for college

and I forgot about '93 and '95. How she said
she'll never find a '93, and shouldn't this
be a great thing to one day put into an oak frame,
but not now, not until we find the missing coin?

How we don't have many traditions left, thanks
to Your Father. These are the things she says
instead of a blessing to our food. These are the words
that stick inside me as I snap off the next head.

Wrap

I don't mean when a movie ends,
as in, *it's a*! Nor tortillas splitting
with the heavy wet of bean.
And I don't mean what you do

with your lavender robe—all fluff
and socks—to snatch the paper
from the shrubs. Nor the promise
of a gift, the curl and furl of red ribbon

just begging to be tugged. What I mean
is waiting with my grandmama (a pause
in the Monsoon) at the Trivandrum airport
for a jeep. Her small hand wraps

again the emerald green pallu of her sari
tucked in at her hips, across her breast,
and coughs it up over her shoulder—a hush
of paprika and burnt honey across my face.

Falling Thirds

We measure our names the same.
Across the world, when children
call out for a friend, their mother,

their favorite white goat—they have
the same intonation, the same fall
and lilt to their voice, no matter

their language: *Jahhn-ee! Mah-ma!*
Pehh-dro! My music teacher friend says
this is *falling thirds*: this is proof we spoke

the same language before Babel, that maybe
a tower did fall into rock and dust, gilding
our tongues slicker past any understanding.

We speak little wants, call little kisses
into our ears across beanfields, sand,
saltwater. Still, we sing the same songs.

Speak

If the Hopi say "ripi"
to mean *notch*, then
for them, *serration*
is "ripiripiripi." I want
to speak like that, fill
your ears and hands
with wet stones, turquoise
and smooth, as if
they had tumbled
in the mouth of a macaw.

Naomi Shihab Nye

Born March 12, 1952, in St. Louis, Missouri. Each year Naomi Shihab Nye spends time as what she calls "a wandering poet" with many various assignments in schools and libraries and communities all over the United States and elsewhere. Her most recent books are *You & Yours* (BOA Editions), *Honeybee* (Greenwillow Books, HarperCollins) and *I'll Ask You Three Times, Are You OK?* (Greenwillow Books), winner of the 2007 Texas Institute of Letters Award for the Best Book for Young Adults. Nye and her family have two large turtles living in their backyard. She admits that she prefers her junky old green bicycle with a basket to the sleek Italian bicycle a kind friend gave to her.

Half-and-Half

You can't be, says a Palestinian Christian
on the first feast day after Ramadan.
So, half-and-half and half-and-half.
He sells glass. He knows about broken bits,
chips. If you love Jesus you can't love
anyone else. Says he.

At his stall of blue pitchers on the Via Dolorosa,
he's sweeping. The rubbed stones
feel holy. Dusting of powdered sugar
across faces of date-stuffed *mamool*.

This morning we lit the slim white candles
which bend over at the waist by noon.
For once the priests weren't fighting
in the church for the best spots to stand.
As a boy, my father listened to them fight.
This is partly why he prays in no language
but his own. Why I press my lips
to every exception.

A woman opens a window—here and here and here—
placing a vase of blue flowers
on an orange cloth. I follow her.
She is making a soup from what she had left
in the bowl, the shriveled garlic and bent bean.
She is leaving nothing out.

My Friend's Divorce

I want her
to dig up
every plant

in her garden
the pansies
the pentas
roses
ranunculus
thyme and lilies
the thing nobody knows
the name of
unwind the morning glories
from the wire windows
of the fence
take the blooming
and the almost-blooming
and the dormant
especially the dormant
and then
and then
plant them in her new yard
on the other side
of town
and see how
they breathe

Guide

My neighbor knew the exact location
of every map   every postcard & pincushion
          every empty basket
that once held chocolate eggs

In her tall house
          a century of spunk & clutter
          Please get me   she would say
guiding from her wheelchair
          in the other room
no, a little to the left of
          the nail clippers
there, that's it,
          in the orange tin
yes, you have it!

a folded essay about artifacts or water conservation
a purple ribbon or a pill that cost 3 dollars
she hated the pill that cost 3 dollars
when her father owned the 6th car
          in the state of Texas

& ran a drugstore
        no pill cost 3 dollars

I tried to memorize charms & Mexican pottery
        dolls & laces crowding the dresser,
                exactly the ways they stood
through wars & revolutions
        calmly   calmly
a glass case of miniature teacups
even clumps of dust on the ceiling
        over the bed
so that after her sudden terrible departure
as the icons were lifted & boxed & bagged
        for the highest bidders
                her voice from the other room
kept describing   what we'd find

Music

When you wanted a piano
everyone wanted something:
your sister wished for a red silk dress
with polka-dots,
your mother, a gold watch
to hold the time
that kept leaving her
before she could find it.
Even your father,
who spent hours calculating
figures in a checkbook,
wanted a green car
with fancy headlights,
a venetian blind
that didn't stick.

That was the first lesson.

You made a paper keyboard
and played it in the dark,
singing the notes.
If you pressed your foot
you could feel a pedal in the carpet,
hear the murmur lasting beyond itself
the way it did when they played
piano at school.
Everyone would leave the music class

while you stood hinged to that last tone
emptying into air. It wasn't gone
if you tilted your head.
Your father found the keyboard
and slapped you for wasting paper.

The second lesson was long.

Read Me

Watch us humans

as we enter our rooms,

remove our shoes and watches

and stretch out on the bed

with a single good book.

It's the honey of the mind time.

Lights shine through our little jars.

Hidden

If you place a fern
under a stone
the next day it will be
nearly invisible
as if the stone has
swallowed it.

If you tuck the name of a loved one
under your tongue too long
without speaking it
it becomes blood
sigh
the little sucked-in breath of air
hiding everywhere
beneath your words.

No one sees
the fuel that feeds you.

Katherine Kayser

Deborah Nystrom

Born July 12, 1954, in Pierre, South Dakota. Debra Nystrom grew up in South Dakota. Her new book of poems, *Bad River Road*, will be out from Sarabande Books in early 2009. She has published two previous books of poetry, *Torn Sky* from Sarabande Books (2003) and *A Quarter Turn* from Sheep Meadow Press (1991). Her current work has appeared or is forthcoming in *Ploughshares, Slate, Agni, Five Points, The Virginia Quarterly Review,* and *TriQuarterly*, and has received awards from The Virginia Commission for the Arts, The Library of Virginia, and The American Anthropological Association. She teaches in the Creative Writing Program at the University of Virginia, and lives in Charlottesville, Virginia, with her husband and daughter.

Twisting Vines

My mother bought a dress once and my dad
said it looked like curtains. Nothing if not honest,
nothing much but me to his name, doing his best
about the trike and baby pool, new triple-speed
living-room fan, her just-landed job as a typist
while her mother baby-sat. There must
have been some wedding, or National Guard
occasion—James-Dean handsome he was,
even in eagle-crest hat, glare-polished shoes—
but the dress went right back in its creased
paper bag, unused. She had modeled it for me first
though, gazing over each shoulder to the longest
mirror before he got home, smeared and hot
from painting houses. *How does it look, hon?*—
that dress I remember more than any other,
off a rack at London's, our two-block downtown's
only clothes store. *Scoop-necked*, she called it,
for summer. Cap-sleeved. White, with a pattern of
little twisting green vines. I touched the satin piping
that showed off her collarbone, tiny waistline.
Made her look like a full grown fairy out of my book.
Those days she still sang when she sifted flour, folded
laundry plucked off the line by the morning
glories and tulips—"Tammy's in Love," "Blue Moon,"
"My Buddy." Never again got herself
what she wished for, if she knew.

My Mother Never Told Me

For years my mother wore special gloves to bed.
Sometimes her hands were so swollen she couldn't

bend her fingers without the cracked skin opening
again and weeping. "Nerves," the doctor had said,

and gave her a lotion she kept on the kitchen counter
by the screen door, where she could reach for it after

raking leaves or scrubbing the floor. Neighbors
commented, my grandmother, my aunts; I'd hear them

sympathize about the pain. No one asked what made
her nervous, except when Dad shouted

WHAT HAVE YOU GOT TO BE NERVOUS
ABOUT—as if even skin could be frightened into

behaving. Yet I remember him now and then down
on the linoleum with a rag, times she couldn't manage.

When I told my mother over the phone about leaving
my second husband, the one she'd hardly known,

she asked me only one thing. I said he saw other
women all the time; he couldn't control himself; he was

molested as a child. Did he hit you? her question
had been, but I hadn't answered, recalling how as a kid,

like a trainer readying a boxer, I'd help pull her gloves on
before bed, over fresh lotion, covering the defiant flesh.

Picture Window: Blizzard

No seeing to the streets, where Dad's out
in a National Guard truck, moving families with no heat

to the cots and blankets and tinned food at the armory.
Our house warm enough, weirdly muffled inside

the wind, but out front the snow-fort we kids packed
and iced with matted mittens just days ago is vanished

into white frenzy. Mom watching too, maybe wondering
when or how he'll be back—guard, rescue squad,

fire crew, he's always getting called to a body in the river,
a lightning-blazed line of haystacks. Any minute

the fire-radio might pitch its squeal from the kitchen, then
the raspy station-voice repeat again and again the address

to rush to—now and then if I've wandered from bed
Dad takes me in pajamas to hook up the blue flasher

while he veers through stop-lights or barrels beyond town
to where I can look out at a life gone suddenly dark—

black-suited divers under the condemned bridge
searching for Linda Frye; Dad shaking upside-down

the Reese boy with the Lincoln Log piece stuck
in his throat. Other nights the radio spells out

its scratchy directions, but only the rest of us wake up—
those nights he's gone already, his own emergency.

Smoke-break Behind the Treatment Center

End of the third week: family weekend.
The smokers, most of the patients, are more

jittery than usual, more anxious just now
than other days to step out this door behind

the cafeteria, where they can look across
to the stubble-field, world of chopped-off stalks

that has ripped them up, that they've needed
too much from. In fifteen minutes they'll see

the ones who've come to find out if
they are changing. Maybe half have family

visiting; fewer than that will leave in another
week without needing to come back, stand

here in a different season and stare at the silo
you set yourself by, imagine walking through

your own cloud of smoke to clean blank sky.

Waitress at a Window

You can feel dusk suck at the heat and clatter
and rhythms of earnest conversations,
standing a minute with the silver pitcher,
letting its sweat collect in your palm
as a secret, something for yourself,
like the thought of diving on a long breath
into the swelling river, then rising to recover
and lie motionless, face upward on the water.

Steve Ladner

Sharon Olds

Born November 19, 1942, in San Francisco, California. Sharon Olds's most recent poetry collection, her ninth, is *One Secret Thing* (Knopf, 2008). Her first, *Satan Says* (University of Pittsburgh Press, 1980), received the inaugural San Francisco Poetry Center Award. *The Dead & the Living* (University of Pittsburgh Press, 1983) received the Lamont Poetry Selection and the National Book Critics Circle Award. Her numerous other honors include fellowships from the National Endowment for the Arts and the Guggenheim Foundation. Olds was New York State Poet from 1998 to 2000. She is on the faculty of New York University's Graduate Creative Writing Program and runs a workshop at Goldwater Hospital on Roosevelt Island in New York.

Self-exam

They tell you it won't make much sense, at first,
you will have to learn the terrain. They tell you this
at thirty, and fifty, and some are late
beginners, at last lying down and walking
the old earth of the breasts—the small,
cobbled, plowed field of one,
with a listening walking, and then the other—
fingertip-stepping, divining, north
to south, east to west, sectioning
the little fallen hills, sweeping
for mines. And the matter feels primordial,
unimaginable—dense,
cystic, phthistic, each breast like the innards
of a cell, its contents shifting and changing,
streambed gravel under walking feet, it
seems almost unpicturable, not
immemorial, but nearly un-
memorizable, but one marches,
slowly, through grave or fatal danger,
or no danger, one feels around in the
two tack-room drawers, ribs and
knots like leather bridles and plaited
harnesses and bits and reins,
one runs one's hands through the mortal tackle
in a jumble, in the dark, indoors. Outside—
night, in which these glossy ones were
ridden to a froth of starlight, bareback.

The Rising Daughter

(b. San Francisco, 1942)

As I sucked life from my mother's body
in the blacked-out room above the sea,
the cream-flecked milk swaying in me
as I swayed in her arms—
                                        off the coast,
underwater, in silence and darkness,
delicate as shrimp, the Japanese frogmen
swam, slowly. They approached from the west,
their gold faces glowing like specks of
mica, in the heavy Pacific,
their flippers the fins of prawns. I lay
and sucked, and in great numbers, like yellow
flakes of butter, they entered me
with my mother's milk, a vocation. I would be
for myself, then, an enemy
to all who do not wish me to rise.

The Talk

In the dark square wooden room at noon
the mother had a talk with her daughter.
The rudeness could not go on, the meanness
to her little brother, the selfishness.
The 8-year-old sat on the bed
in the corner of the room, her irises dark as
the last drops of something, her firm
face melting, reddening,
silver flashes in her eyes like distant
bodies of water glimpsed through woods.
She took it and took it and broke, crying out
I hate being a person! diving
into the mother
as if
into
a deep pond—and she cannot swim,
the child cannot swim.

Toth Farry

In the back of the charm-box, in a sack, the baby
canines and incisors are mostly chaff,

by now, split kernels and acicular down, no
whole utensils left: half
an adz; half a shovel, in its broken
handle a marrow well of the will
to dig and bite. And the enamel hems
are sharp as shell-tools, and the colors go from
salt, to bone, to pee on snow, to
sun on pond-ice embedded with twigs
and chipped-off skate-blade. One cuspid
is like the tail of an ivory chough
on my grandmother's what-not in a gravure on my mother's
bureau in my father's house in my head,
I think it's our daughter's, but the dime Hermes
mingled the deciduals of our girl and boy, safe-
keeping them together with the note that says
Dear Toth Farry, Plees Giv Me
A Bag of Moany. I pore over the shards,
a skeleton-lover—but who could throw out
these short pints of osseous breastmilk,
or the wisdom, with its charnel underside,
and its dome, smooth and experienced,
ground in anger, rinsed in silver
when the mouth waters. From above, its knurls
are a cusp-ring of mountain tops
around an amber crevasse, where in high
summer the summit wildflowers open
for a day—Crown Buttercup, Alpine Flames,
Shooting-Star, Rosy Fairy Lantern,
Cream Sacs, Sugar Scoop.

The Mother

In the dreamy silence after bath,
hot in the milk-white towel, my son
announces that I will not love him when I'm dead
because people can't think when they're dead. I can't
think at first—not love him? The air outside the
window is very black, the old locust
beginning to lose its leaves already . . .
I hold him tight, he is white as a buoy
and my death like dark water is rising
swiftly in the room. I tell him I loved him

before he was born. I do not tell him
I'm damned if I won't love him after I'm
dead, necessity after all being
the mother of invention.

Late

The mist is blowing across the yard
like smoke from a battle.
I am so tired of the women doing dishes
and how smart the men are, and how I want to
bite their mouths and feel their hard cocks against me.

The mist moves, over the bushes
bright with poison ivy and black
berries like stones. I am tired of the children,
I am tired of the laundry, I want to be great.

The fog pours across the underbrush in silence.
We are sealed in. The only way out is through
fire, and I do not want a single
hair of a single head singed.

2007 diomass.com

Mary Oliver

Born September 10, 1935, in Maple Heights, Ohio. Mary Oliver's most recent poetry volume is *Red Bird* (Beacon Press, 2008). *American Primitive*, her first collection, won the 1983 Pulitzer Prize, and she won the National Book Award for *New and Selected Poems* (1992). Oliver has also written two volumes on the craft of writing poetry, *A Poetry Handbook* (1995) and *Rules for the Dance: A Handbook for Writing and Reading Metrical Verse* (1998). She has been the Poet-in-Residence at Bucknell University, the Margaret Banister Writer-in-Residence at Sweet Briar College, and the Catharine Osgood Foster Chair for Distinguished Teaching at Bennington College. She lives in Provincetown, Massachusetts.

Crows

It is January, and there are the crows
like black flowers on the snow.
While I watch they rise and float toward the frozen pond, they have seen
some streak of death on the dark ice.
They gather around it and consume everything, the strings
and the red music of that nameless body. Then they shout,
one hungry, blunt voice echoing another.
It begins to rain.
Later, it becomes February,
and even later, spring
returns, a chorus of thousands.
They bow, and begin their important music.
I recognize the oriole.
I recognize the thrush, and the mockingbird.
I recognize the business of summer, which is to forge ahead, delicately.
So I dip my fingers among the green stems, delicately.
I lounge at the edge of the leafing pond, delicately.
I scarcely remember the crust of the snow.
I scarcely remember the icy dawns and the sun like a lamp without a fuse.
I don't remember the fury of loneliness.
I never felt the wind's drift.
I never heard of the struggle between anything and nothing.
I never saw the flapping, blood-gulping crows.

In the Evening, in the Pinewoods

Who knows the sorrows of the heart?
God, of course, and the private self.
But who else? Anyone or anything else?
Not the trees, in their windy independence.
Nor the roving clouds nor, even, the dearest of friends.

Yet maybe the thrush, who sings
by himself, at the edge of the green woods,
to each of us
out of his mortal body, his own feathered limits,
of every estrangement, exile, rejection—their
  death-dealing weight.

And then, so sweetly, of every goodness also to be remembered.

Everything

I want to make poems that say right out, plainly,
  what I mean, that don't go looking for the
laces of elaboration, puffed sleeves. I want to
  keep close and use often words like
heavy, heart, joy, soon, and to cherish
  the question mark and her bold sister

the dash. I want to write with quiet hands. I
  want to write while crossing the fields that are
fresh with daisies and everlasting and the
  ordinary grass. I want to make poems while thinking of
the bread of heaven and the
  cup of astonishment; let them be

songs in which nothing is neglected,
  not a hope, not a promise. I want to make poems
that look into the earth and the heavens
  and see the unseeable. I want them to honor
both the heart of faith, and the light of the world;
  the gladness that says, without any words, *everything*.

Randy Madsen

Jacqueline Osherow

Born August 15, 1956, in Philadelphia, Pennsylvania. Jacqueline Osherow is the author of five books of poems, most recently *The Hoopoe's Crown* from BOA Editions and *Dead Men's Praise* from Grove Press. She has been awarded grants from the National Endowment for the Arts, the John Simon Guggenheim Foundation, the Ingram Merrill Foundation and the Witter Bynner Prize from the American Academy and Institute of Arts and Letters. She is Distinguished Professor of English and Creative Writing at the University of Utah. She has three daughters, one of whom she can no longer beat at Scrabble, who all make fun of her avid kickboxing.

At the Wailing Wall

I figure I have to come here with my kids,
though I'm always ill at ease in holy places—
the wars, for one thing—and it's the substanceless
that sets me going: the holy words.
Though I do write a note—my girls' sound future
(there's an evil eye out there; you never know)—
and then pick up a broken-backed siddur,
the first of many motions to go through.
Let's get them over with. I hate this women's section
almost as much as that one full of men
wrapped in tallises, eyes closed, showing off.
But here I am, reciting the *Amida* anyway.
Surprising things can happen when you start to pray;
we'll see if any angels call my bluff.

God's Acrostic

What if the universe is God's acrostic?
He's sneaking bits of proverbs into seismic variations;
Abbreviating psalms in flecks of snow.
Try to read them, says a comet,

If you dare.
Fine print. What you've been waiting for.

Twisted in the DNA of marmosets:
Hermetic feedback to your tight-lipped prayer.
Examine indentations left by hailstones in the grass;

Unearth their parallel soliloquies;
Note, too, the shifting patterns of cuneiform
Initiating each communication.

Verify them. Don't take my word.
Eavesdrop on the planets in the outer spheres; they can
Reverse the letters' previous direction.
Silence, as you might imagine, has no bearing here.
Episodes of stillness—however brief—must be

Interpreted as unheard
Sounds,

Gaps that, with any luck, you'll fill in later—
Or so you tell yourself, acknowledging
Delusion's primal status in this enterprise.
Still, that's no reason to slow down.

Abandonments are howling out around you:
Cast-off lamentations from the thwarted drops of rain
Reduced to vapor on their struggle down;
Observe, at the very least, their passing.
Sanctify them. Don't succumb
To anything less vivid than a spelled-out
invitation to a not yet formulated nebula.
Calm yourself. Come quickly. Welcome home.

My Version: Medieval Acrostic

Jealousy? Homage? Longing? Superstition?
All I know is, I want to join those guys
Calling God's name, writing their own
Quietly, in steady pieces, as if praise
Unmasks the giver as it goes along,
Existing and singing simultaneous.
Let me in, guys—even if I'm wrong;
I'm not fit for unremitting chaos.
Nudge me when another cornered word
Escapes as firmament the moment it's uttered.

Villanelle

This chill in spring—my subtle ally—
The elements all blossoming at once—
New snow on the mountains, lupines in the valley,

Like a rare conjunction of planets, ideally
Stationed for a long spell of disturbance.
This chill in spring—my subtle ally—

Will not suffer ice to let go easily
And I envy its immaculate resistance.
New snow on the mountains, lupines in the valley.

Will the air give lessons? See how coolly
It ambushes the lilacs' shrill abundance,
This chill in spring—my subtle ally.

But how has it managed so uncannily
To find me out? I burned the evidence.
And what about snow, lupines, mountains, valley?

The whole earth is unreconciled, unruly.
I'm just one tiny dissonance.
This subtle spring, this chilling ally.
New snow on the mountains, lupines in the valley.

Egrets in Be'ersheva

What language is it
in which egret feathers
mean purity? In which—
my friend swears it—
Isaiah's scarlet sins
go white as egret
feathers, not as snow?
Isaiah could so easily
have mentioned egrets—
I saw them in Be'ersheva,
crowding out the trees,
each slender, graceful
torso white as snow,
so many I thought
the trees would
topple over. Though
it was summer, they
seemed to have no
leaves, just slender,
graceful arcs of blameless
snow, which made,
I have to admit,
an absolute racket.
But, surely, it was
that ecstatic noise

that got me—for
once—to lift my eyes,
the very sound Isaiah's
voice was after:
though your sins be
scarlet, they shall be
white as the egrets
in these trees, but then
he was afraid he'd
divulged his secret:
his immaculate source
wasn't God at all, but
fleet, white arrows
slashing the heavens,
divvying the clouds
among the startled trees,
snow-white feathers
flying as they'd go.
He crossed out "egret"
and wrote "snow."

J.P. Ostriker

Alicia Ostriker

Born November 11, 1937, in Brooklyn, New York. Alicia Ostriker's most recent volumes of poetry are *The Volcano Sequence* (University of Pittsburgh Press, 2002) and *No Heaven* (University of Pittsburgh Press, 2007), and her most recent book of criticism is *Dancing at the Devil's Party: Essays on Poetry, Politics, and the Erotic.* She has twice been a National Book Award finalist, has won the San Francisco State Poetry Center Award and the Paterson Poetry Prize, and has been married (as of this printing) for fifty years to the astrophysicist J.P. Ostriker. They are both workaholics, which keeps life interesting, and they both love to travel, which also helps.

The Marriage Nocturne

Stopped at a corner, near midnight, I watch
A young man and young woman quarreling
Under the streetlamp. What I can see is gestures.
He leans forward, he scowls, raises his hand.
She has been taking it, but now she stands
Up to him, throwing her chin and chest out.
The stoplight purples their two leather jackets.
Both of them now are shouting, theatrical,
Shut up, bitch, or, Go to hell, loser,
And between them, in a stroller,
Sits their pale bundled baby, a piece of candy.

Earlier this evening I was listening
To the poet Amichai, whose language seemed
To grow like Jonah's gourd in a dry place,
From pure humility, or perhaps from yearning
For another world, land, city
Of Jerusalem, while embracing this one,
As a man dreams of the never-obtainable mistress,
Flowery, perfumed, girlish
(But hasn't she somehow been promised to him?)
And meanwhile has and holds the stony wife
Whom the Lord gives him for a long reproach.

I can imagine, when such a husband touches
Such a wife, hating it, in tears,
And helpless lust, and the survivor's shame,
That her eyes gaze back at him like walls
Where you still can see the marks of the shelling.

We make beauty of bitterness. Woman and man,
Arab and Jew, we have arrived at that

Dubious skill. Still, when one of these children,
Having moved like a dancer, smashes the other
One in the face, and the baby swivels its periscope
Neck to look, I will not see it:
The light changes. Fifteen miles down the road,
That will be lined by luminous spring trees,
My husband reads in bed, sleepy and naked;
I am not crying, I step on the gas, I am driving
Home to my marriage, my safety, through this wounded
World that we cannot heal, that is our bride.

A Question of Time

I ask a friend. She informs me it is ten years
From when her mother wrote
"I hope at least you are sorry
For causing your father's heart attack,"
To now, when they are speaking
Weekly on the phone
And almost, even, waxing confidential.
I check my watch. Ten years is rather much,
But I am not a Texas Fundamentalist,
And you are not a red-headed Lesbian,
So it should take us shorter, and I should get
Time off for good behavior
If I behave well, which
I do not plan to do.
No, on the contrary, I plan to play
All my cards wrong,
To pelt you with letters, gifts, advice,
Descriptions of my feelings.
I plan to ask friendly maternal questions.
I plan to beam a steady
Stream of anxiety
Rays which would stun a mule,
Derail a train,
Take out a satellite,
At you in California, where you hack
Coldly away at this iron umbilicus,
Having sensibly put three thousand miles between us.

I remember you told me once, when we were still
In love, the summer before you left
For the hills of San Francisco,
The music of youth,

To stop fearing estrangement:
"Mom, you're not crazy like Grandma."
It was the country. We were on the balcony
Overlooking the pond, where your wiry boyfriend
And the rest of the family swam and drank, unconscious.
False but endearing, dear. I *am* my mother.
I am your mother. Are you keeping up
Your drawing, your reading?
Have you written poems?
Are you saving money? Don't
Do acid, it fries the brain,
Don't do cocaine, don't
Get pregnant, or have you already,
Don't slip away from me,
You said you wouldn't,
Remember that. I remember it was hot,
How lightly we were dressed,
And barefoot, at that time,
And how you let me rest
A half a minute in your suntanned arms.

Bus Station

Those bus station bathrooms are bad,
You would have to be a desperate
Woman with broken shoe heels
A torn jacket lining
And a child whose face
Has to be washed because the tracks
Of its gritty tears make you ashamed,
To use those bathrooms
With their smell of disinfectant
Like a personal insult

Then you would come out
Not very hopeful, the kid
Unready to control himself,
You would get some candy from a machine
Prop the kid on a bench, wait for the bus
And history to repeat themselves

Outside the revolving doors
Somehow rain would probably be falling
Steadily in slow wet crystal globes
Through the inky night the wet streetlights
The taxis, the entire world.

May Rain, Princeton

Green, green, the luminous maples preen,
Swaying like girls at a prom
Waiting to be asked to dance,

The bird feeders need daily refilling, the hot
Azaleas enhance their orange and fuchsia tints,
The rhododendrons puckered dryly inside

Their big buds have begun to force themselves out,
Apple blossoms lie in shallow pools
At the feet of their trunks. All afternoon

Relentless pouring rain soaks the ground,
Beats the roofs, rat-tat,
Races down the gutters.

I imagine it falling into the Hudson River
Around the scows and barges. I imagine it
Splashing the yellow slickers of road crews.

I pretend that I am farms and towns stretched out
The breadth of New Jersey and Pennsylvania
Flat on my back looking up at a gray sky.

The grays shift, it must be windy up there,
I feel the rain batter me, how good it is, cleansing
The air, pocking my skin—

Good, good, like sex after childbirth
When the body is keen
For pleasure again.

Anita K. Boyle

Nancy Pagh

Born September 17, 1963, in Anacortes, Washington. Nancy Pagh was born on Fidalgo Island in Washington State and grew up with a deep connection to place. Her first published poem, "Is a Clam Clammy or Is It Just Wet?" appeared when she was twelve. *No Sweeter Fat*, her first book of poems, won the 2007 Autumn House Press Poetry Prize. Her work also appears in *The Bellingham Review, Rattle, Poetry Northwest, and O (Oprah)* magazine. She is a recipient of an Artist Trust Fellowship. *At Home Afloat: Women on the Waters of the Pacific Northwest* (2001) is her critical study of the language women use when traveling at sea. She teaches at Western Washington University in Bellingham.

Ten Reasons Your Prayer Diet Won't Work

1.
Praying to god that you will be thin
instead of eating
only burns eleven calories
at average fervency.

2.
Jesus had large love handles.
I know in the pictures he is skinny
and White
with slightly Italian-esque features,
but he understood the value
of keeping on a few extra pounds
to tide him over in the desert.
If you are a child of god
this runs in your family.

3.
All food miracles create *more*:
more loaves, more fishes, more wine, more manna . . . .
When you ask god to do something about fat
expect multiplication.

4.
The only time you used to talk to god
was giving thanks before high-caloric meals.
Your fat cells remember this
and begin to swell
even at the mention of his name.

5.
God has stock in Doritos.

6.
Eventually you will tell yourself
that god created you this way
and who are you to disagree?

7.
Contrary to popular belief,
eating is not a mortal sin *per se*
and god believes in free will.

8.
Bread and wine. Communion would suggest
god endorses the Mediterranean Diet
instead.

9.
Blasphemy, to waste German chocolate cake.

10.
God is characterized by excess;
your only proof that god exists
is that the natural world is more than it has to be.

Perhaps the closest you've come
to acting in her perfect image
was building your sacred hips.

I Believe I Could Kneel

I believe I could kneel
in so many quiet places
where the pale sponge of moss
would surely reach above
my hips as I sank down and down
as the deer must in their beds
kneeling once, then once again
to lower themselves front and back
before closing their glistening eyes.

I think I am the kind of person
down on one knee and shifting my weight
my whole life long
but capable of sinking far, and deep,
to the bottom of something
that might replace the religion I discarded
or make me really live in this body
or waste my life.

I would like to live my way into being
someone who stands back up
and runs toward that holy forest.

Fat Lady Reads

A fat lady reads a book
she reads a book all day
and all day
she is not a fat lady

unless she reads a diet book
or Wally Lamb's *She's Come Undone*
and there's a good chance she reads
one of those.

A fat lady reads a book
and enters a world
where there really are no fat people
of consequence

except old Mrs. Manson Mingott
in Edith Wharton's *The Age of Innocence*
whose "immense accretion of flesh
descended on her in middle life
like a flood of lava on a doomed city"

and except the rude person
repeatedly referred to as "the fat man"
(corpulence meant to represent everything
unaware of its own privilege)
in Bharati Mukerjee's "A Wife's Story."

Wealthy matchmaking fat ladies
and chubby men who use more than their half
of an armrest at the theatre
are just useful minor characters;
the fat lady reads
and identifies with the heroine (or hero)
and we all know who they are.
Their pants fit.

The fat lady understands
you cannot expect regular people
to identify with a tubby Ishmael

or believe he could carry that belly
all the way up the *Pequod*'s spars
or to relate with the poet Amy Lowell
who the *Heath Anthology of American Literature* says
was an unattractive, overweight woman,
an old maid, a lesbian
soundly rejected by readers
and reviewed as a failure because
she was "cut off
from the prime biological experiences of life
by her tragic physical predicament."

A fat lady writes a book
she writes a book all year
and all year
she's fat
but never writes about that.

She wants to be a serious writer.
What a tragic literary predicament.

Rounding the Point

Walking the shore trail today
I rounded the point and saw
eight pairs of seals in the bay,
dark wet heads bulbous and nodding
together. I saw the current move
across their thick backs and
slight upwellings shadow their turns.
It is November and last year's pups
are heavy as their mothers now,
or perhaps pairs are reuniting
in the gray monochrome bay.

The maple leaves across the trail
unstitched themselves from stem and form,
relinquished all desire.
Look. There were no seals,
but sixteen bull kelp in the bay.
Each bulb was separate as my head,
empty floats in coiling tide.
Why did I want it otherwise?

Margaretta Mitchell

Linda Pastan

Born May 27, 1932, in New York, New York. Linda Pastan is the author of twelve volumes of poetry, most recently *Queen of a Rainy Country* (W. W. Norton, 2006). Her awards include the Dylan Thomas Award, a Pushcart Prize, the Alice Fay di Castagnola Award from the Poetry Society of America, the Bess Hopkin Prize from *Poetry* magazine, the Maurice English Award, the Charity Randall Citation of the International Poetry Forum, and the 2003 Ruth Lilly Poetry Prize. Two of her collections of poems were finalists for the National Book Award and one for the *Los Angeles Times* Book Prize. She was on the staff of the Bread Loaf Writers' Conference for twenty years, and from 1991 to 1995 she was Poet Laureate of Maryland.

In an Unaddressed Envelope

Dear loves I never met,
dear children I never carried,
you who were here for a while
clothed in the rags of imagination,
who brushed past me without seeing
and sang songs the wind carried away
as if they were so many leaves
to be raked and burned later:
your singing comes back to me now
beneath the dark elusive notes
of someone else's music.

There are so many faces in the world,
each as particular as a snowflake, and yet
I see your smoky hair, your eyes
through the window of a train that rushes past
with the swooshing sound of distances.
Listen. I know you wait for me
at a place I am always seeking.
You are as real as the changelings
in my favorite books, have the tenderness
of the sea on a calm day, and all
the patience of the long invisible.

After a Month of Rain

Everything I thought I wanted
is right here,
particularly when the sun
is making such a comeback,

and the lilac engorged
with purple has recovered
from its severe pruning,
and you will be back soon

to dispel whatever it is
that overtakes me like leaf blight,
even on a day like this. I can still
hear remnants of the rain

in the swollen stream
behind the house, in the faint
dripping under the eaves,
persistent as memory.

And all the things I didn't think
I wanted, cut like the lilac back
to the root, push up again
from underground.

Return to Maple 9

Here I am, back
in my own past, river
and meadows exquisitely
the same, only my face
disguised by 15 years.

In this closet
the very hangers I left—
question marks over the pole—
soon will be clothed
in the livery of age.

The past is the underside
of the future. Remember
the yellow sundress? Remember
the heat of the motorcycle
raging down the road?

Why doesn't the landscape
seem to age? Outside
the old mountain waits
us out, still mute,
still greening.

The Obligation to Be Happy

It is more onerous
than the rites of beauty
or housework, harder than love.
But you expect it of me casually,
the way you expect the sun
to come up, not in spite of rain
or clouds but because of them.

And so I smile, as if my own fidelity
to sadness were a hidden vice—
that downward tug on my mouth,
my old suspicion that health
and love are brief irrelevancies,
no more than laughter in the warm dark
strangled at dawn.

Happiness. I try to hoist it
on my narrow shoulders again—
a knapsack heavy with gold coins.
I stumble around the house,
bump into things.
Only Midas himself
would understand.

Suffocation

for R. J. P.

In Chekhov's *Three Sisters,* everyone
is infected with terminal boredom.
When Irena says her soul is like a locked
piano without a key, I want
to tell her that playing the piano too
the fingers can wander up and down
the scales, going nowhere.
And when the talk leads always back
to Moscow, where she longs to be,
I wish I could remind Olga of the cold,
unyielding streets where even the ice hardens
to the color of stone. Sitting here, watching
someone I love slowly die, I see
how anguish and boredom can be married
for years, an ill-assorted couple, suffocating
in each other's arms. I watched Masha

at the curtain call, the tears still streaming
down her face as she moved from one self
to the other through the wall
of applause, a kind of backwards birth.
And I wondered where all that feeling
came from if not some deep pool
where one can be dragged and dragged
beneath the surface but never quite drown.
Russia . . . I thought, Russia . . . a country
my grandfather thought he had escaped from
but which he wore always
like the heavy overcoat in the story
by Gogol, or the overcoat he wrapped me in
one night when the grown-ups kept on talking,
and I shivered and yawned in an ecstasy
of boredom that made my childhood
seem a vast continent I could only escape from
hidden in a coat, in steerage, and at great risk.

The Almanac of Last Things

From the almanac of last things
I choose the spider lily
for the grace of its brief
blossom, though I myself
fear brevity,

but I choose *The Song of Songs*
because the flesh
of those pomegranates
has survived
all the frost of dogma.

I choose January with its chill
lessons of patience and despair—and
August, too sun-struck for lessons.
I choose a thimbleful of red wine
to make my heart race,

then another to help me
sleep. From the almanac
of last things I choose you,
as I have done before.
And I choose evening

because the light clinging
to the window
is at its most reflective
just as it is ready
to go out.

Don Anders

Kathleen Peirce

Born October 5, 1956, in Moline, Illinois. Kathleen Peirce teaches in the MFA program at Texas State University. Her most recent books are *The Ardors* (Ausable Press), and *The Oval Hour* (University of Iowa Press). Among her awards are The AWP Prize for Poetry, The Iowa Prize, and The William Carlos Williams Award. She has been the recipient of fellowships from the Whiting Foundation, The National Endowment for the Arts, and the John Simon Guggenheim Foundation. She lives in Wimberley, Texas.

Buy Something Pretty and Remember Me

A nun is sliding silver dollars underneath the pillow
of the failed novitiate still lying on her cot,
still looking from the transom to the cross
and back, baffled as when she saw, again, on the convent grounds,
bark on a pin oak twisting in an imitation of a face. Here, inside,
the linen is so clean, and the nun's hand, and the money.
Between the sheet and pillowcase there is a welcome cool
her visitor associates with untouched things,
but to the girl the hand is radiant and tender
as a sleeping robin passing a new egg, oval and delicately
blue, almost a savior's color, if the hand turned over,
if the pillow wasn't there, if the other world could keep
from hanging over everything its constant voluminous hem.

Quiet Lines

We wanted to be seen by our mothers
but our mothers were falling down,
and though we tried to think of falling
as the inversion of ascent, our thinking failed
for we had not ascended very far,
even by middle age, or if we had,
we had been taught to feel our heights discreetly,
as titmice might feel while waiting in a cypress
for the rain to stop, and wasn't fall
beautiful, the cypress leaves more feather-like in brown.
When our mothers entered the familiar rooms
and looked at us, and knew not who we were,
we were not anonymous, we were more shell than pearl
is all, opened to the limit at the hinge: wings for a doll to wear.
No pearl; pearls roll away. So we remember them.

Linen Napkin

Woven for cutting, cut for sewing,
sewn to wear away, yes,
but first worn upon
and again upon, passed across
so many mouths like a middle name spoken
as the first name of other women,
or many times across one mouth
as a middle name quietly worn;
then, years later, sewn into again, with
floss following like a body pulled by love or
someone else's death in moments
sudden and exact and following the memory
of what a lily looked like, or a rose.

Theology of Water

Water is a dampened flame.—Novalis
Water is a burned body.—Balzac

We said that water became holy, blessed by words.
There were closed vials of it, marvelous to hold
and through them the inverted world
was willed. This was the water of duration,
kept more often by the women than the men,
and among them, most often by the mothers.
We seemed as it seemed, more alive
the more time had to do with us,
though we were not preserved. How strange
to be led to thoughts of transformation
by something we ourselves arranged. If we loved to think
the saved water turned to tears, or became sweeter,
jewel-flavored, or more pure, it was to rehearse
our own transparency while moving palpably
across the earth like any night, though night was
uncontainable, was another habit of another thirst
we described as sleep. In our vials was
no sleep. Our holy water never slept;
it waited with our women to need us.

Confession 3.10.18

Of the times I felt myself an ornament
of the world, it was always with the clarity
of my body moving over a larger body,
brought to move as a bracelet rolls upward on the arm
when the hand, without consciousness,
is lifted to the eye or mouth, or as a bracelet falls
to its limit when the arm swings down,
the wearer made aware, pleased by having been so
added to. But if the world had been aware of me,
and had been given pleasure by my moving over it,
I would have known, the way a lover knows the other's arm
as an adornment greater than the silver at its wrist,
and the rock that generates a stone daylight can pass through
would have been obvious to me, and the memory of flowers
exhaled by the interior of the fig would have been as the aperture
a child's body, a man's body could pass through,
and I would have asked for equal mercy
for myself and fragrances.

Becky Liebman

Lucia Perillo

Born September 30, 1958, in New York, New York. Lucia Perillo's recent work includes the forthcoming book of poems *Inseminating the Elephant* (Copper Canyon 2009) and a book of essays, *I've Heard the Vultures Singing* (Trinity University Press 2007). Her 2006 book *Luck is Luck* was nominated for the *Los Angeles Times* Book Prize and won the Kingsley Tufts award from Claremont Graduate School. She currently divides her time between writing poems and training her service dog, who can now pull off her underwear and put it in the laundry basket.

The Van with the Plane

At first I didn't get it: I thought it was just scrap metal roped to the roof
of this dented ancient Econoline van
with its parrot-yellow burden.
Bright mishmash so precarious
my heart twitched whenever I had to tail it down the road
until one day I woke to it: you blockhead that's a *plane*.

I don't know how I missed it—of course it was a plane,
disassembled, with one yellow wing pointing sideways from the roof.
Fuselage dinged by rocks from the road
and two little wheels sticking up from the van—
now when I tally all the pieces, it seems pretty obvious.
And I wonder if toting it around would be a burden

or more some kind of anti-burden.
Because if you drove around with a plane
you might feel less fettered than the rest of us:
say your life hung around your neck like a concrete Elizabethan ruff
you could always ditch that junker van
and take off rattling down the runway of the road.

But my friends said they'd seen that heap for so long on the road
it was like a knock-knock joke heard twice too often.
You'll be sorry they said when I went looking for the guy who drove the van,
whom I found in the library, beating the dead horse of his plane.
Once you got him started it was hard to shut him off:
how, if he had field to rise from, he'd fly to Sitka, or Corvallis—

but how does a guy living in a van get a field, you think the IRS
just goes around giving people fields for free? The road
of his thought was labyrinthine and sometimes ended in the rough
of Cambodia or Richard Nixon.
He said a plane in pieces still counts as a plane,
it was still a good plane, it was just a plane on a van.

And of course I liked him better as part and parcel of the van;
the actual guy could drive you nuts.
All his grace depended on his sitting underneath that plane
as it rattles up and down the road
like train with a missile, a warhead of heavy hydrogen.
Because the van reverts to rubble once the plane takes off.

And if my own life is a plane, it's like the Spirit of Saint Louis—
no windshield, just the vantage of a periscope.
Forward, onward, never look down—at the burden of these roofs and roads.

Shrike Tree

Most days back then I would walk by the shrike tree,
a dead hawthorn at the base of a hill.
The shrike had pinned smaller birds on the tree's black thorns
and the sun had stripped them of their feathers.

Some of the dead ones hung at eye level
while some burned holes in the sky overhead.
At least it is honest,
the body apparent
and not rotting in the dirt.

And I, having never seen the shrike at work,
can only imagine how the breasts were driven into the branches.
When I saw him he'd be watching from a different tree
with his mask like Zorro
and the gray cape of his wings.

At first glance he could have been a mockingbird or a jay
if you didn't take note of how his beak was hooked.
If you didn't know the ruthlessness of what he did—
ah, but that is a human judgment.

They are mute, of course, a silence at the center of a bigger silence,
these rawhide ornaments, their bald skulls showing.
And notice how I've slipped into the present tense
as if they were still with me.

Of course they are still with me.

They hang there, desiccating
by the trail where I walked back when I could walk,
before life pinned me on its thorn.

It is ferocious, life, but it must eat
then leaves us with the artifact.

Which is: these black silhouettes in the midday sun
strict and jagged, like an Asian script.
A tragedy that is not without its glamour.
Not without the runes of the wizened meat.

Because imagine the luck!—to be plucked from the air,
to be drenched and dried in the sun's bright voltage—
well, hard luck is luck, nonetheless.
With a chunk of sky in each eye socket.
And the pierced heart strung up like a pearl.

Cesium (Goiania, Brazil, September 30, 1987)

How can this infinite beauty and sovereign glow
Fail to burn even as I am burning?
Michelangelo Buonarroti

Take the example of the young Buonarroti,
who sees in his marble quarried from Carrara
no beauty in this world the stones might not contain:
this one the voluptuous, stopped climax
of the slave who surrenders to his death in sexual release,
that one the proud bastard de Medici and all his ducats,
and the slab of pinkish opalescence, squarely cut . . .
dare he be so blunt to claim that one is God?

Likewise, the junkman gauges not
the surface appearance of a thing, for a copper pipe
is lighter than an iron one and silver grows
more oxidized than steel. So when he sees
the lead capsule that weighs more than three of him
he knows better than to pass it by.
His men hammer for hours until finally
it splits—and blue light spills out
in dust and lumps the junkman's wife could wear as gems.
Children plaster the sheen to their faces and throats;
his brother paints a blue cross on his skin
as the day decays into a sunset paling
next to this new horde of light. But before
the nausea and the burning come, go back again—

take the example of the old Buonarroti,
who finds nine-tenths of beauty not to be salvation,

but retribution: he can make Christ die
and die again, but never in these stones shall He be risen.
He carves more slaves but leaves the heads and hands and feet
buried inside the rough-hewn blocks,
and the scrotum that was once the sculptor's pride
is left a raw, undifferentiated mass.
Only the rack of the torsos are carved
true enough, the muscles webbing in each chest
so that the figures seem convulsed and strained
against bearing their suffering to this world.

Call this the non-finito: this recognition
that the world encases forms best not brought forth,
no matter what their brilliance. In Goiania,
children run home to sleep with glossy bodies—
for a time they are ethereal: *This is my body,*
eat of me, and even the scrap dealer
spins the isotope in his palms like the globe of God.
All night he's lit by the blue sea of it.
All night he bathes in its phosphorescence.
But when the sun crawls over the horizon,
it ignites his skin, and money that he's dreaming.
He burns, as Buonarroti also left his figures
burning in the rocks' flames,
unfinished because what good is beauty
if it will not save us.

Beige Trash

Who is to blame for there being no tractors
churning the soil into veils
to drape over the telling
where and how I grew, in a suburb
with no men that I could in good conscience adorn
with prosthetic limbs or even crushed straw hats?
Kudzu was something we shouted
jujitsuing air like the Green Hornet's sidekick

whose name still needed some time to ferment
in those years separating the yellow peril
from kung-fu mania, before BRUCE LEE
floated up to the marquee lights.
Like the stripers you could not eat
floating on top of our poisonous river,
to whose bank we never carried our burdens
and let them weep down into Jersey.

Because surely these words would have profited
from at least one silo lording over,
with some earth-moving equipment
parked nearby in a nest of wire
belonging to some good old boy named . . .
what? Leldon? Limuel? But sorry:
in no barn did the whiskey bottles lie
like Confederate casualties at Appomattox—

no tent revivals, no cousins with red hair
and freckled hands, no words as exotic as *po'boy*
or *chifforobe* or *muffaletta*. Which meant
we had no means to wrangle Beauty
into the cathedrals of our mouths,
though on occasion an ordinary cow
could make the car's eight-chambered heart
stop dead beside a pasture, where none of us

dared get out for fear of stampedes or hay fever
or maybe even fangs hidden behind the lips.
Call us ignorant: everything we knew poured out
those two-at-a-time black-and-white TVs—
one for picture, one for sound—& antlered
with coat hangers that gave even *Hawaii Five-O*
the speckling of constant winter. The snow
fell like the fur of our fat white dog

for whom my mother cooked lamb chops every night
in an attempt to cure its baldness,
while we dug our fingers in the chopmeat
before she slapped it into patties.
Then *Star Trek* came on. Then for an hour
the men faded in and out of light.
And there is nothing about this past
it does any service to the language to recall:

Art was what the fire department sold tickets to,
raising money for the hook and ladder.
It took place inside the school auditorium,
where an old Italian couple hid
by donning black and standing
just outside the purple spotlight.
Then music surged that was vaguely familiar
though we'd fail to lure its elaborate name

in from the borders of what we knew,
while the marionette-swan bobbled to its feet
as if newly born. I can say it now:
Tchaikovsky. Of course, the whole time
they worked the sticks and strings,
the puppeteers stood right out in the open.
Yet how silently they moved, how easy
a thing they were to pretend we couldn't see.

Alan Kolc

Lia Purpura

Born February 22, 1964, in Hewlett, New York. Lia Purpura's poetry collections are *King Baby* (Alice James Press) and *Stone Sky Lifting* (Ohio State University Press), and her prose books are *Increase* (University of Georgia Press) and *On Looking* (Sarabande Press), which was short-listed for the National Book Critics' Circle Award. She has won a Pushcart Prize, a National Endowment for the Arts Fellowship, the Beatrice Hawley Award, The Associated Writing Programs Award in Creative Nonfiction, the Ohio State University Press Award, and a Fulbright Fellowship. Purpura teaches in the Rainier Writing Workshop low-residency MFA program and is the Writer-in-Residence at Loyola College in Baltimore, where she lives with her husband, conductor Jed Gaylin, and their son, Joseph.

Red Cluster, Mid-Summer

after a sketch by George Baselitz

One part, darkened, reddened, hangs
until it can no longer

be a bird or shredded nest and I must take it
for something come too soon,

of the tree, but growing more
adamantly

into the available spot of sun
to be lit, as any crown

plotting for future
manifestations and glints of

might—yes, the taller, the more
greenly translucent the tree, mid-summer,

the more that red-brown windfall looks
wholly unaccountable.

Bee

For once I was not bent
on denying the worst scenario
but listened to the bee
get louder as it came closer.
I was still as the rumble moved
into my chest and the machinery
of its wings passed over.

*

The bee kept changing direction, midair,
and the sound diminished or drew close randomly.
I've seen the brightest yellow flicker
do the same in a wet, green field
—take one sip, reverse itself,
and look for some fresh thing because
it so loved the idea of abundance.

*

But I was only part of the abundance.
And who else would I be
so adorned, but clearly
an attractive thing to it,
a singular sweetness
willing to think
like an ornament.

*

Then I saw myself as I was—
not nearly what it wanted.
I did not grow, like the rose,
dangerous and inviting
steps to my heart, and my heart
was not perfect—hidden,
dusty, and small.

*

In place of what it wanted,
I would do. And I saw
my two wild arms
in the air, waving,
not knowing how to say
I was more than that,
in its language.

On Waiting

What is air
but a terrible fishhook
swallowed whole?

And the curve
of your back, striped
rind, path,

what, before you grew
in the cage I am: like faith:
cowl first, head next,

and fit my secret emptiness:
Why are the most violently bent trees
also a habit of growth?

And how does green come on
so softly
and deny that utterly?

At Six Months

Heavy things get seen like this—
not smart, not mean.
I know, I know, inside's a seed
growing, dividing, it should make me
kind in my roundness. It kicks
the heaviness I am, and I
take it all, absorb the blow, the current
circling out in rings: mother
to be, to be, to be: inside
isn't old enough to be known.
In a few more months, this counting
stops, and starts again on the clock's
black dot. Look, in the corner of the yard,
what used to be a weed is measured
in circumference now, whose leaves are broad
and full of intention, tipped
to let the rain course down
the determined path to the determined vein.
Today someone said *rest,*
you deserve it. What does that mean?
And who am I now
if I call that bloom a tree?

Standing Figure with Knife Edge

after Henry Moore

The iron-cool and stationary bone.
Those marrow holes and hollows on the rump end turned
that I might look through, that I might see

how she became all vertebrae
and knife-fine pleat. How she made herself
a perfect solitude: no woman I know
escapes cleaning up, so she, too, must be
—at her age, on her knees.

And there, in the sun, at the end of August,
when heat is a force, oppressive as anger,
she in the courtyard, she the bone skirt
inclined to me. I had come to feel
this wedge of dark patience pass over.

I laid my head upon her bone-apron,
visibly creased to a humble edge,
and asked how many years it takes
to love the full weight of yourself
in a circumscribed courtyard.
I asked how to be as she was, with no cape
for the coming wind, no white deflection
from the sun.

I sat a long time while she ministered
to the light. She was everywhere
stunting all embellishment. And though
wind snagged in the steep pleats she wore,
she shed the wind's fingerings for silence.
She shed the need to be seen for presence.
She told me, soon, that I would be, with my new child,
more alone than I had ever been. And grateful for it.

Fall

Then I think I'll keep the window open
a little longer
and the screen in so I can hear
the leaves turning yellow
so it won't be sudden
the day I sit down
and there's street—truck—that house,
open so I am reminded, chilled,
how slowly empty space grows.

University of Nebraska

Hilda Raz

Born May 4, 1942, in Rochester, New York. Hilda Raz's most recent books of poems are *All Odd and Splendid* (Wesleyan University Press, 2008) and *What Happens* (University of Nebraska Press, 2009). Her memoir *What Becomes You*, written with Aaron Raz Link (University of Nebraska Press, 2007), was a finalist for the Lambda Book Award and won an Outstanding Research/Creative Activity Award from the University of Nebraska. Raz is Professor of English and Women's and Gender Studies at University of Nebraska, where she also serves as Luschei Chair & Editor of *Prairie Schooner* and Founding Director of the *Prairie Schooner* Book Prizes in Poetry and Short Fiction. Often featured at writers' conferences and other universities, when at home she occasionally pets the cat.

Diction

"God is in the details,"
I tell the kids
in the public school
at Milligan, Nebraska.
They wonder what I mean.
I tell them to look
out the window
at the spring fields
the mud coming up
just to the knee
of the small pig
in the far pasture.
They tell me
it's not a knee
but a hock
and I hadn't ought
to say things I know
nothing about. I say
the light on the mud
is pure chalcedony.
They say the mud
killed two cows
over the weekend.
I tell them the pig
is alive and the spring
trees are standing in a green haze.
They tell me school is out
in a week and they have to plant.
The grain elevator at the end
of Main Street stretches out
her blue arms. The kids say chutes.

Widow

I have had this lesson,
not to care for the bones.
The cat in my lap dies,
he is replaced, the man who
casts me out is cast out,
the love that leaves returns
as "a wall of water," she kept
saying, as if the words
were the flood and all she could see
she would repeat: "A wall of water."
Wipe me out. I have been replaced,
supplanted, ignored, cast out,
ground down, spat upon, rejected,
refused, neglected, soiled,
reviled, dismembered.
I have lost husband and children,
beasts and possessions, I am ashes,
an orphan; my dearest self took a gun
into himself and died in the fields.
My breasts are empty pockets.
Pain visits my body; tears
my eyes, my mouth is filled
with wind, I speak nonsense
incessantly, silence is fled
from me, wisdom hides her head.
A feverish energy holds, then drops me down.
My children flee from me. A succession
of bruises bloom on the long bones of my body.
Oh God of the waters, God of the fragile body,
imperfect and weak,
watch over me, care for me,
raise me up out of the plumes of the dust,
the rusty canyons.
Rinse and nourish me. In return I have
nothing but my great and perfect
need.

September 11

My sneakers, having taken me through a bed of poison ivy
to the window, now transfer their oils to the bathroom rug
and no wonder in this time of monstrous trouble
I have knocked five times on the glass, and you have come

to open the door, for which anyone would be grateful,
your bristly head bent to the knob, round glasses reflecting
light from the glass of water that tips as you brush by,
intent on my call, so the spill sprays over the teak

in much the same way as the physics of matter
determined today that marble and steel would vaporize
or turn rubble under such pressure. Meanwhile, I'm inside
the door, returned to our hearth where the fire

place holds ivy, the summer having just closed down
and the grate in the basement covered with dust
isn't ready to be hosed down, isn't ready to open her arms
to keep us far enough, but not too far from the blaze
that we ourselves have set, unwisely,
in a house made of twigs and straw.

Repair

In my house, men tear out the floor:
hammering, then wood splits—
hour on hour. You almost need
safety glasses for this work, the blond says
and truly, as I go for the phone,
the kitchen is now rubble. Delight
a paste bubble in my throat. If anger is tangible
here it is, a danger to these men
who let fly plaster, the smell of something old
letting go. They unmake what I made
with my life, or where I made it.

Not Now

It's not my turn
It's been my turn not
now under the hot shower
everyone safe for the nonce
even the old cat   no cancer
on her nose close to the brain
hoofing it into the spring evening
ice floe at the bottom of the driveway
even that one melting under the juniper hedge
the lilac flushing through its scale.

Letter of Transmittal

Herein find one woman, used, in fair shape,
given to excess, too fond of what's personal
to star in meetings, intuitive
rather than learned as we say,
whose favorite pastime is the job
you've offered (which in our service
she defined), whose greatest accomplishment
is drawing breath.

On the office phone we heard
she heard this counsel, part of her job,
to pet the scar, croon to her body,
the surviving parts, sway and cherish
like a lover all that falls easily
into the upturned palm. Representative
of the job she's done.

Her last assignment is her signature, here
at the bottom of this letter. Take her.
We have voted, given voice to her eulogy.
Where she goes now is her own affair.
Our names are below. Take her.
Everything we have been able to do
for her is done. What's left is truly bone.
If you wish it, take her home.

Tommy Chandler

Paisley Rekdal

Born December 11, 1970, in Seattle, Washington. Paisley Rekdal is the author of a book of essays, *The Night My Mother Met Bruce Lee* (Pantheon, 2000 and Vintage, 2002), and three books of poetry, *A Crash of Rhinos* (University of Georgia Press, 2000), *Six Girls Without Pants* (Eastern Washington University Press, 2002), and *The Invention of the Kaleidoscope* (University of Pittsburgh Press, 2007). Her work has received awards from *The Village Voice*, National Endowment for the Arts, and the Fulbright Foundation. Her poems and essays have appeared in such places as *Michigan Quarterly Review*, *The New York Times Magazine*, *Poetry*, *Denver Quarterly*, and on National Public Radio. She also knits avidly and has a black belt in Tae Kwan Do.

What Was There to Bring Me to Delight but to Love and Be Loved?

I declared, and immediately rejected this. For instance:
a man I loved once liked to hurt women and would tell me
what he did to his lovers. The sight of a woman's slight hips
as she was knocked over a television might give delight. Or the way
bones sounded in skin that bumped or scraped against a wall.
He used to claim he could hear things like this, not
the scratch of a woman's back on a wall, but actual
bone rubbing muscle, skin, joint, the sound
as if sticks rattled in cloth. It frightened him, he said, he found himself
pushing other women to prove he couldn't really hear the sound.
And I loved him. I loved forgiving him. I must admit this
though he never laid a hand on me,
I knew enough about this kind of loss.
There were more significant things
to demand from the world. Such as how
a word could call up more than violence, idea, person, become
reality with only the finest limitations
of meaning. Such as *monster*, perhaps,
or *grave*, or *delicious*. I could say, for instance, that this man
was a *delicious monster* with his strap-colored hair and soft mouth
though where does that place me
in the universe of word? Perhaps you could say *I*
was the monster, searching not for where rivers ran but to the source
of rivers, the frozen nugget of an idea of river: so cold
it almost burns the rock around it. I was the one willing to sacrifice
so many others of my kind; I could listen for hours
to his stories of women whose bones itched within them
and all I could think was *hand, eye, mouth* as if to say the words
was to take his fingers into my mouth, to suck
the warm pink nails between my teeth, or lick the egg taste
from his eye with my tongue. These were more real to me
than the fact he would cry out on the phone or in my bedroom

where we would talk. He would cry and all I could think was
More, let my thighs be another casing for you
if this is the kind of grave you want. I almost thought grace. I almost
gave in once but, and this is the truth, he was afraid of me. I
was the coldness of rivers, he said, I was the source
and when he looked down at me lying on the sheets rumpled
like ruined skin, he called me his destroyer.

Perhaps the real question in the world is not
what to love, but how to forgive.
What does it take for the monstrous
to be delightful in the eye of God? As if beauty itself
wasn't also obscene—a hand really fleshed claw, a peony
a flowering of blood. Or perhaps a word is really all it signifies, all
we can trust in fact; to name a thing
is to make it so. When I called this man a *man*, you must believe
he became one for me. The source of the river,
not its oceangrasp. What happened to the man I loved
is that eventually he choked a woman almost to death.
We weren't speaking then. Even I, it seems, have my limits.
But I can imagine how he would have told me he could hear her spine
crying out to him, an accusation of the flesh. *What more is there*
but to love like this and to be loved? he asked me once.
You are my source of delight, an eternal search
for grace, I answered. I almost said *the grave*.

25% Pressure

"Of course I support
    women's rights," he
        declared, "along with those

of the criminally
    insane." His lower
        lip trembled, a slug

of red, the vegetarian
    hands looking screwed
        into their wrist sockets.

He didn't mean this
    as a joke. This
        was political earnestness

before women intent
on teasing him
at a party—drift of starlings,

our sexual interest
like a seatide of foam.
There is nothing worse

to a man than a woman's
laughter I read once,
the year my grandmother

bought me the pamphlets
on rape. A child
I read with fascination

the story of a teenager
whose date suddenly
pressed her hand

against his jeans' crotch,
then worked her own
jeans off, forcing her

to lie back
on the vinyl seat
that smelled of cigarettes

and breath freshener.
And I will always remember
what she wrote next:

Suddenly his penis
pushed aside my panties
and he was in me.

Then the quote
about a woman's laughter,
its implicit punishment,

its revenge,
like my revenge
at this stranger and his lack

of humor. I should say
he also admitted
he'd been "pushed aside"

from his job
        when the manager,
                a woman, had reached

for a piece of paper
        and touched his groin
                instead. Pressed it,

actually, he said,
        with full
                "25 percent pressure."

As if to demonstrate
        what deliberateness
                felt like he struggled

towards my leg
        and turned his palm
                sideways so that the branching

knuckles, string
        of fat pearls,
                might stroke the skin.

Then thought better
        of it, withdrew
        seeing my eyes fill

with the red light
        of laughter.
                "Don't do that

without—" he began.
        Then he pulled away.
                When I read the account

of the rape
        the first thing I learned
                to believe in was the accident

inherent to sex,
        the pressure
                of thumb or mouth or penis

to act as if knowing
        more than the mind would,
                seeing more than any eye.

I think this man
felt that too, hating
the meats and bloods

and shames of him,
cloistered
behind a wall of rectitudes.

When he raised his hand
up to my leg, hovering
past knee as if to touch

the groin, he stopped
at the place only ruiners,
destroyers, numbly

would-be lovers
would take. He stopped
and did not push

past that scrim
of self-doubt,
refused to invite despair in

for something simple
ruined forever.
What does he know

about his manhood
but that it might be
ashamed?

What do I remember
of the girl in the story?
The moments before she was raped

she had kissed the boy,
had leaned up blushing
to finger his shirt

buttons,
and laughed, gently,
in his face.

Post-Romantic

Yesterday, everything was possible. Today we're good
as married. You don't want to hear that,
do you, thinking I'm going to call you back
in from the rain to fight over the morning paper,
limning my deft and emotional promiscuities?
That we'll sit in our sitting room,
watching the shaggy junipers twirl in winter wind
as a storm closes its throat around the city?
I'm thinking about how to ask God to be nicer.
I'm thinking about that fabled leper colony
where the last, solitary patient waited inside its unlocked tower
three years in the belief she could not step outside.
And how the local doctors visited only
to re-wrap her face, to brush out her last gold strands
of hair, wondering how to save anybody
so willing to kill herself with denial.
They wanted to talk about pain, the doctors, to say,
One day, you'll be half asleep in the dark, listening to a radio
play in another room, and feel yourself
suddenly filling like a jug with the cold
awareness nothing more will ever happen, the disaster
of your old ambivalence, the familiarity
of desire's wolfish teeth sinking into the body.
The body, as if it didn't belong to you anymore.
The doctors said, Fear should never be elevated
to ritual. They told the woman, You must change your life!
One day, I'm on the steps of an office tower losing a shoe,
the next I'm screaming on a gurney, I'm stuffing a baby
into a diaper, I'm wandering the woods
in my scar-dark cape. Every story has an archetype, doesn't it?
And if so, why *aren't* we married? Why can't we be
just like everyone else this fucking, fucking once? God, I hate
the way this tale is turning out: two aged strangers learning
to tuck in their blood, hiding the knives and bread crumbs
deep inside their pockets. Look, this time I swear,
I won't run; really; I'll come and go from my stone room
without a mirror, all my extremities taped in white.
I'll learn to knit with three fingers. I'll learn to read
into the deepening silences, to be nice to your stepsisters,
singing to drown out the tears of their ugliness.
I love you. Can I even say that? In this story,
I want to spend the rest of my life growing quietly bored with you,
locking away loom and spindle, sweeping out the piles
of rose petals and ash. For once, I plan to triumph

over smug experience. I marry you. Don't hit me.
Please, just come in from the stars awhile, sit here
in this sitting room, let me find you another section of the paper
to argue over. The doctors said I get to wear a suit.
They said I'll be released next Thursday. Listen:
even now, the junipers are whispering their dark good-byes,
thin limbs smocked in white. A riderless horse has appeared
on the horizon. And somewhere, out in the meretricious night,
somebody's life is quietly changing.

John R. Rogers

Pattiann Rogers

Born March 23, 1940, in Joplin, Missouri. Pattiann Rogers has published thirteen books, most recently *Wayfare* (Penguin, 2008), *Generations* (Penguin, 2004), and *Firekeeper: Selected Poems, New and Revised* (Milkweed Editions, 2005). Among other awards, Rogers has received five Pushcart Prizes and the Literary Award from the Lannan Foundation. She has two sons and three spirited and robust grandsons. She lives with her husband and their black cat, Pamina, in Castle Rock, Colorado.

Creation Alive

The trick is the trick the wild creature,
captured and caged, remembers and turns to,
staring as he does unmoving, facing,
without seeing, the bars of his cell and us.

He departs this place, enters the circling
archives and depths of his own body,
finds the woven forest, the damp rank
of its layered mat, the shadowed hues
and run of the river, cadence of its current
and cold, subtle peppery scent of cutbanks,
silty richness, soaked mosses, snailey
muds, the forgiving lap and sand of its bar.

He feels the imperceptible rise and fall
of the woods as a breathing he breathes
in sleep, haphazard slip of a leaf, jitter
of a twig, single hairs of hedge rubbish
and withered petals shaken loose by the wind
filling and bolstering all crevices and hollows
with the theology of its coming and going.

He pads slowly beside the moving waters,
sniffs the array of oak, hickory, sour mint,
markings and decay, hears a contrapuntal
play of fading caws in the distance, a closer
creak and rub of branch against branch.

He takes the fancy grasses of the clearing
into his mouth, licks the liquid sugar
of their graces. He is the light of the sun,
its pelt and paw, its crude warmth and rigor.
He creates its story in his passing. He makes

the sound of its soul. This is his name.

Step away and leave him. I know
you understand the trick. Study my eyes.

Seeing the Three Magi

They are country boys, dusty,
barefoot, bumping up a dirt road, one
pulling the wooden wagon, one riding,
the third behind pushing. They pause,
rotate places, continue on.

They are three summer winds—across
the bow, pressing the sails, skimming
the wake—following a ship following
a chart of stars.

On the street, one has a guitar
on his back, one a pair of drumsticks
hanging from his belt, the third
a mouth harp in his pocket.
They are wiser than the city.

(Three four-horned and cloven-footed
demons of the nether world—demon
of blindness, demon of nightmares,
demon of faltering—attempt to track them
by moving beneath them upside down
and in the opposite direction.)

They are brothers sleeping
in a bed together beside an open
window overlooking the sea, a single
blanket pulled to their chins. The star
they dream as an angel of fire finally
rises, dripping and spilling light,
out of the eastern waves.

See those three white herons
descending with the nightfall, one
right behind the other almost like stars
over the black sky of the lake. In the beauty
and angle of their journey, doesn't it
make you wonder?

These three perfect yellow pears
placed on a table outdoors in the shade
of a winged elm—how intently they watch,
as though seeking, how steadfastly they pass
through the shadows of this day
on their way together.

Capturing the Scene

With pen and ink, the artist takes care
To be explicit, each board of the covered bridge
Elucidated, each shingle of the roof. The columns
Of the termites and the holes of the borers to be,
He remembers. He is deliberate to denote those specifics
He understands, filling in the blank with the pause
Of the dragonfly, the scratch of the myrtle weed.
He watches to maintain in his lines exactly
That tedious balance between the river in motion
And the river itself. Like wires, he coordinates
The trees and their affinity for disorder.

How skillfully he locates the woodthrush clearing
The last field beyond the hills, and the worn rocks
Along the bank, each with its own specific hump
Against space. He acknowledges the sunken
And the sucked away, the shadows on the far left
Bearing witness to objects still outside the scene.

And notice how he achieves that incandescence of ink
Around the seed pod. He knows that the scream of the jay,
The odor of the sun-dried wood is entirely in his stroke.
Without making a single mark, he executes the heavens.

And hasn't he understood from the beginning where he must never
Look directly—into the dark hedgerow on the opposite bank,
Among the crossed sticks of the rushes and the spaces between,
How he must not stare steadily at the long fall
Of the sky below the horizon or probe too deeply that area
Lying between the ink and its line on the paper? He knows
There is that which he must draw blindfolded or not at all.
And before he can give to the scene its final name,
He must first identify every facet of its multiplicity
In detail; he must then turn away his face completely
And remember more.

Without Violence

That cat who comes during sleep, quiet
On his cushioned claws, without violence,
Who enters the house with a low warm rattle
In his throat; that cat who has been said
To crawl into a baby's crib without brushing
The bars, to knit his paws on the pale
Flannel of the infant's nightdress, to settle
In sleep chin to chin with the dear one
And softly steal the child's breath
Without malice, as easily as pulling
A silk scarf completely through a gold ring;

The same cat who has been known to nudge
Through castle doors, to part tent flaps,
To creep to the breasts of brave men,
Ease between their blankets, to stretch
Full length on the satin bodices of lovely
Women, to nuzzle their cheeks with his great
Feline mane; it was that cat who leaped last night
Through the west window of father's bedroom.
Who chose to knead his night's rest on my father's
Shoulder, who slept well, breathing deeply,
Leaving just before dawn to saunter toward
The north, his magnificent tail and rump
Swaying with a listless and gorgeous grace.

Anna Crabtree

Mary Ruefle

Born April 16, 1952, in McKeesport, Pennsylvania. Mary Ruefle is the author of ten books of poetry, most recently *Indeed I Was Pleased with the World* (Carnegie Mellon, 2008), and a book of prose, *The Most of It* (Wave Books, 2008). She also makes one-of-a-kind erasure books which have been exhibited in museums and galleries. Among her awards are a Guggenheim, a National Endowment for the Arts Fellowship, and an Award in Literature from the American Academy of Arts and Letters. An avid swimmer (and smoker), she has no other interests beyond her work as a writer and artist. She is unmarried, without children, petless, and unemployed.

Examination

Out of a high prison window
with a long rope on a dark night John of the Cross
let himself down, a shaking branch
against the moon—

And the Sisters he fled to,
faced with feeding the image of death, fed him
pears stewed with cinnamon! It was enough for him
who lay so long without a spoon to break ardently
into the core.

In the same house there was a Sister
who, like a fussy child coming out of her shadow,
insisted on fresh shoes each time she
approached the altar.

Down five hundred years of vanity
these facts have passed. You must never forget them.
If you tell his story—of how later they brought the pen—

Examine your heart and see if you
leave out the arms of a girl shaking like a branch
as she walks in her new shoes to set down the pears,
two half-moons quivering in their own sweet wine.

Dove

1.
One thousand years ago a woman in Japan
with no name

wrote a book without a title.
I can turn the pages
I can rip them out
and fold them,
put them in my pocket
and walk into town. She said
even at the best of times
I am not much good at poetry
and at a moment like this
I feel quite incapable of expressing myself.
But one day the pages will blacken and curl
like singed eyelashes. And that will be
that. So why walk to town?

2.
My heart is full of malice
and it will not burn away.
Of course there was Yeats, *stony*
in front of the fire, but he was
himself and I am mine, I like
to stand in the street
with a large tear
caught in my lashes, like the petit-
bourgeois I am.
I do say this is so
I do say I have seen a black wing
I stood in the street
when the dove of her soul
broke out of the book
and flew from the burning earth.

Funny Story

I don't remember where I was going.
I always worry about driving in the snow.
To the airport I think.
What if my car won't start, cold as it is?
But at five a.m. on the morning of January fifth
I was up and out.
Quite frankly, I can still see it:
the sky a glaze of celadon
with a pink moon set in the corner.
It took my breath away
in small white puffs.

When I get to thinking, I think maybe it was my mood.
But my mood was low-down and mean.
I mean before I saw it.
Afterwards—no, not afterwards:
in the same moment
I realized I have a prerequisite for joy.
It surprised me.
I was surprised to consider everything must be made of glass.
Not only the icy poverty of life on earth
but high, immovable things.
I was afraid to move.
I was afraid I would be late.
I was afraid my car wouldn't start.
What if the moon, awash as it was
in decanted light, was dangerously close
to disappearing altogether
and for good this time?
So I just stood there.
I let it take my breath away.
That's OK I said
take my breath away.
And it was gone.

Instrument of the Highest

—Chaim Soutine (1893–1943)

Ah the truth,
    is the rank lustful lives of men and women
    going after it
in all its *red*—

it is just this nipple exposed beneath the rag
    puce with lava-milk,

it is just this beef-stink in the studio,
the popped-out eyes of rotting salmon,

a particular chicken: the scrawniest one in the shop,
    long neck and blue skin

I'm going to hang it up by the beak with a nail.
In a few days it should be perfect.

It must be *very very* dead.
Even the red gladioli
have passed over into that garden where things shout

don't look at me!

Everything startled into still thinking
it is alive.

What else is spirit but the hectic orifice
of the still unwilling
to admit they are excruciatingly gone?

A conniption fit of fact?

Still nothing new.

What is more beautiful than that?

Kay Ryan

Born September 21, 1945, in San Jose, California. Kay Ryan became the U.S. Poet Laureate in 2008. Her most recent books are *The Niagara River* (2005), *Say Uncle* (2000), and *Elephant Rocks* (1996). Her awards include the 2004 Ruth Lilly Poetry Prize from The Poetry Foundation, a Guggenheim Fellowship, an Ingram Merrill Award, and a National Endowment for the Arts Fellowship. Ryan's work has been selected four times for *The Best American Poetry*. Her poems and essays have appeared in many journals and anthologies, have been used in the funny papers ("Boondocks"), and one was permanently installed at New York's Central Park Zoo. Since 1971 she has lived in Marin County, California.

Blandeur

If it please God,
let less happen.
Even out Earth's
rondure, flatten
Eiger, blanden
the Grand Canyon.
Make valleys
slightly higher,
widen fissures
to arable land,
remand your
terrible glaciers
and silence
their calving,
halving or doubling
all geographical features
toward the mean.
Unlean against our hearts.
Withdraw your grandeur
from these parts.

The Fabric of Life

It is very stretchy.
We know that, even if
many details remain
sketchy. It is complexly
woven. That much too
has pretty well been
proven. We are loath
to continue our lessons,

which consist of slaps
as sharp and dispersed
as bee stings from
a smashed nest,
when any strand snaps—
hurts working far past
the locus of rupture,
attacking threads
far beyond anything
we would have said
connects.

Cut Out for It

Cut out
as a horse
is cut
from the
pack. Peeled
off, but
a long time
back. Now
such a feeling
for the way
they touch
and shift
as one, the
beauty when
they run.

The Best of It

However carved up
or pared down we get,
we keep on making
the best of it as though
it doesn't matter that
our acre's down to
a square foot. As
though our garden
could be one bean
and we'd rejoice if
it flourishes, as
though one bean
could nourish us.

Grazing Horses

Sometimes the
green pasture
of the mind
tilts abruptly.
The grazing horses
struggle crazily
for purchase
on the frictionless
nearly vertical
surface. Their
furniture-fine
legs buckle
on the incline,
unhorsed by slant
they weren't
designed to climb
and can't.

Why We Must Struggle

If we have not struggled
as hard as we can
at our strongest
how will we sense
the shape of our losses
or know what sustains
us longest or name
what change costs us,
saying how strange
it is that one sector
of the self can step in
for another in trouble,
how loss activates
a latent double, how
we can feed
as upon nectar
upon need?

Attention

As strong as
the suction cups
on the octopus
are the valves
of the attention.

If threatened
or pulled off
they leave welts
and pink rings

but also
can unstuck
unfelt
from things.

Forgetting

Forgetting takes space.
Forgotten matters displace
as much anything else as
anything else. We must
skirt unlabeled crates
as though it made sense
and take them when we go
to other states.

David Baddley

Natasha Sajé

Born June 6, 1955, in Munich, Germany. Natasha Sajé grew up in New York and New Jersey. She is the author of two books of poems, *Red Under the Skin* (University of Pittsburgh Press, 1994) and *Bend* (Tupelo Press, 2004), and many essays. Her work has been honored with the Robert Winner Award, a Fulbright fellowship, the Campbell Corner Poetry Prize, and the Utah Book Award. Sajé is an Associate Professor of English at Westminster College in Salt Lake City, and has been teaching in the Vermont College MFA in Writing program since 1996. An avid cook and baker, she is writing a cookbook.

I am peeling four pink grapefruit

to make sorbet with Campari, for a party,
removing the bitter white pith,
but I am also eating so many sweet globules
that the I who is doing the work
is clearly not the I swallowing the fruit.
Soon there's no hope of sorbet for six,
only enough for two; one of us
boils the rind and sugar into syrup,
freezes the small mound into dessert.

The self who hops to conclusions
like popcorn, who falls in love on the basis
of a bare arm, the self always
drunk with the pleasure at hand, shares a body
with the woman who has been true to one man,
who even at midnight when the other I wants
only to roll into bed, is reaching for chocolate and eggs,
melting and separating, envisioning the faces
of her guests at the first mouthful of mousse,
dark as the heart of a faithless wife.

Alibi

I was treading on yellow primroses in their limestone beds.
I was eating langoustines and saffron fettuccine with my fingers.
I was learning not to smile at strangers.
I was jaywalking.
I was hanging out the window waiting for lightning to strike.
I was having tooth #12 drilled to death.
I was up to my elbows in buckwheat.
I was charmed.
I was pumicing my heels.
I was apologizing for my government.

I was lost in Reverdy.
I was listening to the sunset.
I was mispronouncing the names of my cousins.
I was shown the old slaughterhouse by some cats.
I was practicing being blind, cobblestones under my soles.
I was buying poisons whose labels I couldn't read.
I was massaging my thumbs.
I was drinking liqueur made from the dead poet's family recipe.
I was using the clock tower of St. Joseph's to tell time.
I was allowing boiled dough to rise in my stomach.
I was making a list of famous syphilitics.
I was comparing egg yolks to pumpkins.
I was thinking about Flaubert putting in commas, then taking them out.
I was planning the next time I could travel here
and wrap solitude around me like cashmere.

E

essay, to try, from *exagiare,* to weigh out, examine

I was eleven and watching the Galloping Gourmet with his British-Australian accent and his glass of wine

learning how to get juice out of a lemon by rolling it hard on the counter

when the doorbell rang

my hair around cans to make it straight

the man next door, his receding hair combed back

erminea, the weasel whose fur turns from brown to white in winter

asked if anyone else were home

I said no

edentate, lacking teeth

asked if he could come in

electric, from Greek, *elektron,* amber, because it produces sparks when rubbed

I said no, I'm sorry

euphemism, to speak with good words

we stood   eye to eye

eutrophic: a body of water with so much mineral & organic matter the oxygen is reduced

until I slowly shut the door in his face

Eve, from Hebrew, living

pushing with both hands

V

veritas: not behind the veil of sky
but the moving veil itself
fox and its ears hanging upside down
virus carried say by civet cats from animal to human
and back in the form of vaccines
Van Dyck moved from Belgium
to England to Italy to England carrying
some melancholy elegance intact
his royal subject later deposed by the very principle
that permits a husband to divorce a wife
permits a country to divorce its rulers
beheading merely a cruel flourish
Milton's *vade mecums* were faith
and verse, from *vertere,* to turn
two fingers spread as a sign
or digits severed at the joints
any search for abiding truth doomed
as a beautiful city built on water
viewed through windows on the way to the dungeon

Kathy Haas

Ruth L. Schwartz

Born February 22, 1962, in Geneva, New York. Ruth L. Schwartz's fifth book, *Dear Good Naked Morning*, won the 2004 Autumn House Press Poetry Prize. Her other books of poems are *Edgewater*, a 2001 National Poetry Series winner; *Singular Bodies*; and *Accordion Breathing and Dancing*. She has published a memoir, *Death in Reverse*, and her creative nonfiction has appeared in *Utne Reader, The Sun*, and numerous anthologies. Recipient of over a dozen national writing awards, including fellowships from the National Endowment for the Arts, the Ohio Arts Council, and the Astraea Foundation, Schwartz teaches in the low-residency MFA program at Ashland University. She has a private practice in psychospiritual healing, and leads Conscious Relationship workshops.

Sex

It's the church of pleasure and sorrow.
All its intricate windows have been smashed.
It holds the places where the stars
opened inside us, blood on shattered glass.
It holds the light between us,
brighter than anything—
except for the equal measure of darkness,
sealed inside our bodies,

which eclipses it.
O stubborn animal, celestial, transforming.
O spasm which loves nothing but itself,
aware of nothing but itself, grateful to nothing.
O firefly which asks, What do you most want?
as it sputters out.

Tangerine

It was a flower once, it was one of a billion flowers
whose perfume broke through closed car windows,
forced a blessing on their drivers;
then what stayed behind grew swollen, as we do;
grew juice instead of tears, and small hard sour seeds,
each one bitter, as we are, and filled with possibility.
Now a hole opens up in its skin, where it was torn from the
branch; ripeness can't stop itself, breathes out;
we can't stop it either. We breathe in.

Perseid

August meteor shower

While they're here I hold them
like my breath. They deepen the sky
like blood in my body, I'm glad to offer
my body like this—a small craft
over fields of water,
where light can fall, be lost, be caught,
be held.
I'm naked in my chair,
facing the window.
If I were outside I'd want to look up
and see someone naked in every window.
I think we need
the difficult river, we need the absence of tenderness
so love can come like shooting stars
if it comes.

When They Know

for H., who tested positive

"The man sitting next to me just disappeared," said one passenger.
News item, February 25, 1989

We are talking about the plane:
the nine who followed the fuselage,
the sky which sucked them up lit by the jet's parts going up,
debris storming the hole—
the three hundred and forty-six who remained,
firmly buckled in their seats,
bolted to the floor, fused
to the wings and frame.

And it is not surprising that I think mostly of
the three hundred and forty-six:
their lives gleaming ahead of them,
some of them turning to religion, others finally able to love,
how they will continue belting themselves
into their seats, as if it keeps them safe,
how they will think there is some reason they survived—

while you can't stop thinking about the nine:
those few, randomly plucked from their lives,
radiance hurtling into dark—
you are with them in that instant,
just when they know they are leaving

Melissa Buckheit

Rebecca Seiferle

Born December 14, 1951, in Denver, Colorado. Rebecca Seiferle was awarded a Lannan Foundation Poetry Fellowship in 2004. She is the author of four poetry collections, most recently *Wild Tongue* (Copper Canyon, 2007), and two book-length translations: *The Black Heralds* (Copper Canyon, 2003) and *Trilce* (Sheep Meadow, 2002). Her collection, *Bitters* (Copper Canyon, 2001), won the Western States Book Award and a Pushcart Prize. Her poetry, translations, and essays have appeared in over twenty-five anthologies, including *Best American Poetry 2000*, and her poetry has been translated into several languages. She is the founding editor of *The Drunken Boat*, www.thedrunkenboat.com. She teaches at the Art College in Tucson, Arizona.

The Shearing

Each hour they grow fewer, the splayed
lipped, white drift of the apple blossoms
falling to wind, late frost, and 90 lumens
of the brilliance of paper falling, shredded
to the floor, even incised with the black burning
of someone else's sacred defoliation, love is not
transitory enough but snail-like shapes
self to shell, or hooks like scorpion tail
in crevice or niche, long past luck or life.
Who wants to love forever? Love should fall
like the apple blossoms, die at the kiss
of a bee, learn to perish, come to an end.

Bitter Herb

I had to lie down in the earth myself,
plowing the sand
with my belly, propelling myself
under the wire fence
that kept us apart. I'd stood there,
for a long time on the other side, just
clinging to a post, until the sheriff said
someone would have to cross over
and identify the body. Through
the gauntlet of the earth—the scrambling
weeds, the willows striking my shoulders
like whips—I crawled and bent
and shuffled until I was beside my brother—
his face as if someone had taken it apart
and put it back together in an awry
riddle of wood. Death was a riddle

to Gilgamesh when he went looking for a way
to bring his brother, Enkidu, back to life.
He was told to find *the plant*
of opening, a mysterious herb
that grew by the banks of a stagnant pond,
like this one, at the edge of a desert waste,
and was warned that it would prick his own hand
as he cut free its bitter root. On the way back
Gilgamesh stopped to rest and bathe;
as he drifted back into himself, full
of relief, reverie, and rescue,
a snake came out of the grasses
and swallowed the herb of eternal life.
But these waters, near where my brother lay,
were still and empty. The plant of opening,
rose-colored, ambrosial, did not shimmer
like a prism in the murky depths. My brother
had aimed at his own heart, not once,
but twice, firing down that pathway
of the soul. And the only sign
of a snake was his discarded skin.
When I said "Yes, that is
my brother, Clinton Seiferle,"
I heard the fingers of the dead snapping
around me. They would not let me touch him.
He was still evidence, the last witness
to the story they thought they would find
in the gleanings of his fingernails,
in his shirt as if shredded by a swarm of bees
from the powder burns, in the ground seething
with ants, the flies swarming and settling
upon him, his dead dog that lay at his feet.
He had come to the edge of that abyss
where fear came out of the water
and consumed whatever could have
brought him back. Three days later,
I'm the only one who comes back
to life, realizing that I'm still
wearing the same clothes, my jeans
prickly with nettles. As I slip out
of the black and stinging fabric, I find
the pockets are full of sand. How can
I give this earth to the waters? For touching
these fine grains, these sparkling abrasions,
it seems I touch all that remains
of the lost face of my brother.

Homophobia

I could say that discovering such ugliness
in a friend is like standing on my own porch,
barefooted, ready to jump into the sweet grass,
still soft with spring newness, and finding coiled—
its outline broken by fractals of sand—the blunt
venomous head of a prairie rattler,
lying in wait, striking out at whatever
comes within range of its desire or fear.
Throwing itself forward, the snake
would be as certain of its normality as my friend is,
coiled around the memory of the man who died,
rattling with indignation at the news
that he died of AIDS, and I, I could be the mouse,
frozen with timidity, having blundered
on an exceptionally beautiful morning
into this toxic stare, struck dead on the spot,
the hypodermic lullaby poisoning my conscience
as much as muscles of my throat and heart. But
the snake is beautiful, those diamonds etched
along its spine as newly green as the fragrant sage,
and the mouse, the mouse being swallowed
would become of use, its cells, mother
and father of new snakeskins, and I could turn
back, refrain from jumping off the step, and the snake
would slide into the grass, its body a long sigh
breathing itself away, leaving me to thank heaven
for such a glimpse, and such a narrow escape.
The snake would not, as my friend does,
keep flinging itself at a dead man, talking about
how repulsive it must have been, how shocking
to imagine the lovemaking of two people
of the same sex, though she keeps imagining
it again and again. As if she held her soul
in an artificial grip, forcing its jaws open
to the naked drip and chill—though a snake,
so pried upon a petri dish,
would be milked of all its poison.

Muse

In later years, my daughter said to me
that when she was little and before
sister and brother, growing up in that trailer
that bordered the desert, she thought there was someone
else who lived with us, and it was only later that she knew
there was no one else, just the poetry, that other child that I was always singing to,
nursing in my arms, chanting, as I passed back and forth between those rooms.

Face Photography

Heather Sellers

Born September 10, 1964, in Orlando, Florida. Heather Sellers is the author of a children's book and three volumes of poetry, including *Drinking Girls and Their Dresses* (Ahsahta Press) and *The Boys I Borrow* (New Issues Press). Her multi-genre textbook is *The Practice of Creative Writing* (Bedford/St. Martins). *Georgia Under Water*, linked stories, won a Barnes & Noble Discover Great New Writers award. She's just completed a memoir about her experience with prosopagnosia, or, face blindness. She's a professor of English at Hope College in Michigan. Heather is a cyclist and studying Spanish. Her blog on teaching creative writing is heathersellers.com/blog.

SAT Words with David Jr. in His Father's Bed

We are on his dad's bed
On the comforter
Which is inimical
To our comfort and
David Jr. is pusillanimous.
And irascible. And petulant.
"These are all you," I say.
He says, "Stop talking, stop
Trying to help." He's afraid
Of these words, rightly so.
They scare their recipients.
Hard to pronounce, these words
Snootify and do not truly
Amplify the meanings they
Promise. "I already know,"
He says, "Give me 'stipend.'
Stop shuffling the pack."
"Hazard," I say. "Maul, copious."
I call out the words looking
For an order that makes sense,
At least foretells, or just pleases
Me. He says, "This is not how I learn.
Stop giving me clues.
Stop moving the flashcards.
Stop talking. Stop using
Words in sentences.
That is not how I remember.
Stop saying 'good job!'
After every single word.
Cease." He says, "Heather.
You have a hole in your shirt."

The definition of which is
You are drinking wine.
You are not helping me.
You are Dad's girlfriend
I was listening outside the door
Last night and for some
Of the things that happen
In this house, there are not words.
But you pretend it can all be said.

I Know What I Saw Last Summer

Mostly his back. We were on the motorcycle leaning
Into the speed limit dreaming of whole
Other nights, happiness, Florida, the unreconstructed
Shangrai-La Motel. Moon well-hung, low-slung.
I stuck my neck up around his, banging swan.
Our giant plastic heads clanking. Hanging on.
That moon: cold orange plastic ball foretelling *fall fall.*
I was pointing. But it was behind clouds, gone.

Fall. That was the first second of the end of it all.
So long, summer. Tonight I look up and see a slice
And remember there were two names for the moon
That month, names which no longer apply.

Dating Men with Children

I'm the girlfriend.
The dad works

Late. Jake is the kid and
We play

Nintendo.
He is talking to priests

In peril all over the world,
He's at melee level.

It's a very difficult level
(We know from experience).

I wish my life
Was more like this:

Little dialog boxes,
Strange figures in Mauritania

In monks' robes, giving
Me light. My friend

Liz is getting a divorce.
They have three

Kids. She said:
His lips burned.

Every time.
They kissed.

I'm scratching my lips.
Clicking Up C. No, Jacob says.

You just gave away
Your cloaking power.

I love the dad, but maybe
It's killing me. I like the kid.

Levelling up to Family.
Power me to the castle.

You want out of that room,
Jake says. Laser now.

There are dragons here.
(There were dragons there, too.)

Palm Sunday in Pew with Ex

I can't hold hands with him. Steal the song book.
I can sing in Spanish. Love his new shoes.
It's our anniversary—which we lose
When we divorce—a date. Kids with palms look

For those of us unpalmed; I hide my first
Take three, four more. Minister, amped, selects
Death Where Is Thy Sting, a damp hymn my ex
Wholly knows: note, word, breath. I slit my wrist

Accidentally; blood beads. I knit, braid
What I divided, make a fan of what I frayed
While we sing. I have looked back inside
My old ring: today's date, I was a bride.

I forget it will always be ending,
Ends over again and again. And stings.

Beth Kelly

Enid Shomer

Born February 2, 1952, in Washington, DC. Enid Shomer's work has appeared in *New Yorker, Atlantic, Poetry, Best American Poetry, Best New Stories from the South,* and elsewhere. She's the author of four poetry collections and two fiction collections, most recently *Tourist Season: Stories* (Random House, 2007), chosen for Barnes & Noble's Discover Great New Writers program. Recent awards include *Virginia Quarterly Review*'s Balch Prize and *Southern Poetry Review*'s Guy Owen Prize. The recipient of grants from the National Endowment for the Arts and the Florida Arts Council, since 2002 she has edited the University of Arkansas Press Poetry Series. She lives in Florida and is writing a novel for Random House.

"Gowned Waiting"

is the name of the room where we sit, clutching
rouge-pink robes with flimsy ties. One flips

through fashion mags. Her cubicle door ajar,
another rehearses a script, while two friends,

scheduled together, compare injustices
at work. I'm writing this in my journal, trying

for calm against the terror at hand, this visit
a truce with disease I negotiate twice

a year. A woman enters speaking broken
English, weeping. We understand—tears

are the native idiom here in "Gowned Waiting."
Minutes ago, she was swept aboard

the diagnosis express, where everything blurs
like a landscape rushing past, though at the moment

her train creeps so slowly that seconds
freeze, refusing to pass, trapping her

in the instant of discovery, the words
that struck like fangs—*malignant, invasive . . .*

bad. The brochure they gave her—support
groups and hotlines, survivors beribboned in pink—

lists on her lap like a shipwrecked paper boat.
She wants to run the day backwards,

as I did last year. To walk back
out through the clinic door to the subway stop,

to my block, to pause in reverse for the breakfast I grabbed
on the run until I'm standing wreathed with steam

in the morning shower, completely clean.

King David Memorial Gardens

I went to help put my father
in the ground, the way you lock
something in a box
but don't throw away the key.
I went to see that he was really
gone, that the cruelty
would turn simple and green,
that he would at last receive
the riches of the rain and be rendered
unharmable and harmless—cut
by a mower blade and not bleed
and not warp the steel.

Black Drum

At last the fish thrashed
out of the water
as if to break the black
bars on his side. One eye
felt the air, the dry

death of it, then he plunged again
in downward spirals.
We had been struggling for ten
minutes—a lifetime—over whose world
would prevail: his, with its purled

edges and continuous center, or mine
with its yin and yang,
its surface incised into sky
and sea, the land like a scar
between.

A crowd had gathered, you could sense
their excitement
the way you feel tension
on the line when something strikes.
You could hear the awe when they looked

at what I was battling—a creature
who belonged farther out, an ocean
liner in a backwater
bayou. My arms ached with happiness,
my sight narrowed to the place

where the line disappeared, the rod
bent to a hairpin, the fish pulling
at me like religion or god
with the strength of what can't be
seen.

Finally, like all saints, he tired,
he became more flesh than force,
flapping on his side, heaving for air,
the marble eye lidless against the sun,
the green water gilding the silver bands

between the black. I have not missed
my father since he died, but now
I want to tell him about the tackle, test,
bait, how the drag was set, though he'd disparage
my catch, remind me of the snook he bragged

of courting for seven years
by the pilings of his condo.
My father, gone entirely sour
by the time I was five, lived for
two things: the racetrack and the pier.

And I was nothing to him, I was only
a noise that shattered his nerves
a mouth chewing too loudly.
Whatever kept him together was thin and taut
as this line. Now someone lowers a basket net

to cradle the fish as we hoist
him to the dock, hooked through the lip,
a gash in the beautiful tail like a broken wish
bone. And there the scarlet blood.
I had forgotten his blood. I had

forgotten that every beauty involves a wound.
Now I pull the fish
from the mournful sound
in which he lived. His gills beat
like stubby wings, the red plush pleats

turning pink, all the fight gone
out of him. And now the fish
is like a man whose agony
was mysterious, whose every gesture,
every silence, was a roar.

For the Women of the All-Female Bookkeeping Department at H. G. Smithy's

I think of them with summer,
polka-dot dresses and white
enamel jewelry, a petal
on each ear. The rest of the year
while I was in school,
they must have worn drabber garb,
but I never saw them bundled up
against a cold world, only displayed
like a bucket of tulips for sale,
their bangle bracelets clinking like laughter.

My family looked down on women
who worked, but I, a trainee at fifteen,
was in awe of the magic
wands tucked in their bags—
mascaras, lip brushes, pink-tonged
lash curlers that caged their eyes!
I loved their seamed stockings,
the way they turned
to check them, one leg slightly raised,
the made-up face set back on the shoulder
like a clock on a mantel.

And their clothes—tight
sheath skirts, Doris Day shirtwaists.
A silk scarf at the neck
like a snippet of lingerie inviting
a man to carry them off
to someplace besides the department
stores where they shopped the sales

at lunch: Hecht's, Woodward & Lothrop's,
even chandeliered Garfinkle's,

where the wives of diplomats wandered
in saris and pearls. The bookkeepers
bought the best, believing a French
hat might be the key
accessory to a different life. It could happen
anywhere—on a streetcar or bus, walking
the long breezy blocks to the office
and back, chatting with the men who visited
our corridor from Real Estate and Rent.

I loved them the way I loved all my teachers—
so that in memory they seem more
adult than I will ever be.
O Miss Dottie, Miss Helen, Miss Elaine,
ambition had not yet been given
to you or to me. I wish I could
remember you simply as women
who worked for a living,
not as thwarted pilots and judges,
not as perpetual ingénues
swatting at fate with a kidskin glove.

Steve Cummings

Deborah Slicer

Born October 9, 1953, in Carbondale, Pennsylvania. Deborah Slicer's *The White Calf Kicks* won the 2003 Autumn House Press Poetry Prize. She has most recently published in *Red, White, and Blues* (University of Iowa), *The Spoon River Review*, and *Orion*. Her poems have been featured several times on Garrison Keillor's radio program, "The Writer's Almanac." She teaches philosophy at the University of Montana and lives peaceably with her horses and cats near Missoula, Montana.

I Loved the Black Cat

Who stayed in the woodshed with me
During sudden summer thunderstorms late at night.

I miss the man who stayed in our house
Afraid, but I think I did not love him

So much as I loved that cat.
Darkness came undone at seams of lightning.
Black cat sat. Still.

You know how wind leaps on top a bull pine's back, rides it nearly to the ground?

Well, cat just flared his leather nose a little,
Paws Buddha-tucked.
Watched on.

When thunder cracked its thirty knuckles, helved its three free fists, when rain spat sideways at us—

Cat snuffed—*Pfsss—*
So what?

Some storms were so sudden and spectacularly
Terrible, I'd run half-dressed to the woodshed from our house,

Where I'd find my black cat
Staring down my terrible,
When the man inside the house could not.

Pastoral

Let the roadside go to chicory
and gall-
of-the-earth, and the hillside go
to clover
and everlasting
pea, and the road itself
to the barred belly of the blacksnake
and the tarot belly
of the tortoise,
while burdock and poke
choke the corn
out of the fields,
and morning glories run wild
over the immaculate gardens—
let thistle grow tall
and defiantly purple.
And let there be no noise,
just the pileated woodpecker
screeching
like a wild monkey,
heat,
and the wind stumbling through a long row of pines,
the unabashed turning
of leaves
asking
the wind's *blessings, blessings, blessings.*

Shiners

I climb toward the headwaters of Mill Creek
and where the Appalachian Trail crosses the creekbed
squat down in the path of the midmorning sun,
so they can see me in my shadow,
so I can see them.

Because two-legs are supposed to keep walking in the direction of afternoon,
because something that's different is something gone wrong,
it takes a long time,
an almost graveside stillness
before they will come out from under the rocks.

Jesus bugs are oblivious.
Two one-armed crayfish sling silt at woozy moss.

I sit with my mind tucked under my wing like a sleepy heron

until the first shiner melts out of a silvery rock,

then more shiners
in a shallows so clear they seem to levitate just above the gold pea gravel,
shy as new silk.

When I sink my limp fist to the muddy bottom
shiners scatter-burst,
a darting scream, filmy chaos
in which I lose myself, again.

But after some time a shiner enters the hand-house I've built,
and the current in there contracts and expands and it feels as though I have hold
of the first pulse of Adam.

Then my own heart beats once less lonely,
ashes in my mouth taste less bitter,
and I remember how even his God had to rebuild covenants with life like this.

Sunflowers, Wyoming

Wednesday, west of Sheridan, sky
flattens out like a dinner plate,

distance
runs a marathon into Montana,
never gets winded, never turns for a backward glance at the Big Horns,

wind
undresses the unleavened west two hundred miles to Stillwater.

Joy-running, a red balloon crisscrosses the highway in front of my truck.

Then caught in forty-mile-an-hour gusts it turns panicked
circles, seeking
some tether, clutch
of creekside willow, chokecherry,
bitterbrush.

Have I been this reckless with my life?
During all those years I walked with my hands behind my back

did I strangle every opportunity
for love, pick-pocket pity on street corners, pray
to a beautiful but indifferent grievance,
waiting for a rose thorn to bloom?

Yesterday, east of Sheridan,
fields of September sunflowers hung their collared heads, multitudes
at the Vatican, miles
of humility.
Drove faster.

Tina Chang

Tracy K. Smith

Born April 16, 1972, in Falmouth, Massachusetts. Tracy K. Smith is the author of *Duende* (Graywolf Press, 2007), which received the 2006 James Laughlin Prize of The Academy of American Poets. Her first collection, *The Body's Question* (Graywolf Press, 2003), won the 2002 Cave Canem Poetry Prize. She has also received awards from the Rona Jaffe Foundation, the Mrs. Giles Whiting Foundation, *Essence Magazine* and elsewhere. She has been a member of the Creative Writing faculty at Princeton since 2005. Smith travels for inspiration. She lives in Brooklyn with a dog, a cat, and Raphael Allison.

After Persephone

At a certain point, it didn't matter.
I commanded him to lead.
Farther. So far I was no longer me
Long before I was no longer safe.

I shed everything, save being.
There is a moment, even in the face
Of defeat, when the chase alone
Is enough. I lived quickly,

My whole life disappearing
From around me like a sound
That rises into the air and is gone
Without even an echo. After song

There is a pang. The heart in clench.
Then memory. Then retreat
Into the present. That silence.
Not emptiness, but weight.

I felt my steps marking the space
Where I must tread. Then it was I
Who led. Dragging us both
Into his world. It was real. More real

Even than what came after.

I Don't Miss It

But sometimes I forget where I am,
Imagine myself inside that life again.

Recalcitrant mornings. Sun perhaps,
Or more likely colorless light

Filtering its way through shapeless cloud.

And when I begin to believe I haven't left,
The rest comes back: Our couch. My smoke

Climbing the walls while the hours fall.
Straining against the noise of traffic, music,

Anything alive, to catch your key in the door.
And that scamper of feeling in my chest,

As if the day, the night, wherever it is
I am by then, has been only a whir

Of something other than waiting.

We hear so much about what love feels like.
Right now, today, with the rain outside,

And leaves that want as much as I do to believe
In May, in seasons that come when called,

It's impossible not to want
To walk into the next room and let you

Run your hands down the sides of my legs,
Knowing perfectly well what they know.

A Hunger So Honed

Driving home late through town
He woke me for a deer in the road,
The light smudge of it fragile in the distance,

Free in a way that made me ashamed for our flesh—
His hand on my hand, even the weight
Of our voices not speaking.

I watched a long time
And a long time after we were too far to see,
Told myself I still saw it nosing the shrubs,

All phantom and shadow, so silent
It must have seemed I hadn't wakened,
But passed into a deeper, more cogent state—

The mind a dark city, a disappearing,
A handkerchief
Swallowed by a fist.

I thought of the animal's mouth
And the hunger entrusted it. A hunger
So honed the green leaves merely maintain it.

We want so much,
When perhaps we live best
In the spaces between loves,

That unconscious roving,
The heart its own rough animal.
Unfettered.

The second time,
There were two that faced us a moment
The way deer will in their Greek perfection,

As though we were just some offering
The night had delivered.
They disappeared between two houses,

And we drove on, our own limbs,
Our need for one another
Greedy, weak.

Fire Escape Fantasy

This is a city of tunnels and great heights,
Fierce tracks where you find yourself
Just going, face fixed, body braced
Against questions, against knowing,
The lights below and out across proof
Of the thin liquid we float in.

Windows open to the faint breath
Of the inevitable, I pray
To my god of smoke, of science,

Of the people I despise. I draw
The strings of my life tighter,
Feeling nothing. There are small men

Whose small fists rattle, spilling dice
Onto the pavement like teeth, so that our night
Is a kind of agitated music. That's why women
Wear worry and cover their heads, let their words
Drop like shot birds from the higher windows.
Every night here one of us is sliced open.

A woman lifts her arm and brings it down.
Or a cop. This is obviously a question.
The child that cries out from below
Repeats the answer again and again: obedience.
This century was not designed to be felt. Still, I test
Like a girl determined to break herself apart.

Success must hurt. Must yield sharp evidence.
I'll have to lie to get to it.
                                        Like love.

Credulity

We believe we are giving ourselves away,
And so it feels good,
Our bodies swimming together
In afternoon light, the music
That enters our window as far
From the voices that made it
As our own minds are from reason.

There are whole doctrines on loving.
A science. I would like to know everything
About convincing love to give me
What it does not possess to give. And then
I would like to know how to live with nothing.
Not memory. Nor the taste of the words
I have willed you whisper into my mouth.

Teake Zuidema

Sheryl St. Germain

Born July 28, 1954, in New Orleans, Louisiana. Sheryl St. Germain's work has received several awards, including two National Endowment for the Arts Fellowships. Her most recent books are *Swamp Songs: The Making of an Unruly Woman*, a memoir about growing up in Louisiana, and *Let It Be a Dark Roux: New and Selected Poems* (Autumn House Press, 2007). Born and raised in New Orleans, she has written extensively about the culture and environment of Louisiana. She is a devotee of New Orleans music and cooking, and loves to make rich, dark-rouxed gumbos for friends. She directs the MFA Creative Writing Program at Chatham University in Pittsburgh.

Addiction

in memory of my brother, Jay St. Germain, 1958–1981

The truth is I loved it,
the whole ritual of it,
the way he would fist up his arm, then
hold it out so trusting and bare,
the vein pushed up all blue and throbbing
and wanting to be pierced,
his opposite hand gripped tight as death
around the upper arm,

the way I would try to enter the vein,
almost parallel to the arm,
push lightly but firmly, not
too deep,
you don't want to go through
the vein, just in,
then pull back until you see
blood, then

hold the needle very still, slowly
shoot him with it.
Like that I would enter him,
slowly, slowly, very still,
don't move,
then he would let the fist out,
loosen his grip on the upper arm—

and oh, the movement of his lips
when he asked that I open my arms.
How careful,

how good he was, sliding
the needle silver and slender
so easily into me, as though
my skin and veins were made for it,
and when he had finished, pulled
it out, I would be coming
in my fingers, hands, my ear lobes
were coming, heart, thighs,
tongue, eyes and brain were coming,
thick and brilliant as the last thin match
against a homeless bitter cold.

I even loved the pin-sized bruises,
I would finger them alone in my room
like marks of passion;
by the time they turned yellow,
my dreams were full of needles.

We both took lovers who loved
this entering and being entered,
but when he brought over the
pale-faced girl so full of needle holes
he had to lay her on her back

like a corpse and stick the needle
over and over in her ankle veins
to find one that wasn't weary
of all that joy, I became sick
with it, but

you know, it still stalks my dreams,
and deaths make no difference:
there is only the body's huge wanting.

When I think of my brother
all spilled out on the floor
I say nothing to anyone.
I know what it's like to want joy
at any cost.

Cajun

I want to take the word back into my body, back
from the northern restaurants with their neon signs
announcing it like a whore. I want it to be private again,

I want to sink back into the swamps that are nothing
like these clean restaurants, the swamps
with their mud and jaws and eyes that float
below the surface, the mud and jaws and eyes
of food or death. I want to see my father's father's
hands again, scarred with a life of netting and trapping,
thick gunk of bayou under his fingernails,
staining his cuticles, I want to remember the pride he took
gutting and cleaning what he caught; his were nothing
like the soft hands and clipped fingernails that serve us
in these restaurants cemented in land, the restaurants nothing
like the houses we lived and died in, anchored in water,
trembling with every wind and flood.

And what my father's mother knew:
how to make alligator tail sweet, how to cut up
muscled squirrel or rabbit, or wild duck,
cook it till it was tender, spice it and mix it all up
with rice that soaked up the spice and the game so that
it all filled your mouth, thick and sticky, tasting
like blood and cayenne. And when I see the signs
on the restaurants, *Cajun food served here,*
it's like a fish knife ripping my belly, and when I see
them all eating the white meat of fat chickens
and market cuts of steak or fish someone else
has caught cooked *cajun* style, I feel it
again, the word's been stolen, like me,
gutted.

The Lake

I think it was always polluted,
even as a child I remember that gray-peppered foam
mouthing the shore. Some days it had a rotten smell to it,
especially hot days when the fish that had tried so hard
to filter shit through their gills gave up
and floated open-eyed to the surface.
I used to be amazed at what could thrive in that lake,
scavengers, shellfish, how white and sweet their meat was.
Its name was French like mine: *Pontchartrain,*
St. Germain, and the names echo each other nights
when I feel those waters rising, and the dead fish all rise up,
the dark waters swelling higher and higher
until I have to give it up or drown,
swim for whatever hard-shelled goodness I can find.

What We Found in our Mother's Shed After the Hurricane

Broken tools, chairs from the sixties,
two broken bikes, a broken lawnmower,

eight moldy boxes of books, tax information
from the seventies. Lots of cat shit.

Piles of stockings, Maw Maw's walker,
Maw Maw's toilet, Mother's maternity clothes,

three letters to Santa Claus, lizards, roaches,
one dead squirrel, one unrecognizable skeleton.

Wisteria, mold, lots of sun.

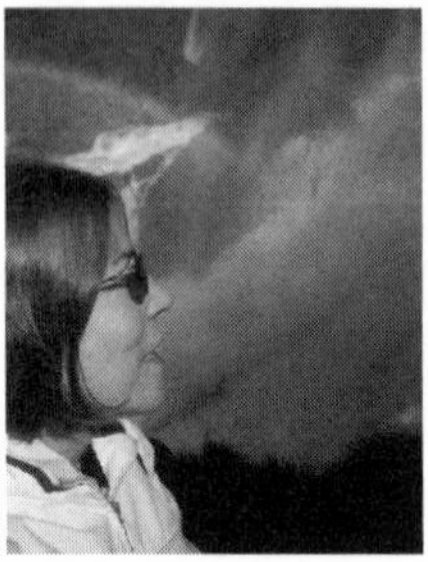
Susan Terris

Susan Terris

Born May 6, 1937, in St. Louis, Missouri. Susan Terris's poetry books include *Contrarwise* (Time Being Books, 2008), *Natural Defenses* (Marsh Hawk Press), *Fire Is Favorable to the Dreamer* (Arctos Press), *Poetic License* (Adastra Press), and *Eye of the Holocaust* (Arctos Press). Recent work appears in *The Iowa Review, Beloit Poetry Review, FIELD, Calyx, The Journal, Colorado Review, Prairie Schooner, Shenandoah, Denver Quarterly*, and *Ploughshares*. For seven years she was editor of *RUNES, A Review of Poetry*. She is also the winner of a Pushcart Prize for a poem published in *FIELD*. In her spare time, she likes to kayak and to bake.

Pantoum for a Member of the Wedding

It was the summer of fear. A jazz sadness quivered her nerves.
She was an unjoined person. A member of nothing.
The world, she said, *is certainly a sudden place.*
A green sick dream. I wish I was somebody else except me.

She was an unjoined person. A member of nothing.
Too tall for the arbor, she stared into a tangle of vines
A green sick dream. I wish I was somebody else except me.
Remembrances were sudden, each colored by its own season.

Too tall for the arbor, she stared into a tangle of vines
Sun-drunk bluejays screamed and murdered among themselves.
Remembrances were sudden, each colored by its own season.
But in the corner of her eye. Love. A thing not spoken.

Sun-drunk bluejays screamed and murdered among themselves.
The wedding was like a dream outside her power.
But in the corner of her eye. Love. A thing not spoken.
She was a wild girl. Strange words flowered in her throat.

The wedding was like a dream outside her power.
In blue light, she felt as a person drowning.
She was a wild girl. Strange words flowered in her throat.
She heard a chord then, a bell, an unfinished tune.

In blue light, she felt as a person drowning.
It was the summer of fear. A jazz sadness quivered her nerves.
She heard a chord then, a bell, an unfinished tune.
The world, she said, *is certainly a sudden place.*

Goldfish: A Diptych

Science has proven the goldfish has a memory of a second and a half.

1.
Tale of the Goldfish

Look, there's a castle,
submerged so its world magnifies
in water hazed with algae,
but I see willow, sun, a dragonfly.

Look, a castle—
rays of sunlight through its doorway,
a mermaid on a rock
amid roots and burnished shells.

Look, there's a castle,
and I angle through the door, out the window,
everything static,
yet behind I sense a shadow.

Look—
its distorted world is pooling,
until I see a rock with no mermaid,
sense jaws of darkness.

Look, there's . . .

2.
A Man Is a Goldfish with Legs

Look, there's a castle,
where Circe turns seamen to swimming pigs
while the universe expands,
so watch out for solar glare.

Look, there's . . .
and at its hearth, a clockwise flame,
but below continents of ice,
stress lines.

Look, a castle—
and a pearl at my throat to keep me alive,
yet if there's heat lightning,
Venus will wink at daybreak.

Look—
how Circe takes up the pearl,
and Venus, in morning sun, floats fire and ice,
and may her lightning give you pause.

Some days—it's less than a second.

I Speak in My Mother's Voice

This is what is meant by old—older than my mother.
And my body, heavy these days, not fat
just slow, hard to move; and here in my summer house,
the children, my guests, breeze through rooms
as if I'm gone. They cook in my kitchen,
whisper about my TV. Once, before they were
born, or as Harold (yes . . . dead now for
more than twenty years) always said, *a gleam*
in his eye, I was a considered a beauty—
seductive, smart, and everyone paid attention.
Now, though, I'm failing and afraid of falling,
I still hear, see, win at Scrabble, do a puzzle faster . . .
ort . . . pariah-dog . . . mai-tai . . . play better bridge
than any of them. For my 80th, they gave me
a computer and stick-on tattoos. Now my 90th is
coming. But, except for manicures, massages,
a few forced kisses, no one touches me;
and my nerve endings are dying. For pleasure,
I think about the next meal and the next. Try to forget
hospitals, swollen legs, bruises. The children
find me as aggravating . . . *Trigger . . . Bermuda Triangle* . . .
as I once found my aging mother. Everything is
being taken away, except the present tense
of food and TV sports. The children, you ask?
Well, my youngest sleeps too much and does too little.
My son thinks only about money. My oldest
moves in her own world and has her secrets,
but she knows my spark and my drive,
my need to travel, to dance the night away.
Yes, even with a walker, I dance. In the hospital, too.
The last time, the discharge nurse gave me a list.
Its final item: *Sexual Activity*, and she wrote in:
As tolerated. While my daughter and I laughed,
I thought of someone stroking my breasts, of a man
inside me. Not Harold, though he was only 70,
and, right now, 70 sounds about right. Of us, I remember

mostly our travels . . . *largo* . . . *West Nile* . . . *espresso* . . .
his temper, yet little about how he touched me.
My daughter touches everyone yet seldom me as if old age
is contagious, as if one day she'll wake and find
herself with my arms, my feet, my sack-of-potatoes
belly. And slow, as I am. "Myrtle the Turtle"
Harold called me. But my daughter's always moved fast,
fast runner, whitewater girl. Now, still, she speeds
as if she can keep age from catching her. The writer,
the spark, and, here up north: the camp counselor.
But I know words she doesn't . . . *dik-dik* . . . *palimpsest* . . .
After the stroke, they asked me the steps to change a tire;
and I said I'd call the Auto Club and that Hamlet lived
at Elsinore and Rosalind in the Forest of Arden.
My daughter is an aging Rosalind, sharp,
but she doesn't know a five letter word for soap plant.
She doesn't know the beach at Rarotonga. Yes, I'm
an adventurer who hangs elephant bells
on my walker. And, still, some days when I wake,
I think I am already dead. Those mornings, I don't
feel my body at all—not hot or cold, pleasure
or pain. My daughter's daughter always says people
need to get a life. Well, I still have one. But look
at me. Body dying faster than mind; and if I
can't keep traveling, I think I *will* die. My last
freedom. To my daughter, I gave more freedom
than I ever had. Harold loved me, but I made
the compromises. My eldest makes few,
was never the beauty I was, but freedom keeps her
exotic. My legacy, and she uses it—sometimes
even against me. But that's okay. When she skims by,
I pretend to go with her, see her secret life as mine.
And this morning, when I move from my back, from
this numb, turtled state, I'll sit on my shower stool
until the hot water is drained from the tank.
Then I'll phone about a foot massage,
butter myself two slices of wild rice bread
from Bemidji, and do my crossword . . .
Song of Solomon . . . *ai* . . . *Arthur Ashe* . . . as I watch
the Open and make plans for my next world cruise.

Stuart Parnes

Sue Ellen Thompson

Born July 19, 1948, in Glen Ridge, New Jersey. Sue Ellen Thompson is the author of four books, most recently *The Golden Hour* (Autumn House Press, 2006), and editor of *The Autumn House Anthology of Contemporary American Poetry* (2005). Her work has been featured in Ted Kooser's column, "American Life in Poetry," and in *Best American Poetry 2006.* A former Robert Frost Fellow at the Bread Loaf Writers' Conference and resident poet at The Frost Place, she now lives a block from the Chesapeake Bay on Maryland's Eastern Shore, where she works as a freelance lexicographer and is trying to re-establish her identity as a poet after a lifetime in New England.

How to Tell a True Love Story

Say he pulled her face roughly to his,
the way he once grasped a coconut

on the black sand beach, pausing to take
its sweetness in first through the eyes;

or say he pulled her down like a rare book,
his face dissolving in wonder

as he fingered the leaves of her smile.
We will bring our own urgencies to the scene.

Put some obstacle in the way of their lovemaking:
have her wearing those tapered jeans

he must pick at her heels to remove;
or let their bodies impede,

his elbow snagging a silken breast,
her teeth meeting his in a kiss

that clacks like bone. Let them fail
to get it right, so there will be something unfinished

between them, something that blights
the small green fruit of their meeting

and fades into correspondence. Then let
their correspondence drop off,

a misunderstanding, a failure of passion
or nerve. But end where love

as I would have you tell it ends,
with him opening the door to the retreating light

and her falling without seeing where she is going,
or who it is that trembles there above her.

With My Second Husband, Thinking of My First

He knew light and how to bend it.
He could hold a glass of rum
up to the milky winter sky
and turn the kitchen autumn.

He bought me silks whose colors lay
like filtered lamplight on my skin.
I danced upon my crystal stem
until the room turned scarlet.

He drank too much, but he was young,
his face still luminous with years unspent,
with late nights tossed in twisted sheets,
with morning's ravenous argument,

his body always six months shy
of spoiling. To my Tantalus he played
the rising water, ripened peach. I can't deny
I dreamed of him long after he was gone—

I'd see him slinking down the driveway
in his profligate black car, his bike
and skis and all his treasures on a rack
while you lay bearded, patient, as unlike

him as any man could be—
or that I'm thinking of him now, your hand
upon our ripening daughter as we stand
before the ancient cider press like pilgrims

paying homage to the fall. We watch the pulp
pour down the chute until it's spread
in layers between burlap-covered frames.
The generator clears its throat and bends its head

to the task, bearing down like truth
upon the flesh of those who were betrayed,
pressing sweetness from the bruised and bitter,
pressing it right through the light of day.

After the Accident

the old rose-colored Buick turns in
past the rows of slush-covered cars
with webbed windshields and wrinkled doors.
My father steps out, unfolding himself
on the ice-slick asphalt with an old bird's grace
and stands, hands at the back of his waist,
leaning against the sky. My mother,
buoyed along by her puffed blue coat,
is all scurry and search as she hurries
toward me through the glass door marked
"Service," her arms already rising
from her sides. Swept up into

the car's small warmth, I let myself
be taken to lunch, I let them order for me—
a cheeseburger in the golden arms
of mounded onion rings, a cookie the size
of my own spread palm
weighted with chocolate. I eat
and I eat, as if I'd been trapped
in that snow-choked ravine for days,
as if food were love and I could absorb it,
turning it into flesh the way
they turned their love into me.
But seeing all that is left—a thinnish woman
in her forties without a car, without
even a purse, they must think
it is not enough. So they feed me and I
eat, and all that keeps me from an infant's sleep
is who will carry me home when they are gone?

The American Hotel

We caught a bargain flight to Amsterdam
from our chilly flat in London for a honeymoon.
The hotel clerk didn't understand
English, and we found ourselves in a room

with twin beds. Should we complain?
I had a fever and a sore throat,
and we'd been living together for seven
years. Then I remembered my mother's boast

that she and my father had never spent a night
apart. As she dozed off during those final days
of her illness, my father would be curled beside
her, sunlight setting the bed ablaze.

Never sleep apart if you have a choice:
My mother's words, in my mother's voice.

Helping My Daughter Move into Her First Apartment

This is all I am to her now:
a pair of legs in running shoes,

two arms strung with braided wire.
She heaves a carton sagging with CDs

at me and I accept it gladly, lifting
with my legs, not bending over,

raising each foot high enough
to clear the step. Fortunate to be

of any use to her at all,
I wrestle, stooped and single-handed,

with her mattress in the stairwell,
saying nothing as it pins me,

sweating, to the wall. Vacuum cleaner,
spiny cactus, five-pound sacks

of rice and lentils slumped
against my heart: up one flight

of stairs and then another,
down again with nothing in my arms.

Natasha Trethewey

Born April 26, 1966, in Gulfport, Mississippi. Natasha Trethewey is the author of three collections of poetry, *Domestic Work* (Graywolf, 2000), *Bellocq's Ophelia* (Graywolf, 2002), and *Native Guard* (Houghton Mifflin, 2006), for which she won the Pulitzer Prize. At Emory University she is Professor of English and holds the Phillis Wheatley Distinguished Chair in Poetry. She is the daughter of poet Eric Trethewey.

Southern History

Before the war, they were happy, he said,
quoting our textbook. (This was senior-year

history class.) *The slaves were clothed, fed,*
and better off under a master's care.

I watched the words blur on the page. No one
raised a hand, disagreed. Not even me.

It was late; we still had Reconstruction
to cover before the test, and—luckily—

three hours of watching *Gone with the Wind.*
History, the teacher said, *of the old South—*

a true account of how things were back then.
On screen a slave stood big as life: big mouth,

bucked eyes, our textbook's grinning proof—a lie
my teacher guarded. Silent, so did I.

Incident

We tell the story every year—
how we peered from the windows, shades drawn—
though nothing really happened,
the charred grass now green again.

We peered from the windows, shade drawn,
at the cross trussed like a Christmas tree,
the charred grass still green. Then
we darkened our rooms, lit the hurricane lamps.

At the cross trussed like a Christmas tree,
a few men gathered, white as angels in their gowns.
We darkened our room and lit hurricane lamps,
the wicks trembling in their fonts of oil.

It seemed the angels had gathered, white men in their gowns.
When they were done, they left quietly. No one came.
The wicks trembled all night in their fonts of oil;
by morning the flames had all dimmed.

When they were done, the men left quietly. No one came.
Nothing really happened.
By morning all the flames had dimmed.
We tell the story every year.

Taxonomy

after a series of Casta *paintings by Juan Rodríguez Juárez, ca. 1715*

1. *De Español y de India Produce Mestizo*

The canvas is a leaden sky
        behind them, heavy
with words, gold letters inscribing
        an equation of blood—

this plus this equals this—as if
        a contract with nature, or
a museum label,
        ethnographic, precise. See

how the father's hand, beneath
        its crown of lace,
curls around his daughter's head;
        she's nearly fair

as he is—*calidad*. See it
        in the brooch at her collar,
the lace framing her face.
        An infant, she is borne

over the servant's left shoulder,
        bound to him
by a sling, the plain blue cloth
        knotted at his throat.

If the father, his hand
        on her skull, divines—
as the physiognomist does—
        the mysteries

of her character, discursive,
        legible on her light flesh,
in the soft curl of her hair,
        we cannot know it, so gentle

the eye he turns toward her.
        The mother, glancing
sideways toward him—
        the scarf on her head

white as his face,
        his powdered wig—gestures
with one hand a shape
        like the letter C. *See,*

she seems to say,
        what we have made.
The servant, still a child, cranes
        his neck, turns his face

up toward all of them. He is dark
        as history, origin of the word
native: the weight of blood,
        a pale mistress on his back,

heavier every year.

2. *De Español y Negra Produce Mulato*

Still, the centuries have not dulled
the sullenness of the child's expression.

If there is light inside him, it does not shine
through the paint that holds his face

in profile—his domed forehead, eyes
nearly closed beneath a heavy brow.

Though inside, the boy's father stands
in his cloak and hat. It's as if he's just come in,

or that he's leaving. We see him
transient, rolling a cigarette, myopic—

his eyelids drawn against the child
passing before him. At the stove,

the boy's mother contorts, watchful,
her neck twisting on its spine, red beads

yoked at her throat like a necklace of blood,
her face so black she nearly disappears

into the canvas, the dark wall upon which
we see the words that name them.

What should we make of any of this?
Remove the words above their heads;

put something else in place of the child—
a table, perhaps, upon which the man might set

his hat, or a dog upon which to bestow
the blessing of his touch—and the story

changes. The boy is a palimpsest of paint—
layers of color, history rendering him

that precise shade of in-between.
Before this, he was nothing: blank

canvas—before image or word, before
a last brush stroke fixed him in his place.

4. *The Book of Castas*

Call it the catalogue
          of mixed bloods, or

          the book of naught:
                    not Spaniard, not white, but

mulatto-returning-backwards, (or
hold-yourself-in-midair) and

the *morisca*, the *lobo*, the *chino*,
sambo, *albino* and

the *no-te-entiendo*, the
I don't understand you.

Guidebook to the colony,
record of each crossed birth,

it is the typology of taint,
of stain: blemish: sullying spot:

that which can be purified,
that which cannot—Canaan's

black fate. How like a dirty joke
it seems: *what do you call*

that space between
the dark geographies of sex?

Call it the *taint*—as in
T'aint one and t'aint the other—

illicit and yet naming still
what is between. Between

her parents, the child,
Mulatto-returning-backwards,

cannot slip their hold,
the triptych their bodies make

in paint, in blood: her name
written down in the *Book*

of Castas—all her kind
in thrall to a word.

Emma Dodge Hanson

Chase Twichell

Born August 20, 1950, in New Haven, Connecticut. Chase Twichell is the author of six books of poetry, most recently *Dog Language* (Copper Canyon, 2005). A *New & Selected* is forthcoming in 2009. She has received fellowships from the National Endowment for the Arts and the John Simon Guggenheim Memorial Foundation, and a Literature Award from the American Academy of Arts and Letters. After teaching for many years (Hampshire College, the University of Alabama, Warren Wilson College, Princeton University), she resigned in 1999 to start Ausable Press, which publishes contemporary poetry. Twichell is a student of Zen Buddhism. She lives in the Adirondacks with her husband, the novelist Russell Banks.

The Givens

One side of the dialogue
I have by heart,
but learned it so long ago
each phrase seems
sullenly dangerous now, in that
it withholds something I once knew.
The words go forth,
sleek pigeons into the wild sky,
smaller and smaller and smaller,
like pictures trapped in a telescope,
shrinking it-ward segment by segment.

I had as a child a mind
already rife with sacred greens
I could neither harvest nor ignore.
They sprang up everywhere:
from the black dirt of memory—
the old farm, its raspberries
diamonded with dew, etc.—
even from bodiless fantasy,
and from the mailbox full of letters
standing in for the various
emotions and kinds of news.

Part of myself must have
courted and married another part.
I don't know when it happened.
I know I heard both voices early on.
But one now drags its half of the duet
off into a scary song about

its intimations of the time ahead:
love, lost love, and love again,
and I dislike the long-drawn,
melancholy music that it makes.

But it's beautiful here
in this house above the valley,
close to the crumpled
paper of the clouds.
Birds return from invisible worlds.
Their feet print words on my sills.
And words weigh down the long,
soft-spoken branches of the evergreens,
weigh the unpruned
branches of abandoned orchards
down into the blond grass
where the pears,
grown small and hard with wildness,
soften and disappear.

And yet,
sometimes sick of the orderly,
pallid little stars,
I hear the stray heart's careless noise,
its tears and mysteries of laughter
close outside. It calls to me,
that voice, its ragged sweetness
intimate with everything I fear.

Centaur

The first typeface I loved
was Centaur, cut by Bruce Rogers
in 1914. It had animal bones,
and reminded me
of skinny-dipping at night,
baptized in star water so cold
I suddenly became another
animal from the waist down.

In our family, we knew
all about the Minotaur,
Cyclops, and centaurs.
My father read to me
about the man-horses,
so I had an inkling

of their danger,
and thereafter leaned
toward the horse part
and away from the man.

Sorry

I'm to press the pad of my thumb
against the trout's upper jaw,
its teeth surprisingly sharp,
more like berry cane than teeth,
its eyes already beginning to look back
from the afterlife. It's limbless,
like a whole soul in my hands,
and slimy, so I clamp it
with my knees to get a better grip,
and use both thumbs
to force back the jaw until the spine
breaks slowly, like a green stick,
and the jaws half close
as if by failing memory.
Then later in the sink we slit
open the belly, strip out the guts,
see if it's male or female,
see what it's eaten. If it's female
Dad clicks *sorry* with his tongue.

Infant Pearls

On the subjects of poetry and love,
I ask a lot of questions that are
the children of the questions
I should be asking,
but S. just dances out there
with her new escort,
in her string of infant pearls
and a black bra showing
through white eyelet.
I want to be just like her,
half bride, half martyr
going to God in my mind.

Erotic Energy

Don't tell me we're not like plants,
sending out a shoot when we need to,
or spikes, poisonous oils, or flowers.

Come to me but only when I say,
That's how plants announce

the rules of propagation.
Even children know this. You can
see them imitating all the moves

with their bright plastic toys.
So that, years later, at the moment

the girl's body finally says yes
to the end of childhood,
a green pail with an orange shovel

will appear in her mind like a tropical
blossom she has never seen before.

Road Tar

A kid said you could chew road tar
if you got it before it cooled,
black globule with a just-forming skin.
He said it was better than cigarettes.
He said he had a taste for it.

On the same road, a squirrel
was doing the Watusi to free itself
from its crushed hindquarters.
A man on a bicycle stomped on its head,
then wiped his shoe on the grass.

It was *autumn*, the adult word for fall.
In school we saw a film called *Reproduction*.
The little snake-father poked his head
into the slippery future,
and a girl with a burned tongue was conceived.

To the Reader: If You Asked Me

I want you with me, and yet you are the end
of my privacy. Do you see how these rooms
have become public? How we glance to see if—
who? Who did you imagine?
Surely we're not here alone, you and I.

I've been wandering
where the cold tracks of language
collapse into cinders, unburnable trash.
Beyond that, all I can see is the remote cold
of meteors before their avalanches of farewell.

If you asked me what words
a voice like this one says in parting,
I'd say, *I'm sweeping an empty factory*
toward which I feel neither hostility nor nostalgia.
I'm just a broom, sweeping.

Sandra Usui

Amy Uyematsu

Born October 18, 1947, in Pasadena, California. Amy Uyematsu is a *sansei* (third-generation Japanese American) poet and teacher from Los Angeles, California. Her poetry collections are *Stone Bow Prayer* (Copper Canyon Press, 2005), *Nights of Fire, Nights of Rain* (Story Line Press, 1998), and *30 Miles from J-Town* (Story Line, 1992), winner of the 1992 Nicholas Roerich Prize. She was an editor of the widely-used *Roots: An Asian American Reader* (UCLA Asian American Studies Center, 1972). For over thirty years Amy has taught high school mathematics, currently at Venice High School. Her interests include jazz, "old school" R&B music, woodblock prints, folk art, and stones.

Lexicon

try not to be insulted
when they call us oriental.
let exotic be a compliment.
even the most educated among them
will ask how long we've been here,
be genuinely surprised we speak English so well.
don't expect other wrongnamed people to be any better.
immigrants from Guatemala and Mexico
will keep calling us Chino,
even when we explain we were born here.
"you know what we mean," they'll say,
and we'll tell them our parents were born here too.
"you know what we mean," they'll insist,
so we'll tell them our grandparents came from Japan.
they'll nod their heads,
still calling us Chino when they talk among themselves.
don't let these daily misunderstandings get to you.

learn how to differentiate.
slanted eyes is o.k.
but not you slanteyes, tighteyes, sliteyes, zipperheads.
to most of them Jap, Chink, or Gook all mean the same.
don't let them tell us that "kill
the fuckin Gook," spoken in combat,
is separate from "too many Chinks moving in"
to Anaheim, California, or Biloxi, Mississippi.
watch the mouth and eyes carefully as they say the words
maybe our closest friends can call us crazy Japs,
but be cautious when their talk turns
to those sneaky Japs who attacked Pearl Harbor,
who deserved to be put away in camps,
bombed at Hiroshima and Nagasaki.

pay close attention to headlines
which warn about "influx," "imbalance," "invasion."
don't consider any place safe anymore.
watch what they hide in their hands.
in Raleigh, North Carolina, Ming Hai Loo
was gunned down by two brothers
who hated Vietnamese. Loo was Chinese.
and it didn't matter if Vincent Chin
was clubbed to death
by two Detroit autoworkers
who mistook him for Japanese.

don't expect them to ask us our real names.
don't even try.

Muchas Gracias

Just about everyone in California
knows the phrase, *Muchas gracias*—not just
thank you, but *muchas* for very much. I never
expected to find *mucha* in Japanese, which stretches
the meaning to so much more. It fits the way my life's
been going lately—*mucha*, defined as absurd, rash,
excessive, unreasonable, blindly or recklessly. And even
this doesn't go far enough. I had to smile when
I found *mucha-kucha* just below *mucha*
in my Japanese dictionary. It means exactly
how it sounds to my ears—confused, topsy-turvy,
madly, utterly making a mess of things—as in still
being in love with the wrong man,
muchas mucha-kucha.

Wintertide

Some part of me never left the snow country—
where my lover and I chase each other on a white mountain,
feeling nothing but our heat in the icy air,
where I have known the smell of fish broth and fire in the winter,
can remember standing by myself, surrounded by ice and sky,
not needing answers. There is a field of snow
where a woman can stand alone and hear everything.

Under the Wave of Kanagawa

from Hokusai's "36 Views of Mt. Fuji"

i
We who have witnessed
a wave that dwarfs mountains
cannot stay away from your waters.

We who are fed
by armfuls of seaweed and fish
sew garments of blue deep as indigo.

We who are swept away
in your furious white claws
keep coming back in our light yellow boats.

ii
I am your granddaughter but your words were lost
by the time I was born. I couldn't hear your stories
of how you crossed the ocean,
you couldn't tell me the names.

I don't even know if you ever climbed Mt. Fuji.
You loved me as only grandparents can—
without really knowing who I am,
without expecting me to understand you.

How could you guess this yearning I hold
for a language I was never taught, this delight
in putting woodblock prints on my walls,
or this reverence for stones?

I can only guess what you gave up
during those long years in Manzanar and Gila.
You didn't waste time on bitterness
or anger—strange, that I should harbor

So much, thinking that's what mattered—
my years of noisy outrage telling the world
how much you suffered unfairly.
But now I'm not so sure if you needed

Vindication. I think what mattered more
were the small green shoots which
you watered in your gardens,
or the platters of hand-made sushi

You prepared for holidays and special picnics.
Would you feel gratified that a president
apologized, or that you became
heroes to my generation?

I wish you could know I'd grow weary of anger
and finally really understand "shikataganai"—
that certain tragedies cannot be avoided—
to make the best of it, like you.

Gene Pittman

Katrina Vandenberg

Born January 15, 1971, in Wyandotte, Michigan. Katrina Vandenberg is the author of *Atlas* (Milkweed Editions) and, with poet Todd Boss, co-author of the fine-arts letterpress chapbook *On Marriage* (Red Dragonfly Press). She has won fellowships and grants from the MacDowell Colony, and the Fulbright, Bush, and McKnight foundations. She teaches in the MFA program at Hamline University and at the Loft Literary Center. In the fall of 2008 she will be the poetry fellow in residence at the Amy Clampitt House near Lenox, Massachusetts. She is a volunteer at the Center for Victims of Torture and lives with her husband in Saint Paul, Minnesota.

New Words

When the skyscrapers fell, I learned the word
burqua: draped in mystery, veiled threat.
Then *jihad* with its ready fist of stones;
Herat erected a mosque with onion domes
on a cerebral ridge. Do all new words
come out of suffering? The older ones fall
more lightly from my lips, having unpacked
their meanings long ago, when they moved in
to English. *English*: variant of the name
of the tribe that landed on Britannia's shores
around the time the *Vandals*—whose name evokes
cartoon graffiti now—first shook Rome's gates
demanding land and sacks of peppercorns.
Still the iambic poems trot on, ignorant
of the Norman Conquest and the burning barn
in which a syllabic forefather first raped the accentual line.
The knowledge rests inside my words, but not me,
I write. Thanksgiving is not far away,
and John bakes pumpkin cheesecake
for a potluck. Dutch spice traders taught my tongue
of cloves; Cortez, *vanilla*—from *vagina*:
black seeds scattered in a free-love frenzy
that ended in smallpox and ruin. I don't know
how many of our words of love arrived
on slave ships, foreign and our own—and now
this new handful flung from the sky. I'll save
this small change, these new words. They are no trade
for a friend or father, but will become my own.

Nineteen

Carrie and I were hanging our wash on the roof
of the hostel in Riomaggiore—all we had carried

in our packs while remaining half-dressed—when
the Italian couple came up to shower. They shared
a stall, not caring about us and our sodden rainbow
of underwear on the line. From the roof
we could see the Mediterranean bang the cliffs,
and other roof gardens, with cats and coral
geraniums like this one. In the shower that morning,
I had sudsed my hair under the open sky,
the fingers of the sun electric, like God's
on the Sistine Chapel ceiling I'd been herded in
to see the week before. Now the cotton partitions
trembled, and the couple's feet danced
in the spray, her small red-painted toes digging
into the tops of his feet. When she cried out,
Carrie looked at me, and I know we were thinking
the same thing, as the couple caterwauled in the tongue
we wanted to learn, and the inbred cats basked,
and our clothes released the grime of early spring,
and the son of the hostel owner went to scout another train.

Diptych: Open Me Carefully

1. Reading the Complete Emily Dickinson, Years Later

Opaque shades half-drawn on every window,
          she makes me think of you: her brevity,
                    intensity, all she left unsaid—her dashes

diving planks over lakes where no one has yet
          found bottom. How she leaves me at
                    the door. On the morning I stood

outside your closed bedroom while you cried,
          I asked *Should I come in or leave?* She is
                    your long pause before *I don't know*

and how I come back to the closed door again and again.

2. Not Going with You to Amherst Overnight to See Her House Soon After His Death

Separate hotel rooms, you said,
if you want, and still
I could not let myself go,

though since then I have grown
less proud to have dodged
the need that rises

in all of us in grief
to be touched, to be sure
we are still alive. If we

had stood on the landing
where she sat in the dark,
piano and company tinkling

laughter in the next room—
touched her desk where
rhymes came slant, not

true—seen the paperwhite
dress I hear would fit—
I might have heeded

their warnings. To hell
with lowering the heart
from a window, in a basket

noosed by a rope, she would
say—with the letters I mailed
until the end. *The heart wants*

what it wants, she would say—
she would say that I should
have let you take me.

January 6

The town baker took a dozen paintings
        to settle Vermeer's bread bill at his death.

Before I knew this meant the man who owned
        the bakery, not the man who made bread,

I thought the paintings hung in a narrow shop
        at night as candles were blown out all over Delft.

Canals froze. Snow fell. The watchman called out
        All is well. I still want it to be true,

that these paintings waited for a man who worked
with his hands when, before anyone was awake,

he walked through his dim kitchen to start baking,
past the few seeded loaves left on the shelves

from the day before, faint white lines on the floor
where he had swept spilled flour and missed.

That for him loaves and paintings were the same.
Four hundred years after this did not happen,

my Dutch father repairs an assembly line
in Detroit. A poem has machinery, too,

and when I watch snow sift through this poem, glittering
its brick streets, it does not make me think

of Currier & Ives or Michael Furey, but
of the diamond factory in Amsterdam

where once my great-grandfather was ten
and swept floors, where his dust

was saved at the end of each day for inspection.

First Snowfall in Saint Paul

This morning in the untouched lots
of Target, St. Agnes, and Lake
Phalen, girls all over the city
in the first snowfall
of their sixteenth year are being asked
by brothers, fathers—my cousin
Warren—to drive too fast then lock
their brakes, to teach them how to right
themselves. The whine of the wheels, the jerk
when they catch—from Sears to Como Park
to Harding High, the smoke
that bellows from their lungs,
the silver sets of jagged
keys, the spray of snow,
the driver's seat, the encouraging *Go*

Barry Goldstein

Ellen Bryant Voigt

Born May 9, 1943, in Danville, Virginia. Ellen Bryant Voigt's seven volumes of poetry include *Kyrie* (1995), a finalist for the National Book Critics Circle Award; *Shadow of Heaven* (2002) and *Messenger: New and Selected Poems* (2007), both finalists for the National Book Award; and *The Flexible Lyric* (1999), a collection of craft essays. Former Vermont Poet Laureate, she is a Chancellor of the Academy of American Poets, and an elected member of both The Academy of Arts and Sciences and the Fellowship of Southern Writers. Voigt's many awards include fellowships from the National Endowment for the Arts and the Guggenheim Foundation. She teaches in the MFA Program at Warren Wilson College and lives in Cabot, Vermont.

The Hen

The neck lodged under a stick,
the stick under her foot,
she held the full white breast
with both hands, yanked up and out,
and the head was delivered of the body.
Brain stuck like a lens; the profile
fringed with red feathers.
Deposed, abstracted,
the head lay on the ground like a coin.
But the rest, released into the yard,
language and direction wrung from it,
flapped the insufficient wings
and staggered forward, convulsed, instinctive—
I thought it was sobbing to see it hump the dust,
pulsing out those muddy juices,
as if something, deep in the gizzard,
in the sack of soft nuggets,
drove it toward the amputated member.
Even then, watching it litter the ground
with snowy refusals, I knew it was this
that held life, gave life,
and not the head with its hard contemplative eye.

The Farmer

In the still-blistering late afternoon,
like currying a horse the rake
circled the meadow, the cut grass ridging
behind it. This summer, if the weather held,
he'd risk a second harvest after years

of reinvesting, leaving fallow.
These fields were why he farmed—
he walked the fenceline like a man in love.
The animals were merely what he needed:
cattle and pigs; chickens for a while; a drayhorse,
saddle horses he was paid to pasture—
an endless stupid round
of animals, one of them always hungry, sick, lost,
calving or farrowing, or waiting slaughter.

When the field began dissolving in the dusk,
he carried feed down to the knoll,
its clump of pines, gate, trough, lick, chute
and two gray hives; leaned into the Jersey's side
as the galvanized bucket filled with milk;
released the cow and turned to the bees.
He'd taken honey before without protection.
This time, they could smell something
in his sweat—fatigue? impatience,
although he was a stubborn, patient man?
Suddenly, like flame, they were swarming over him.
He rolled in the dirt, manure and stiff hoof-prints,
started back up the path, rolled in the fresh hay—
refused to run, which would have pumped
the venom through him faster—passed the oaks
at the yard's edge, rolled in the yard, reached
the kitchen, and when he tore off his clothes
crushed bees dropped from him like scabs.

For a week he lay in the darkened bedroom.
The doctor stopped by twice a day—
the hundred stings "enough to kill an ox,
enough to kill a younger man." What saved him
were the years of smaller doses—
like minor disappointments,
instructive poison, something he could use.

Stone Pond

Driving over the limit
on a mountain road,
the mist rising, Stone Pond
white with ice and white mist
inside its circle
of birch and black fir:

driving home after
seeing friends, the radio
complicitous and loud,
Beethoven's braided musical line,
a sonata I recall
playing well:

passing the tiny houses
on the hillside, woodsmoke
rising among the budded trees,
then passing within inches
of someone's yard:
I circle Stone Pond, and despair

seems like something I can set aside.
The road bends again, the morning
burns through the mist.
Sufficient joy—
what should I have done to make it last?

The Last Class

Put this in your notebooks:
All verse is occasional verse.
In March, trying to get home, distracted
and impatient at Gate 5 in the Greyhound station,
I saw a drunk man bothering a woman.
A poem depends on its detail
but the woman had her back to me,
and the man was just another drunk,
black in this case, familiar, dirty.
I moved past them both, got on the bus.

There is no further action to report.
The man is not a symbol. If what he said to her
touches us, we are touched by a narrative
we supply. What he said was, "I'm sorry,
I'm sorry," over and over, "I'm sorry,"
but you must understand he frightened the woman,
he meant to rob her of those few quiet
solitary moments sitting down,
waiting for the bus, before she headed home
and probably got supper for her family,
perhaps in a room in Framingham,
perhaps her child was sick.

My bus pulled out, made its usual turns
and parted the formal gardens from the Common,
both of them camouflaged by snow.
And as it threaded its way to open road,
leaving the city, leaving our sullen classroom,
I postponed my satchel of your poems
and wondered who I am to teach the young,
having come so far from honest love of the world;
I tried to recall how it felt
to live without grief; and then I wrote down
a few tentative lines about the drunk,
because of an old compulsion to record,
or sudden resolve not to be self-absorbed
and full of dread—
                                        I wanted to salvage
something from my life, to fix
some truth beyond all change, the way
photographers of war, miles from the front,
lift print after print into the light,
each one further cropped and amplified,
pruning whatever baffles or obscures,
until the small figures are restored
as young men sleeping.

Lesson

Whenever my mother, who taught
small children forty years,
asked a question, she
already knew the answer.
"Would you like to" meant
you would. "Shall we" was
another, and "Don't you think."
As in, "Don't you think
it's time you cut your hair."

So when, in the bare room,
in the strict bed, she said
"You want to see?" her hands
were busy at her neckline,
untying the robe, not looking
down at it, stitches
bristling where the breast
had been, but straight at me.

I did what I always did:
not weep—she never wept—
and made my face a freshly
white-washed wall: let her
write, again, whatever
she wanted there.

Prayer

Artemis—virginal goddess of the hunt, thus
        goddess of childbirth, protector of children, to whom
                agonized women can cry out—

was not a name I thought of, a place to send
        those sharp gasps, when you descended sideways,
                still swimming against the narrow walls of me;

or later, after, the low moans, the mews,
        as I throbbed like something flung from a great height
                and could not be appeased; or in between,

a keening, you by then presenting, the cord—
        the lifeline, tether, leash—lashed like a noose
                round and round your neck by so much swimming.

I think what I said, if saying is what I did,
        was *Sweet Jesus*, another virgin who knew
                the body is first and last an animal,

it eats, shits, fucks, expels the fetus—or doesn't.
        Midnight, lamplight in the barn, the farmer,
                arm deep in the cow, turning, turning the calf;

and my father, a farmer, phoning up to ask
        what had gone wrong, he could not keep his worry
                out of his voice. Perhaps I should have prayed

to him, or to some other powerful god
        assigned to *me*, when you were stalled
                inside the birth canal; and also:

when they ripped you out and cut us free.

Robert Vollmer

Judith Vollmer

Born July 1, 1951, in Pittsburgh, Pennsylvania. Judith Vollmer's most recent book, *Reactor* (University of Wisconsin Press), was featured in the *Los Angeles Times* Book Review and was a nominee for the National Book Critics Circle Award. Her other books are *The Door Open to the Fire, Black Butterfly,* and *Level Green,* which was awarded the Brittingham Prize. Vollmer's essay on Baudelaire is included in the *Cambridge Companion to Baudelaire.* She co-edits the national poetry journal *5 AM* and lives in Pittsburgh's Regent Square neighborhood, near the Nine Mile Run aquatic and wetland restoration project, the largest ecological undertaking of its kind in a major metropolitan area in the United States.

She Kept Me

wrapped & close & fragrant
in her incense of strange lemon soap.
She carried me down, all the way down
into her solitude, lace & bones was all
she was under the t-shirt
faded to watered black silk, thin
as her night veils, dreams

of wet earth, spring, Amsterdam
where she hung with the houseboat boys,
loading bricks of blond hash safely on;
she nursed their sore throats with concentrations
of aspirin & oranges. Spent her money on
artcards & books with blue wrappers.
Whores in windows moved
their lips like bright candies
and petals drifted down

onto my dark woven shoulders
& the three weeks we had,
hotels, of course, also her parents'
canal-side perch where I held her
while she read her Stendhal, her Colette,
the stitches of my devotion
weight she counted on
for *quiet, let's find the exact point of focus, now that's desire,*
isn't it? O it is sex, mother
of all creative energies, books, & companion views.

I liked her
in the cool air of her balcony nights.
I was left on a train and once in a musty café.

I was handed down, yes, but never
taken up so fondly.

Port of Entry

The world breathes
its generous display: You can have this! And this!
Look mama, a fish tail! A child cries at the icy
seafood window, and in the blip before hearing
her mother's *Yes!* She's gone, time
is silk, burning, eyes out of nowhere open petals, pages
—she's through, she's peeking
onto the tip of the flat-wavy universe,
a world rushes forward and up through
her feet, palms & fingertips.
Ecstasy
move us, each first time.

House Spiders

Streetlights out again I'm walking in the dark
lugging groceries up the steps to the porch
whose yellow bulb is about to go too, when a single
familiar strand intersects my face,
the filament slides across my glasses which seem suddenly
perfectly clean, fresh, and my whole tired day slows down
walking into such a giant thread
is a surprise every time,
though I never kill them, I carry them outside
on plastic lids or open books, they live
so plainly and eat the mosquitoes.
Distant cousins
to the scorpion, mine are pale & small,
dark & discreet. More like the one
who lived in the corner of the old farm kitchen
under the ivy vase and behind the single
candle-pot—black with curved
crotchety legs.
Maya, weaver of illusions,
how is it we trust the web, the nest,
the roof over our heads, we trust the stars
our guardians who gave us our alphabet?
We trust the turtle's shell because
it, too, says house and how can we read

the footprints of birds on shoreline sand,
and October twigs that fall to the ground
in patterns that match the shell & stars?

I feel less and less like
a single self, more like
a weaver, myself, spelling out
formulae from what's given
and from words.

Early Snow

It was coming down hard so the teacher motioned the flute
then the piano quiet and the children sang

a cappella, teacher's voice was gone, they screaked and worked
their lungs & shoulders like gulls, they swooped and cranked

it up, it was wonderful being all alone,
they could hear pauses, one by two by one, then she

ran to the edge of the world, opened it and thrust the dark
sleeve of her dress out & down into the whirlpools

and when a flake landed crisp & complete on the black
wool she ran to every desk then back for more until

she showed every voice a new jewel, an alien, autotelic
shape. What would you like to be, or who, or would you

go with the wind sweeping the parking lot & small bank of trees.

Besie-Nyesuah Wesley

Patricia Jabbeh Wesley

Born August 7, 1955, in Liberia, West Africa. Patricia Jabbeh Wesley immigrated to the United States in the 1990s during the Liberian civil war. Her three books of poetry include *The River is Rising* (Autumn House Press, 2007), *Becoming Ebony* (Southern Illinois University Press, 2003), and *Before the Palm Could Bloom: Poems of Africa* (New Issues Press, 1998). Her awards include a 2002 Crab Orchard Award, the Irving S. Gilmore Emerging Artist Grant from the Kalamazoo Foundation, and a World Bank Fellowship. She teaches creative writing at Penn State Altoona. After three years, Patricia has finally learned how to drive through the winding, hilly roads of Pennsylvania without holding her breath.

Bringing Closure

Closure is such a final thing—the needle in the arm,
one last word or no last word at all, a death chamber

where the supposed convict lies waiting so the poison
will descend or ascend to the heart, a final beat,

and then sleep, that eternal thing none of us living
has ever seen. In California, today, a man is being

put to death, but outside, his supporters wait; candles,
flames, anger—the cold chill of death and life,

and a country that waits for all the arguments to die
or live on. The victim's mother will see closure today,

they say, and move on after the murderer or the supposed
murderer is laid to rest with her son, side by side.

Death is such an ironic thing to know. To know death
is to know rot, hush, the lack of pain. It is 3 a.m.

in Pennsylvania. Time, so deceptive, and arbitrary
and imperfect. Around the world, we all wait, for

the executioner's poke into vein, blood meeting poison.
We are such civilized people, I'd say, dishing out death

in small poking needles. The newsmen tell us they
cannot find his vein. The awkwardness of asking the one

awaiting death to find his own vein so they can murder
him too—the executioner's awkward fingers, the knowing

fingers—afraid of both the man and the art of killing the man.
I hate death. I hate the dying, the ugly process of dying,

the ritual of murder. So I too keep vigil on my carpet.
Tomorrow, I'll tell my eleven-year-old daughter how

we have all murdered another human being. An eye
for an eye, so far away from my bedroom of dim lights,

a comforter or two, the surrounding hills in close view.
There is always a mountain here in Pennsylvania,

always that looming presence of life and death and the
far away feeling of the valley below, of being so far away

from home. There is no closure, I see, after the poison
has reached the heart, and the accused, stretched out, finally.

The victim's mother begins to weep all over again—
as if this were just the beginning of the dying.

Lamentation After Fourteen Years

If you can sit beside the river long enough,
the tide will come in. You'll be there
for the river's rising—that urgent leaping
only a river can make.
You'll see how the coming tide departs,
leaving behind herring, catfish, *gbuga*,
snappers, where river meets swamp,
where swamp meets land, meeting you.

You'll see the crab or fish or lobsters or clams,
forgotten in the river's rush back to sea.
The poor used to wait on Monrovia's beaches
with bowls or baskets for the fishermen at sea.
Give-away catch can now feed a household.
Today we wait with straw baskets
and buckets, long lines,
we wait, all over the world, we wait;

not for *gbuga* fish or snails, not for the river's
refuse or the fisherman's *dash*—
Instead, we wait for peace, days of quiet,
ocean nights. They say, "if you set your eye

on the moon, you can see right through it."
So I clip away tree branches around my house,
from my front way, so when night finally
comes, I can sit under the sky
and watch the moon come home.

We do not long for yams or rice or oil. We do not
long for clothes or beds or babies; we sigh, not
for lack of tears or lack of laughter. We sit here,
my family and I, reliving the war—Charles Taylor's
cruel warfare haunts us like weeds left so long,
they eat up the yard. We sit here, God,
and we say, give us peace. We ask for

those quiet nights where only the Atlantic's
waves can roar. After so many years,
we long only for the end of war—
not for bread or beef; not for gin or rice,
not for roads or guns, not for street lights—
the sun comes out, and we say, God,
just give us the moon, the big blue moon.

Blessed Are the Sinful for They Shall See God

Blessed are the sinful, for they shall see God
in his plainness without makeup,
for he has no need to be God to them.
They are devils and villains, man-mongers and woman-mongers,
whores and prostitutes, vampires and robbers.
Baby killers and smokers of vampires,
who shall stand before the throne without flip-flops or sandals,
and he shall look at them without blinking or winking
or pretending that they are even righteous.
Blessed are sinners who come into a swinging door
singing Amazing Grace.
For what use is grace without anyone to grace
and what use is sin without a song?
I will be there, waiting to see what God has to say
to people like all of us, one bag
of iron rocks and sin—plain simple sin.
They shall be as blessed as the ocean waves
after twilight—as sinful as the righteous.

Something Death Cannot Know

My husband and I stole away from the camp one day
to see if it was now safe to come back home, from the war.

We pushed open double oak doors, and in our living
room, a few pots laid here and there; no water,
no lights, no clothing—everything gone.

Outside, you could count the deep rocket holes.
Splinters from fallen rockets could fill buckets
after months of bombing.

I stood in the middle of what used to be my hallway, my
house, my world, counting holes on the walls;
the house now leaked. Windows, partly blown out.

On the floor, my Sunday dresses laid trashed about, where
looters had dropped them in that sudden rush.
I watched the sun come in, through cracked glass

of windows, through the holes in the walls, where
only missile splinters could have passed—
But I was home again.

When I saw the birds, they chirped and began to fly
from overgrown brushes. Then the wind blew
in from the river, cold November winds from the river.

The Atlantic's moist winds from the other side over
the hills from the beach, where the ocean's restless waves
howl away days.

The scent of sweet blossoms, oregano mix,
and mint in the air. Flowers in what used to be my yard,
wild. I sat on the floor,

on the cold ceramic tiles of what used to be my living room
and laughed loud, hard, until my husband rushed inside
to see if I was still okay.

I laughed until I began to weep. Glad to be alive, to be here,
to know a town that had become ghost, to get acquainted
with the birds and the flowers and the river

and the winds for the first time. To know life
in its subtle creeping—when only crickets matter.

To know that after all this, my children were still alive,
that Mama was alive still, and life remembered
I used to live here.

The sun touching my now flabby arms told me I was here.
After all that bombing, here was I.
To know that there is something death cannot know—

Todd Budy

Cecilia Woloch

Born November 5, 1956, in Pittsburgh, Pennsylvania. Cecilia Woloch is the author of *Sacrifice*, a BookSense selection; *Tsigan: The Gypsy Poem*; *Late*, for which she was named Georgia Author of the Year in Poetry; and *Narcissus*, winner of the Tupelo Press Snowbound Prize. She serves on the faculty of the BA program in Creative Writing at the University of Southern California, as well as the MFA Program in Writing at Western Connecticut State University. An inveterate traveler, in recent years she has divided her time between Los Angeles and Idyllwild, California; Shepherdsville, Kentucky; Paris, France; and a small village in the Carpathian mountains of southeastern Poland.

Why I Believed, as a Child, That People Had Sex in Bathrooms

Because they loved one another, I guessed.
Because they had seven kids and there wasn't
a door in that house that was ever locked—
except for the bathroom door, that door
with the devil's face, two horns like flame
flaring up in the grain of the wood
(or did we only imagine that shape?)
which meant the devil could watch you pee,
the devil could see you naked.
Because that's where people took off their clothes
and you had to undress for sex, I'd heard,
whatever sex was—lots of kissing and other stuff
I wasn't sure I wanted to know.
Because at night, when I was scared, I just
climbed into my parents' bed. Sometimes
other kids were there, too, and we slept
in a tangle of sheets and bodies, breath;
a full ashtray on the nightstand; our father's
work clothes hung over a chair; our mother's
damp cotton nightgown twisted around her legs.
Because when I heard babies were made from sex
and sex was something that happened in bed,
I thought: *No, the babies are already there*
in the bed. And more babies came.

Because the only door that was ever locked
was the bathroom door—those two inside
in the steam of his bath, her hairspray's mist,
because sometimes I knocked and was let in.
And my father lay in the tub, his whole dark body

under water, like some beautiful statue I'd seen.
And my mother stood at the mirror, fixing her hair,
or she'd put down the lid of the toilet
and perched there, talking to him.
Because maybe this was their refuge from us—
though they never tried to keep us away.
Because my mother told me once
that every time they came home from the hospital
with a brand new baby, they laughed
and fell in love all over again
and couldn't wait to start making more.
Should this have confused me? It did not.
Because I saw how he kissed the back of her neck
and pulled her, giggling, into his lap;
how she tucked her chin and looked up at him
through her eyelashes, smiling, sly.
So I reasoned whatever sex they had, they had
in the bathroom—those steamy hours
when we heard them singing to one another
then whispering, and the door stayed locked.

Because I can still picture them, languid, there,
and beautiful and young—though I had no idea
how young they were—my mother
soaping my father's back; her dark hair
slipping out of its pins . . .
Because what was sex, after that? I didn't know
he would ever die, this god in a body, strong as god,
or that she would one day hang her head
over the bathroom sink to weep. I was a child,
only one of their children. Love was clean.
Babies came from singing. The devil was wood
and had no eyes.

43 rue de Saintonge

There was a book full of fallen leaves that had not been read
There was a chance
There was a chair near a window, a lamp
There was a sky of hammered tin with a few thin clouds in it, some birds

There was a chance
A noise in the courtyard like rain, and rain, and the clatter of keys
There was a sky of hammered tin with a few thin clouds in it, some birds
And several clocks at once and, everywhere, bridges, a river like smoke

A noise in the courtyard like rain, and rain, and the clatter of keys
A stairway being climbed in both directions, curved and steep
And several clocks at once and, everywhere, bridges, a river like smoke
There was a taxi moving slowly through the streets, the city blurred

A stairway being climbed in both directions, curved and steep
A door behind which jazz was playing softly, candles burned
There was a taxi moving slowly through the streets, the city blurred
A rosary of longing being fingered, bead by bead

A door behind which jazz was playing softly, candles burned
And little tongues of flame cast into mirrors and thrown back
A rosary of longing being fingered, bead by bead
Dusk: the curtains gathering their shadows, and a bed

And little tongues of flame cast into mirrors and thrown back
There was a chair near a window, a lamp
Dusk: the curtains gathering their shadows, and a bed
There was a book full of fallen leaves that had not (that still has not) been read

On Faith

How do people stay true to each other?
When I think of my parents all those years
in the unmade bed of their marriage, not ever
longing for anything else—or: no, they must
have longed; there must have been flickerings,
stray desires, nights she turned from him,
sleepless, and wept, nights he rose silently,
smoked in the dark, nights that nest of breath
and tangled limbs must have seemed
not enough. But it was. Or they just
held on. A gift, perhaps, I've tossed out,
having been always too willing to fly
to the next love, the next and the next, certain
nothing was really mine, certain nothing
would ever last. So faith hits me late, if at all;
faith that this latest love won't end, or ends
in the shapeless sleep of death. But faith is hard.
When he turns his back to me now, I think:
disappear. I think: *not what I want*. I think
of my mother lying awake in those arms
that could crush her. That could have. Did not.

Bareback Pantoum

One night, bareback and young, we rode through the woods
and the woods were on fire—
two borrowed horses, two local boys
whose waists we clung to, my sister and I

and the woods were on fire—
the pounding of hooves, the smell of smoke and the sharp sweat of boys
whose waists we clung to, my sister and I,
as we rode toward flame with the sky in our mouths—

the pounding of hooves, the smell of smoke and the sharp sweat of boys
and the heart saying: *mine*
as we rode toward flame with the sky in our mouths—
the trees turning gold, then crimson, white

and the heart saying: *mine*
of the wild, bright world;
the trees turning gold, then crimson, white
as they burned in the darkness, and we were girls

of the wild, bright world
of the woods near our house—we could turn, see the lights
as they burned in the darkness, and we were girls
so we rode just to ride

through the woods near our house—we could turn, see the lights—
and the horses would carry us, carry us home
so we rode just to ride,
my sister and I, just to be close to that danger, desire

and the horses would carry us, carry us home
—two borrowed horses, two local boys,
my sister and I—just to be close to that danger, desire—
one night, bareback and young, we rode through the woods.

East India Grill Villanelle

Across the table, Bridget sneaks a smile;
she's caught me staring past her at the man
who brings us curried dishes, hot and mild.

His eyes are blue, intensely blue, hot sky;
his hair, dark gold; his skin like cinnamon.
He speaks in quick-soft accents; Bridget smiles.

We've come here in our summer skirts, heels high,
to feast on fish and spices, garlic naan,
bare-legged in the night air, hot and mild.

And then to linger late by candlelight
in plain view of the waiter where he stands
and watches from the doorway, sneaks a smile.

I'd dress in cool silks if I were his wife.
We try to glimpse his hands—*no wedding band?*
The weather in his eyes is hot and mild.

He sends a dish of mango-flavored ice
with two spoons, which is sweet; I throw a glance
across the shady patio and smile.

But this can't go on forever, or all night
—or could it? Some eternal restaurant
of longing not quite sated, hot and mild.

And longing is delicious, Bridget sighs;
the waiter bows; I offer him my hand.
His eyes are Hindu blue and when he smiles
I taste the way he'd kiss me, hot and mild.

The Pick

I watched him swinging the pick in the sun,
breaking the concrete steps into chunks of rock,
and the rocks into dust,
and the dust into earth again.
I must have sat for a very long time on the split rail fence,
just watching him.
My father's body glistened with sweat,
his arms flew like dark wings over his head.
He was turning the backyard into terraces,
breaking the hill into two flat plains.
I took for granted the power of him,
though it frightened me, too.
I watched as he swung the pick into the air
and brought it down hard
and changed the shape of the world,
and changed the shape of the world again.

Cupid's Hunting Fields

Taste this, he said
and I thought I saw his dark eyes move
through the blindfold.
The field was impossibly gold;
I didn't know my face from the other faces,
my dress from the sky's great dress.

Taste it, he said
and it wasn't my voice that answered,
that said *yes* to him;
but my mouth came open, as if in prayer
and the liquid did not pour into me,
my body poured into the field.

Acknowledgments

KIM ADDONIZIO: "My Heart" was originally published in *New Letters 74:1* (2007). Copyright © 2007 by Kim Addonizio. Reprinted with the permission of the author. "The Moment," "Onset," and "Collapsing Poem" are reprinted from *Tell Me*, BOA Editions, Ltd., copyright © 2000 by Kim Addonizio, with the permission of BOA Editions, Ltd. and the author.

PAMELA ALEXANDER: "What We Need," "Look Here," and "Manners" are reprinted from *Inland*, University of Iowa Press, copyright © 1997 by Pamela Alexander, with the permission of the University of Iowa Press and the author. "Crossing" and "Letter Home" are reprinted from *Slow Fire*, Ausable Press. Copyright © 2007 by Pamela Alexander. Reprinted with the permission of Ausable Press, www.ausablepress.org, and the author.

GINGER ANDREWS: "How to Talk About Jesus" is reprinted from *Hurricane Sisters*, Story Line Press. Copyright © 2004 by Ginger Andrews, with permission of the author. "What the Cleaning Lady Knows," "The Housewife," "Home Alone,"and "O That Summer" are reprinted from *An Honest Answer*, Story Line Press. Copyright © 1999 by Ginger Andrews, with permission of the author.

JULIANNA BAGGOTT: "Blurbs" is from *This Country of Mothers*, Southern Illinois University Press. Copyright © 2001 by Julianna Baggott. "Helen Keller Dying in Her Sleep," "Marie Laurent Pasteur Addresses Louis in Her Mind While She Scalds the Sheets," and "For Sylvia: Come Winter. Come, Winter." are from *Lizzie Borden in Love*, Southern Illinois University Press. Copyright © 2006 by Julianna Baggott and reprinted with her permission.

JAN BEATTY: "Cruising with the Check-out Girls" is from *Boneshaker*, University of Pittsburgh Press. Copyright © 2002 by Jan Beatty. Reprinted with the permission of University of Pittsburgh Press and the author. "Procession," "The Long White," and "Dreaming Door" are from *Red Sugar*, University of Pittsburgh Press. Copyright © 2008 by Jan Beatty. Reprinted with the permission of University of Pittsburgh Press and the author.

JEANNE MARIE BEAUMONT: "Going by Taxi" is reprinted from *The Journal 28:1* (2004) and is reprinted with permission from Jeanne Marie Beaumont. "Chapter One," "Rock Said," and "Bonnard" are reprinted from *Curious Conduct*, BOA Editions, Ltd. Copyright © 2004 by Jeanne Marie Beaumont. Reprinted with the permission of BOA Editions, Ltd. and the author.

ROBIN BECKER: "The Lover of Fruit Trees" and "The Return" are from *Giacometti's Dog*. Copyright © 1990 by Robin Becker. Reprinted by permission of the University of Pittsburgh Press and the author. "Hold Back" is from *All-American Girl*. Copyright © 1996 by Robin Becker. Reprinted by permission of the University of Pittsburgh Press and the author. "Salon" and "The New Egypt" are from *Domain of Perfect Affection*. Copyright © 2006 by Robin Becker. Reprinted by permission of the University of Pittsburgh Press and the author.

ROBIN BEHN: "Hydrangea" first appeared in *Perihelion* on-line and is reprinted with permission of the author. "My Hair" was published in *Poetry* (2008) and is reprinted with permission of the author. "Unabashed," "Three Horses," and "Elegy: Cook County" are previously unpublished and appear here with the permission of Robin Behn.

TERRY BLACKHAWK: "The Dawn of the Navajo Woman," "Leda," "Little Red," and "At Silver Creek Presbyterian Church" are from *Body & Field*, Michigan State University Press. Copyright © 1999 by Terry Blackhawk. Reprinted with permission of Michigan State University Press and the author.

CHANA BLOCH: "Act One" and "Twenty-Fourth Anniversary" are from *Mrs. Dumpty*, University of Wisconsin Press. Copyright © 1998 by Chana Bloch. Reprinted with permission of University of Wisconsin Press and the author. "The Lesson" is from *The Past Keeps Changing*, Sheep Meadow Press. Copyright © 1992 by Chana Bloch. Reprinted with permission of the author. "'And the Darkness He Called Night'" and "The New World" were first published in *Michigan Quarterly Review*. Copyright © 2003 by Chana Bloch. Reprinted with permission of the author.

MICHELLE BOISSEAU: "Counting" and "Eavesdropping" are from *No Private Life*, Vanderbilt University Press. Copyright © 1990 by Michelle Boisseau and reprinted with her permission. "Tariff" and "Dog's Ars Poetica" are from *Trembling Air*, University of Arkansas Press. Copyright © 2003 by Michelle Boisseau. Reprinted with permission from University of Arkansas Press and the author.

MARIANNE BORUCH: "O Gods of Smallest Clarity" and "The Garden" are from *Grace, Fallen From*, Wesleyan University Press. Copyright © 2008 by Marianne Boruch. Reprinted with permission from Wesleyan University Press and the author. "The Driveway," "Elegy," and "Double Double" are from *Poems: New & Selected*, Oberlin College Press. Copyright © 2004 by Marianne Boruch. Reprinted with permission from Oberlin College Press and the author.

LAURE-ANNE BOSSELAAR: "English Flavors" is from *The Hour Between Dog and Wolf*, BOA Editions, Ltd. Copyright © 1997 by Laure-Anne Bosselaar. Reprinted with permission from BOA Editions, Ltd. and the author. "Belong," "Taller, Wider," and "The Pleasures of Hating" are from *Small Gods of Grief*, BOA Editions, Ltd. Copyright © 2001 by Laure-Anne Bosselaar. Reprinted with permission from BOA Editions, Ltd. and the author.

CATHY SMITH BOWERS: "Learning How to Pray" and "Easter" are from *Traveling in Time of Danger*, Iris Press. Copyright © 1999 by Cathy Smith Bowers. Reprinted with permission from Iris Press and the author. "The Napkin," "Last Day," and "The Notes" are from *The Candle I Hold Up to See You*, Iris Press. Copyright © 2008 by Cathy Smith Bowers. Reprinted with permission from Iris Press and the author.

FLEDA BROWN: "Language" is from *Breathing In, Breathing Out*, Anhinga Press. Copyright © 2002 by Fleda Brown. Reprinted with permission from Anhinga Press and the author. "Knot Tying Lessons: The Slip Knot," "Makeup Regimen," "No Heron," and "Red Paint" are from *Reunion*, University of Wisconsin Press. Copyright © 2007 by Fleda Brown. Reprinted with permission of University of Wisconsin Press and the author.

DEBRA BRUCE: "Divorced Women," "Divorced Men," and "Fasting" are from *Pure Daughter*, University of Arkansas Press. Copyright © 1983 by Debra Bruce. Reprinted with permission from University of Arkansas Press and the author. "Prognosis" and "Infertility" are from *What Wind Will Do*, Miami University Press. Copyright © 1997 by Debra Bruce. Reprinted with permission from Miami University Press and the author.

SHARON BRYAN: "Esque," "Weird Niece," and "Be-" from *Flying Blind*. Copyright © 1996 by Sharon Bryan. Reprinted with the permission of the author and Sarabande Books, www.sarabandebooks.org.

ANDREA HOLLANDER BUDY: "Firmly Married" and "When She Named Fire" are from *House Without a Dreamer*, Story Line Press. Copyright © 1993, 1995 by Andrea Hollander Budy and reprinted with her permission. "Nineteen-Thirty-Eight," "My Grandmother Taking Off My Grandfather's Shoes," and "Living Room" are from *Woman in the Painting*, Autumn House Press. Copyright © 2006 by Andrea Hollander Budy. Reprinted with permission from Autumn House Press and the author.

KELLY CHERRY: "First Marriage" is from *Death and Transfiguration*, Louisiana State University Press. Copyright © 1997 by Kelly Cherry. Reprinted with permission from Louisiana State University Press and the author. "Welsh Song" first appeared in *Welsh Table Talk*, Book Arts Conservancy. Copyright © 2008 by Kelly Cherry and reprinted with her permission. "Truth and Tolerance," "On the Soul," and "Fair Is Fair: A Dialogue Between Husband and Wife," copyright © 2008 by Kelly Cherry, are previously unpublished and appear with the permission of the author.

MARILYN CHIN: "Moon and Oatgrass" is from *The Phoenix Gone, The Terrace Empty*, Minneapolis: Milkweed Editions, 1994. Copyright © 1994 by Marilyn Chin. Reprinted with permission from the author and from Milkweed Editions. www.milkweed.org. "The Half Is Almost Gone," "Blues on Yellow (#2)," "Family Restaurant (#1)" and "Family Restaurant (#2)" are from *Rhapsody in Plain Yellow*, W. W. Norton. Copyright © 2002 by Marilyn Chin. Used by permission of W. W. Norton and the author.

MARTHA COLLINS: "After" is from *A History of Small Life on a Windy Planet*, Sheep Meadow Press. Copyright © 1998 by Martha Collins. Reprinted with permission from the author. "Likes" is from *Some Things Words Can Do*, Sheep Meadow Press. Copyright © 1998 by Martha Collins. Reprinted with permission from the author. "Alone, One Must Be Careful" is from *The Catastrophe of Rainbows*, Cleveland State University Press. Copyright © 1985 by Martha Collins. Reprinted with permission from the author. "There were trees," "Birmingham" and "drag" are from *The Blue Front*, Graywolf Press, Saint Paul, Minnesota. Copyright © 2007 by Martha Collins. Reprinted with permission of Graywolf Press and the author.

DEBORAH CUMMINS: "The Bisbee Donkeys" and "Passage" are from *Beyond the Reach*, BkMk Press. Copyright © 2002 by Deborah Cummins. Reprinted with permission of BkMk Press and the author. "Before It's Too Late" and "'Tidy'" are from *Counting the Waves*, Word Press. Copyright © 2006 by Deborah Cummins. Reprinted with permission of Word Press and the author.

TOI DERRICOTTE: "Black Boys Play the Classics," "Shoe Repair Business," "After Reading at a Black College," "For Black Women Who Are Afraid," "Bird," and "Not Forgotten" are from *Tender*, University of Pittsburgh Press. Copyright © 1997 by Toi Derricotte. Reprinted with permission of University of Pittsburgh Press and the author.

RITA DOVE: "Ö" and "Geometry" from *The Yellow House on the Corner*, Carnegie Mellon University Press. Copyright © 1980 by Rita Dove. Reprinted by permission of the author. "Daystar" is from *Thomas and Beulah*, Carnegie Mellon University Press. Copyright © 1986 by Rita Dove. Reprinted by permission of the author. "Testimonial" is from *On the Bus with Rosa Parks*, W. W. Norton & Co., Inc. Copyright © 1999 by Rita Dove. Reprinted by permission of the author. "Soprano" is from *American Smooth*, W. W. Norton & Co., Inc. Copyright © 2004 by Rita Dove. Reprinted by permission of the author.

DENISE DUHAMEL: "Feminism," "Ego," and "From the Shore" are from *Queen for a Day: Selected and New Poems*, University of Pittsburgh Press. Copyright © 2001 by Denise Duhamel. Reprinted with permission of the University of Pittsburgh Press and the author. "Noah and Joan" is from *Two and Two*, University of Pittsburgh Press. Copyright © 2005 by Denise Duhamel. Reprinted with permission of the University of Pittsburgh Press and the author.

CAMILLE T. DUNGY: "Language," "Before My History Class," "Vo-Tech," "In His Library," "Depression," and "From Someplace" are from *What to Eat, What to Drink, What to Leave for Poison*, Red Hen Press. Copyright © 2006 by Camille T. Dungy. Reprinted with permission of the Red Hen Press and the author.

LYNN EMANUEL: "Frying Trout While Drunk," "Ordinary Objects," "The Sleeping," and "After Your Letter of Elegant Goodbye" are from *Dig* and *Hotel Fiesta*, University of Illinois Press. Copyright © 1984, 1992, 1995 by Lynn Emanuel. Used with permission of the University of Illinois Press and the author. "Soliloquy of the Depressed Book" is from *Then, Suddenly*, University of Pittsburgh Press. Copyright © 2007 by Lynn Emanuel. Reprinted with permission of the University of Pittsburgh Press and the author.

CLAUDIA EMERSON: "Zenith" was published in *Poetry East* (2008). Copyright © 2008 by Claudia Emerson and reprinted with her permission. "Animal Funerals, 1964" was published in *Tar River Poetry* (2008). Copyright © 2008 by Claudia Emerson and reprinted with her permission. "After Hours: A Glimpse of My Radiologist" was published in *Hopkins Review* (2008). Copyright © 2008 by Claudia Emerson and reprinted with her permission. "The Spanish Lover" and "Aftermath" are from *Late Wife*, Louisiana State University Press. Copyright © 2005 by Claudia Emerson. Reprinted with permission from Louisiana State University Press and the author.

BETH ANN FENNELLY: "Mother Sends My Poem to Her Sister with Post-its" is from *Open House*, Zoo Press. Copyright © 2001 by Beth Ann Fennelly. Reprinted with permission of the author. "Interpreting the Foreign Queen" is from *Tender Hooks*, W. W. Norton. Copyright © 2004 by Beth Ann Fennelly. Reprinted with permission from W. W. Norton and the author. "First Warm Day in a College Town," "Cow Tipping," and "People Ask What My Daughter Will Think of My Poems When She's 16" are in *Unmentionables*, W. W. Norton. Copyright © 2008 by Beth Ann Fennelly. Reprinted with permission from W. W. Norton and the author.

ANN FISHER-WIRTH: "Rain Stick" appears for the first time here with permission from the author. Copyright © 2008 by Ann Fisher-Wirth. "Blue Window" and "Ice Storm" are from *Blue Window*, Archer Books. Copyright © 2003 by Ann Fisher-Wirth. Reprinted with permission from Archer Books and the author.

ALICE FRIMAN: "Silent Movie" first appeared in *The Georgia Review 59:1* (2005). Copyright © by Alice Friman and reprinted with her permission. "Autobiography: The Short Version" first appeared in *The Georgia Review 61:1* (2007). Copyright © 2007 by Alice Friman and reprinted with her permission. "Vinculum" first appeared in *The Georgia Review 61:3* (2007). Copyright © 2007 by Alice Friman and reprinted with her permission. "Snow" first appeared in *The Georgia Review 54: 4* (2000). Copyright © 2000 by Alice Friman and reprinted with her permission. "Diapers for My Father" first appeared in *The Ohio Review 57* (1998). Copyright © 1998 by Alice Friman and reprinted with her permission.

CAROL FROST: "Sin" is from *Love & Scorn: New and Selected Poems*, Northwestern University Press. Copyright © 2000 by Carol Frost. Reprinted with permission from Northwestern University Press and the author. "Wild Rose" is from *I Will Say Beauty*, Northwestern University Press. Copyright © 2003 by Carol Frost. Reprinted with permission from Northwestern University Press and the author. "Egret" and "Apiary II" are from *The Queen's Desertion*, Northwestern University Press. Copyright © 2006 by Carol Frost. Reprinted with permission from Northwestern University Press and the author. "Apiary VIII" is from *Poetry 191:1* (2007). Copyright © 2007 by Carol Frost and reprinted with her permission. "Man of War" is from *Poetry 191:4* (2008). Copyright © 2008 by Carol Frost and reprinted with her permission.

ALLISON FUNK: "The Lake" and "Forms of Conversion" are from *Forms of Conversion*, Alice James Books. Copyright © 1986 by Allison Funk. Reprinted with permission from Alice James Books and the author. "Women" is from *Living at the Epicenter*. Copyright © 1995 by Allison Funk. Reprinted with permission by University Press of New England, Hanover, New Hampshire. "After Ovid" is from *The Knot Garden*, The Sheep Meadow Press. Copyright © 2002 by Allison Funk. Reprinted with permission from the author. "The Escape Artist in the Prairie" first appeared in *Natural Bridge 16* (2006). Copyright © 2006 by Allison Funk and reprinted with her permission.

BECKIAN FRITZ GOLDBERG: "Prologue as Part of the Body," "Open," "List," "Wren," and "Mimesis as Part of the Body" are from *Lie Awake Lake*, Oberlin College Press. Copyright © 2005 by Beckian Fritz Goldberg. Reprinted with permission from Oberlin College Press and the author.

LINDA GREGG: "I Wage My Life Against This Your Body" is from *The Sacraments of Desire*, Graywolf Press, Saint Paul, Minnesota. Copyright © 1991 by Linda Gregg. Reprinted with permission from Graywolf Press. "Asking for Directions" is from *Chosen by the Lion*, Graywolf Press, Saint Paul, Minnesota. Copyright © 1994 by Linda Gregg. Reprinted with permission from Graywolf Press. "The Precision," "Like Lot's Wife," and "She Writes to the Man Who Writes of Her in His Poems" are from *Things and Flesh*, Graywolf Press, Saint Paul, Minnesota. Copyright © 1999 by Linda Gregg. Reprinted with permission from Graywolf Press. "Elegance" is from *In the Middle Distance*, Graywolf Press, Saint Paul, Minnesota. Copyright © 2006 by Linda Gregg. Reprinted with permission from Graywolf Press.

MARILYN HACKER: "Glose [Staying put provides the solidest]" first appeared in *Water~Stone Review, Volume 9* (2006). Copyright © 2006 by Marilyn Hacker and with her permission to reprint. "1953: The Bus to Menton" first appeared in *Prairie Schooner 81:1* (2007). Copyright © 2007 by Marilyn Hacker and with her permission to reprint. "Glose [Once out of the grip of desire]" first appeared in *Bloom* (2005) and in *Pushcart XXXI: Best of the Small Presses* (2006). Copyright © 2005, 2006 by Marilyn Hacker and with her permission to reprint. "Ghazal: min al-hobbi ma khatal" first appeared in *Modern Poetry in Translation UK* (2007). Copyright © 2007 by Marilyn Hacker and with her permission to reprint. "Ghazal: Myself" first appeared in *PN Review: UK* (2007). Copyright © 2007 by Marilyn Hacker and with her permission to reprint.

RACHEL HADAS: "The Red Hat" and "Riverside Park" are from *Halfway Down the Hall*, Wesleyan University Press. Copyright © 1998 by Rachel Hadas. Reprinted with permission from Wesleyan University Press and the author. "Skirts" is from *Indelible*, Wesleyan University Press. Copyright © 2001 by Rachel Hadas. Reprinted with permission from Wesleyan University Press and the author. "Conklin 455, 3:55 PM, Wednesday, March 3, 2004," "Crystal Lake," and "The Bond" are from *The River of Forgetfulness*, David Roberts Books. Copyright © 2006 by Rachel Hadas. Reprinted with permission from David Roberts Books and the author.

BARBARA HAMBY: "Betrothal in B Minor" and "The Language of Bees" are from *Delirium*, University of North Texas Press. Copyright © 1995 by Barbara Hamby. Reprinted with permission from the author. "Ode to My 1977 Toyota" is from *Babel*, University of Pittsburgh Press. Copyright © 2004 by Barbara Hamby. Reprinted with permission from University of Pittsburgh Press and the author. "I Beseech Thee, O Yellow Pages" first appeared in *Nightsun 23* (2004). Copyright © 2004 by Barbara Hamby. Reprinted with permission from the author.

LOLA HASKINS: "To Play Pianissimo" and "Fortissimo" are from *Forty-four Ambitions for the Piano*, University of Central Florida Press. Copyright © 1990 by Lola Haskins. Reprinted with permission from the author. "For Someone Considering Death" is from *Hunger*, University of Iowa Press. Copyright © 1993 by Lola Haskins. Reprinted with permission from the author. "Dogwood, December," "For Mother, After the Vision Fire," and "Words" are from *Desire Lines: New and Selected Poems*, BOA Editions, Ltd. Copyright © 2004 by Lola Haskins. Reprinted with permission from BOA Editions, Ltd. and the author.

JANE HIRSHFIELD: "The Lost Love Poems of Sappho" first appeared in *Water~Stone Review 9* (2006). Copyright © 2006 by Jane Hirshfield and reprinted with her permission. "The Heat of Autumn" and "The Woodpecker Keeps Returning" are from *After*, HarperCollins. Copyright © 2006 by Jane Hirshfield and reprinted with her permission. "Critique of Pure Reason" previously appeared in *Ploughshares* (2006) and in *Best American Poetry 2007*. Copyright © 2006, 2007 by Jane Hirshfield and reprinted with her permission. "Shadow: An Assay" first appeared in *Nightsun* (2006). Copyright © 2006 by Jane Hirshfield and reprinted with her permission. "Rainstorm Visibly Shining in the Left-out Spoon of a Leaf" and "All Day the Difficult Waiting" first appeared in *Five Points 10:3* (2006). Copyright © 2006 by Jane Hirshfield and reprinted with her permission. "A Hand Is Shaped for What It Holds or Makes" first appeared in *The Georgia Review 61:4* (2007). Copyright © 2007 by Jane Hirshfield and reprinted with her permission.

MARIE HOWE: "What the Living Do" is from *What the Living Do*, W. W. Norton. Copyright © 1997 by Marie Howe. Used by permission of W. W. Norton. "What the Woman Said," "Hurry," and "Non-violence 2" are from *The Kingdom of the Ordinary*, W. W. Norton. Copyright © 2008 by Marie Howe. Used by permission of W. W. Norton.

LINDA HULL: "Adagio," "The Charmed Hour," "Midnight Reports," and "At Thirty" are from *Collected Poems*, Graywolf Press. Copyright © 2008 by the estate of Linda Hull. Used by permission of Graywolf Press, St. Paul, Minnesota.

ALLISON JOSEPH: "Falling Out of History" and "The Valley of the Shadow" are from *What Keeps Us Here*, Ampersand Press. Copyright © 1992 by Allison Joseph and reprinted with her permission. "The Inner Life" is from *Soul Train*, Carnegie-Mellon University Press. Copyright © 1997 by Allison Joseph and reprinted with her permission.

JULIA SPICHER KASDORF: "Eve's Striptease," "Sinning," "A Pass," and "The Knowledge of Good and Evil" are from *Eve's Striptease*, University of Pittsburgh Press. Copyright © 1998 by Julia Kasdorf. Reprinted with permission from University of Pittsburgh Press and the author.

BRIGIT PEGEEN KELLY: "Harmony Stoneworks, Late Winter," "After Your Nap," and "The Thief's Wife" are from *To the Place of Trumpets*, Yale University Press. Copyright © 1988 by Brigit Pegeen Kelly. Reprinted with permission from Yale University Press and the author. "Song" is from *Song*, BOA Editions, Ltd. Copyright © 1995 by Brigit Pegeen Kelly. Reprinted with permission from BOA Editions, Ltd. and the author.

SUSAN KELLY-DEWITT: "Roller Derby, 1958," "Pomegranates," "Why I Don't Like to Travel," "Crossing the Mojave at Night," and "Egrets at Bolinas Lagoon" are from *The Fortunate Islands*, Marick Press. Copyright © 2007 by Susan Kelly-DeWitt and reprinted with permission from Marick Press and the author.

JANE KENYON: "Prognosis," "Happiness," "Coats," "After an Illness, Walking the Dog," and "Otherwise" are from *Otherwise: New & Selected Poems*, Graywolf Press, Saint Paul, Minnesota. Copyright © 1997 by the estate of Jane Kenyon. Reprinted with the permission of Graywolf Press, Saint Paul, Minnesota.

LYNNE KNIGHT: "Eighteen" and "Her Story" are from *Dissolving Borders*, Quarterly Review Press. Copyright © 1996 by Lynne Knight and reprinted with her permission. "Now There Were More of Them" is from *The Book of Common Betrayals*, Bear Star Press. Copyright © 2002 by Lynne Knight and reprinted with her permission. "Living Apart" is from *Night in the Shape of a Mirror*, David Roberts Books. Copyright © 2006 by Lynne Knight and reprinted with her permission.

MAXINE KUMIN: "Nurture" is from *Selected Poems 1960–1990*. Copyright © 1989,1997 by Maxine Kumin. "Watering Trough" is from *Selected Poems 1960–1990*. Copyright © 1970, 1997 by Maxine Kumin. Used by permission of W. W. Norton and the author. "Death, Etc." and "Waiting to be Rescued" are from *Still to Mow*, W. W. Norton. Copyright © 2007 by Maxine Kumin. Used by permission of W. W. Norton and the author. "A Brief History of English Romanticism" and "Coleridge's Laundry," copyright © 2008 by Maxine Kumin, appear with permission from the author.

LAURIE KUTCHINS: "Daughter" is from *Between Towns*, Texas Tech University Press. Copyright © 1993 by Laurie Kutchins. Reprinted with permission from Texas Tech University Press [1-800-832-4042] and the author. "Heartbeat" and "The Placenta" are from *The Night Path*, BOA Editions, Ltd. Copyright © 1997 by Laurie Kutchins. Reprinted with permission from BOA Editions, Ltd. and the author. "Skin," "River Keeper," and "Joy" are from *Slope of the Child Everlasting*, BOA Editions, Ltd. Copyright © 2007 by Laurie Kutchins. Reprinted with permission from BOA Editions, Ltd. and the author.

DORIANNE LAUX: "Return," "What My Father Told Me," and "Bird" are from *Awake*, BOA Editions, Ltd., (later reissued by Eastern Washington University Press). Copyright © 1990 by Dorianne Laux. Reprinted with permission of the author and BOA Editions, Ltd. "Dust" and "Fast Gas" are from *What We Carry*, BOA Editions, Ltd. Copyright © 1994 by Dorianne Laux. Reprinted with permission of the author and BOA Editions, Ltd. "Family Stories" is from *Smoke*, BOA Editions, Ltd. Copyright © 2000 by Dorianne Laux. Reprinted with permission of the author and BOA Editions, Ltd.

ADA LIMÓN: "Selecting Things for Vagueness," "Miles Per Hour," "The Different Ways of Going ," "Centerfold," and "The Firemen Are Dancing" are from *lucky wreck*, Autumn House Press. Copyright © 2006 by Ada Limón. Reprinted with permission of the author and Autumn House Press.

SUSAN LUDVIGSON: "Hush, for the Night Is Stealthy," "Dear Sharon," "Always Paris," "What I Think It Is," and "The House," copyright ©2008 by Susan Ludvigson, appear with permission from the author.

KATHLEEN LYNCH: "Soaps Fan," "Observation," "Yard Work," and "How to Build an Owl" are from *Hinge*, Black Zinnias Press. Copyright © 2006 by Kathleen Lynch. Reprinted with permission of the author.

ANNE MARIE MACARI: "Sunbathing" and "Palace of Longing" are from *Gloryland*, Alice James Books. Copyright © 2005 by Anne Marie Macari. Reprinted with the permission of Alice James Books and the author. "Their Eyes Were Opened: I (We Always Ate from that Tree)," "Their Eyes Were Opened: XII (Paradise Came Over Me Once)," "Their Eyes Were Opened: XXVIII (What I Wake To)," and "Their Eyes Were Opened: XXXVI (She Heads into the Wilderness)" are from *She Heads into the Wilderness*, Autumn House Press. Copyright © 2008 by Anne Marie Macari. Reprinted with the permission of Autumn House Press and the author.

GAIL MAZUR: "Desire" and "Bluebonnets" are from *The Common*, University of Chicago Press. Copyright © 1995 by Gail Mazur. Reprinted with the permission of the author. "Young Apple Tree,

December" and "They Can't Take That Away from Me" are from *They Can't Take That Away from Me*, University of Chicago Press. Copyright © 2001 by Gail Mazur. Reprinted with the permission of the author.

REBECCA McCLANAHAN: "Visit with the Newlyweds," "Autobiography of the Cab Driver who Picked Me up at a Phoenix Hotel to Catch a Four A.M. Flight and Began to Speak in (Almost) Rhyming Couplets," "Good Fences," and "To the Absent Wife of the Beautiful Poet at the Writers' Conference" are from *Deep Light: New &Selected Poems 1987-2007*, Iris Press. Copyright © 2007 by Rebecca McClanahan. Reprinted with the permission of Iris Press and the author.

JO McDOUGALL: "Labor Day" is from *The Woman in the Next Booth*, BkMk Press, Copyright © 1987 by Jo McDougall. Reprinted with the permission of BkMk Press and the author. "Dirt," "Parlors," and "Boyfriend" are from *Dirt*, Autumn House Press. Copyright © 2001 by Jo McDougall. Reprinted with the permission of Autumn House Press and the author. "Mammogram" and "Dumb" are from *Satisfied With Havoc*, Autumn House Press. Copyright © 2004 by Jo McDougall. Reprinted with the permission of Autumn House Press and the author.

JANE MEAD: "Concerning That Prayer I Cannot Make" and "Passing a Truck Full of Chickens at Night on Highway Eighty" from *The Lord and the General Din of the World*. Copyright © 1996 by Jane Mead. Reprinted with the permission of Sarabande Books, www.sarabandebooks.org. "The Laden Henceforth Pending" first appeared in *Poetry 191:1* (2007). Copyright © 2007 by Jane Mead and reprinted with her permission.

MARILYN NELSON: "Drifter" and "The Perceiving Self" are from *Carver, A Life in Poems*, Front Street, Boyds Mills Press. Copyright © 2001 by Marilyn Nelson and reprinted with her permission and that of the publisher. "Fire from the Gods," "All Night Melodies," and "Unmentionables" are from *Miss Crandall's School for Young Ladies & Little Misses of Color*, Wordsong, Boyds Mills Press. Copyright © 2007 by Marilyn Nelson and reprinted with her permission and that of Boyds Mills Press.

AIMEE NEZHUKUMATATHIL: "My Name," "Fishbone," "Wrap," "Falling Thirds," and "Speak" are from *Miracle Fruit*, Copyright © 2003 by Aimee Nezhukumatathil. Reprinted with permission from the author and Tupelo Press. "Hippopotomonstrosesquipedaliophobia" is from *At the Drive-In Volcano*, Tupelo Press. Copyright © 2007 by Aimee Nezhukumatathil. Reprinted with permission from the author and Tupelo Press.

NAOMI SHIHAB NYE: "Hidden," "Half-and-Half," and "My Friend's Divorce" are from her collection *Fuel*, BOA Editions, Ltd., Copyright © 1998 by Naomi Shihab Nye; used with permission of both author and publisher. "Guide" and "Music" are from *You & Yours*, BOA Editions, Ltd., Copyright © 2005 by Naomi Shihab Nye; used with permission of both author and publisher. "Read Me" first appeared in *Water~Stone Review* and is reprinted with permission of the author. Copyright © 2007 by Naomi Shihab Nye.

DEBRA NYSTROM: "Twisting Vines" and "Waitress at a Window" are from *Torn Sky*. Copyright © 2003 by Debra Nystrom. Reprinted with the permission of Sarabande Books, www.sarabandebooks.org and the author. "Picture Window: Blizzard," "Smoke-break Behind the Treatment Center" and "My Mother Never Told Me" are from *Bad River Road*. Copyright © 2008, 2009 by Debra Nystrom. Reprinted with the permission of the author and Sarabande Books, www.sarabandebooks.org.

SHARON OLDS: "The Talk," "Late," "The Mother," and "The Rising Daughter" are from *Satan Says*, University of Pittsburgh Press. Copyright © 1980 by Sharon Olds. Reprinted with permission from University of Pittsburgh Press and the author. "Toth Farry" appeared in *Poetry* (February 2005) and is reprinted with permission of the author. "Self-exam" appeared in *The New Yorker* (January 7, 2008) and is reprinted with permission of the author.

MARY OLIVER: "Crows" is from *House of Light*, Beacon Press. Copyright © 1990 by Mary Oliver. Reprinted with permission from Beacon Press. "Everything" is from *New and Selected Poems Volume Two*, Beacon Press. Copyright © 2005 by Mary Oliver. Reprinted with permission from Beacon Press. "In the Evening, in the Pinewoods" is from *Red Bird*, Beacon Press. Copyright © 2008 by Mary Oliver. Reprinted with permission from Beacon Press.

JACQUELINE OSHEROW: "My Version: Medieval Acrostic," "At the Wailing Wall," "Villanelle," "Egrets in Be'er Sheva," and "God's Acrostic" are from *The Hoopoe's Crown*, BOA Editions, Ltd., Copyright © 2005 by Jacqueline Osherow; used with permission of BOA Editions, Ltd. and the author.

ALICIA OSTRIKER: "A Question of Time" and "The Marriage Nocturne" are from *The Imaginary Lover*, University of Pittsburgh Press. Copyright © 1986 by Alicia Suskin Ostriker. Reprinted with permission from University of Pittsburgh Press and the author. "May Rain, Princeton" and "Bus Station" are from *No Heaven*, University of Pittsburgh Press. Copyright © 2005 by Alicia Suskin Ostriker. Reprinted with permission from University of Pittsburgh Press and the author.

NANCY PAGH: "I Believe I Could Kneel," "Fat Lady Reads," "Rounding the Point," and "Ten Reasons Your Prayer Diet Won't Work" are from *No Sweeter Fat*, Autumn House Press. Copyright © 2007 by Nancy Pagh. Reprinted with permission from Autumn House Press and the author.

LINDA PASTAN: "The Obligation to Be Happy," Copyright © 1998 by Linda Pastan, "The Almanac of Last Things," Copyright © 1998 by Linda Pastan, and "Suffocation" Copyright © 1985 by Linda Pastan, are from *Carnival Evening: New & Selected Poems 1968–1998*, W. W. Norton. Used by permission of W. W. Norton and the author. "After a Month of Rain" appeared in *Five Points 8:3* (2006). Copyright © 2006 by Linda Pastan and reprinted with her permission. "In an Unaddressed Envelope" appeared in *The Georgia Review 61:3* (2007). Copyright © 2007 by Linda Pastan and reprinted with her permission. "Return to Maple 9" appeared in *The Gettysburg Review 20:3* (2007). Copyright © 2007 by Linda Pastan and reprinted with her permission.

KATHLEEN PEIRCE: "Buy Something Pretty and Remember Me" is from *Mercy*, University of Pittsburgh Press. Copyright © 1991 by Kathleen Peirce and reprinted with permission from University of Pittsburgh Press and the author. "Confession 3.10.18" is from *The Oval Hour*, University of Iowa Press. Copyright © 1999 by Kathleen Peirce and reprinted with permission from University of Iowa Press and the author. "Quiet Lines," "Linen Napkin," and "Theology of Water" are from *The Ardors*, Ausable Press. Copyright © 2004 by Kathleen Peirce and reprinted with permission from Ausable Press and the author.

LUCIA PERILLO: "Cesium" is from *Dangerous Life*, Northeastern University Press. Copyright © 1989 by Lucia Perillo and reprinted with her permission. "Beige Trash" is from *The Oldest Map with the Name America: New & Selected Poems*, Random House. Copyright © 1999 by Lucia Perillo and reprinted with her permission. "Shrike Tree" is from *Luck Is Luck*, Random House. Copyright © 2006 by Lucia Perillo and reprinted with her permission. "The Van with the Plane" appeared in *The American Poetry* (2004) and will be collected in *Inseminating the Elephant*, Copper Canyon Press (2009). Copyright © 2004 by Lucia Perillo and reprinted with her permission.

LIA PURPURA: "Bee," "On Waiting," "At Six Months," and "Standing Figure with Knife Edge" are from *Stone Sky Lifting*, Ohio State University Press. Copyright © 2000 by Lia Purpura and reprinted with permission from Ohio State University Press and the author. "Red Cluster, Mid-Summer" appeared in *Prairie Schooner 79:4* (2005). Copyright © 2005 by Lia Purpura and reprinted with her permission. "Fall" appeared in *FIELD 77* (2007). Copyright © 2007 by Lia Purpura and reprinted with her permission.

HILDA RAZ: "Widow" is from *What Is Good*, Thorntree Press. Copyright © 1988 by Hilda Raz and reprinted with her permission. "Diction" is from *The Bone Dish*, State Street Press. Copyright © 1989 by Hilda Raz and reprinted with her permission. "Letter of Transmittal" and "Repair" are from *Divine Honors*, University Press of New England. Copyright © 1997 by Hilda Raz. Reprinted with permission from University Press of New England and the author. "Not Now" is from *Trans*, Wesleyan University Press. Copyright © 2001 by Hilda Raz. Reprinted with permission from Wesleyan University Press and the author. "September 11" is from *All Odd and Splendid*, Wesleyan University Press. Copyright © 2008 by Hilda Raz. Reprinted with permission from Wesleyan University Press.

PAISLEY REKDAL: "What Was There to Bring Me to Delight But to Love and Be Loved?" and "25% Pressure" are from *Six Girls Without Pants*, Eastern Washington University Press. Copyright © 2002 by Paisley Rekdal. Reprinted with permission from Eastern Washington University Press and the author. "Post-Romantic" is from *The Invention of the Kaleidoscope*, University of Pittsburgh Press. Copyright © 2007 by Paisley Rekdal. Reprinted with permission, University of Pittsburgh Press and the author.

PATTIANN ROGERS: "Seeing the Three Magi" first appeared in *Gettysburg Review* and "Creative Alive" in *FIELD*, copyright © 2007 by Pattiann Rogers; both will be included in *Wayfare*, Penguin, 2008, reprinted with the permission of the author. "Without Violence" and "Capturing the Scene" are from *Song of the World Becoming: New and Collected Poems*, Milkweed Editions, copyright © 2001 by Pattiann Rogers. Reprinted with the permission of the author.

MARY RUEFLE: "Examination," "Instrument of the Highest," "Funny Story," and "Dove" are from *Apparition Hill*, CavanKerry Press, Ltd. Copyright © 2002 by Mary Ruefle. Reprinted with permission from CavanKerry Press, Ltd. and the author.

KAY RYAN: "Blandeur," "Grazing Horses," "Forgetting," "The Fabric of Life," "Why We Must Struggle" and "Attention" are from *Say Uncle*, Grove Press. Copyright © 2000 by Kay Ryan. Reprinted with permission from Grove Press and the author. "The Best of It" is from *The Niagara River*, Grove Press. Copyright © 2005 by Kay Ryan. Reprinted with permission from Grove Press and the author. "Cut Out for It" appeared in *Poetry 191:4* (2008). Copyright © 2008 by Kay Ryan and reprinted with her permission.

NATASHA SAJÉ: "I am peeling four pink grapefruit" is from *Bend*, Tupelo Press. Copyright © 2004 by Natasha Sajé. Reprinted with permission of Tupelo Press and the author. "E" and "V" first appeared in

Prairie Schooner (2006). Copyright © 2008 by Natasha Sajé are reprinted with permission of the author. "Alibi," copyright © 2008 by Natasha Sajé, is reprinted by permission of the author.

RUTH L. SCHWARTZ: "When They Know" is from *Accordion Breathing and Dancing*, University of Pittsburgh Press. Copyright © 1996 by Ruth L. Schwartz. Reprinted with permission of University of Pittsburgh Press and the author. "Tangerine," "Perseid," and "Sex" are from *Dear Good Naked Morning*, Autumn House Press. Copyright © 2005 by Ruth L. Schwartz. Reprinted with permission of Autumn House Press and the author.

REBECCA SEIFERLE: "The Shearing" is from *Wild Tongue*, Copper Canyon Press. Copyright © 2007 by Rebecca Seiferle. Reprinted with permission of Copper Canyon Press and the author. "Bitter Herb," "Homophobia," and "Muse" are from *Bitters*, Copper Canyon Press. Copyright © 2001 by Rebecca Seiferle. Reprinted with permission of Copper Canyon Press and the author.

HEATHER SELLERS: "SAT Words with David Jr. in His Father's Bed," "Dating Men with Children," "I Know What I Saw Last Summer," and "Palm Sunday in Pew with Ex" are from *The Boys I Borrow*, New Issues Press. Copyright © 2007 by Heather Sellers. Reprinted with permission of New Issues Press and the author.

ENID SHOMER: "Black Drum," "For the Women of the All-Female Bookkeeping Department at H. G. Smithy's" and "King David Memorial Gardens" are from *Black Drum*, University of Arkansas Press. Copyright © 1997 by Enid Shomer. Reprinted with permission of University of Arkansas Press and the author. "Gowned Waiting" appeared in *Southern Poetry Review 44:2* (2006). Copyright © 2006 by Enid Shomer and reprinted with her permission.

DEBORAH SLICER: "Sunflowers, Wyoming," "Shiners," "Pastoral," and "I Loved the Black Cat" are from *The White Calf Kicks*, Autumn House Press. Copyright © 2003 by Deborah Slicer. Reprinted with permission of Autumn House Press and the author.

TRACY K. SMITH: "Fire Escape Fantasy," "A Hunger So Honed," and "Credulity" are from *The Body's Question*, Graywolf Press. Copyright © 2003 by Tracy K. Smith. Reprinted with permission of Graywolf Press, Saint Paul, Minnesota, and the author. "I Don't Miss It" and "After Persephone" are from *Duende*, Graywolf Press. Copyright © 2007 by Tracy K. Smith. Reprinted with permission of Graywolf Press, Saint Paul, Minnesota, and the author.

SHERYL ST. GERMAIN: "What We Found in Our Mother's Shed After the Hurricane," "Cajun," "The Lake," and "Addiction" are from *Let It Be a Dark Roux: New and Selected Poems*, Autumn House Press. Copyright © 2008 by Sheryl St. Germain. Reprinted with permission of Autumn House Press and the author.

SUSAN TERRIS: "Pantoum for a Member of the Wedding" is from *Natural Defenses*, Marsh Hawk Press, 2004. Copyright © 2004 by Susan Terris and reprinted with her permission. "Goldfish: A Diptych" appeared in *FIELD* (2005). Copyright © 2005 by Susan Terris and reprinted with her permission. "I Speak in My Mother's Voice" appeared in *Water~Stone Review 8* (2005). Copyright © 2005 by Susan Terris and reprinted with her permission.

SUE ELLEN THOMPSON: "With My Second Husband, Thinking of My First," "How to Tell a True Love Story," and "After the Accident" are from *The Leaving: New and Selected Poems*, Autumn House Press. Copyright © 2001 by Sue Ellen Thompson. Reprinted with permission of Autumn House Press and the author. "The American Hotel" and "Helping My Daughter Move into Her First Apartment" are from *The Golden Hour*, Autumn House Press. Copyright © 2006 by Sue Ellen Thompson. Reprinted with permission of Autumn House Press and the author.

NATASHA TRETHEWEY: "Southern History" and "Incident" are from *Native Guard: Poems* by Natasha Trethewey. Copyright © 2006 by Natasha Trethewey. Reprinted by permission of Houghton Mifflin Harcourt Publishing Company. All rights reserved. "Taxonomy: De Español y de India Produce Mestizo," "Taxonomy: De Español y Negra Produce Mulato," and "Taxonomy: The Book of Castas," copyright © 2008 by Natasha Trethewey, are printed with permission of the author.

CHASE TWICHELL: "The Givens" is from *Perdido*, Farrar, Straus, and Giroux. Copyright © 1991 by Chase Twichell and reprinted with her permission. "To the Reader: If You Asked Me," "Road Tar," and "Erotic Energy" are from *The Snow Watcher*, Ontario Review Press. Copyright © 1998 by Chase Twichell and reprinted with her permission. "Centaur," "Sorry," and "Infant Pearls" are from *Dog Language*, Copper Canyon Press. Copyright © 2005 by Chase Twichell. Reprinted with permission from Copper Canyon Press and the author.

AMY UYEMATSU: "Wintertide" is from *30 Miles from J-Town*, Story Line Press. Copyright © 1992 by Amy Uyematsu and reprinted with her permission. "Lexicon" and "Muchas Gracias" are from *Nights of Fire, Nights of Rain*, Story Line Press. Copyright © 1998 by Amy Uyematsu and reprinted with her permission. "Under the Wave of Kanagawa," copyright © 2008 by Amy Uyematsu, appears with her permission.

The Autumn House Poetry Series

Michael Simms, Executive Editor

Snow White Horses, Selected Poems 1973–88 by Ed Ochester
The Leaving, New and Selected Poems by Sue Ellen Thompson
Dirt by Jo McDougall
Fire in the Orchard by Gary Margolis
Just Once, New and Previous Poems by Samuel Hazo
The White Calf Kicks by Deborah Slicer • 2003, selected by Naomi Shihab Nye
The Divine Salt by Peter Blair
The Dark Takes Aim by Julie Suk
Satisfied with Havoc by Jo McDougall
Half Lives by Richard Jackson
Not God After All by Gerald Stern (with drawings by Sheba Sharrow)
Dear Good Naked Morning by Ruth L. Schwartz • 2004, selected by Alicia Ostriker
A Flight to Elsewhere by Samuel Hazo
Collected Poems by Patricia Dobler
The Autumn House Anthology of Contemporary American Poetry edited by Sue Ellen Thompson
Déjà Vu Diner by Leonard Gontarek
lucky wreck by Ada Limon • 2005, selected by Jean Valentine
The Golden Hour by Sue Ellen Thompson
Woman in the Painting by Andrea Hollander Budy
Joyful Noise: An Anthology of American Spiritual Poetry edited by Robert Strong
No Sweeter Fat by Nancy Pagh • 2006, selected by Tim Seibles
Unreconstructed: Poems Selected and New by Ed Ochester
Rabbis of the Air by Philip Terman
Let It Be a Dark Roux: New and Selected Poems by Sheryl St. Germain
Dixmont by Rick Campbell
The River Is Rising by Patricia Jabbeh Wesley
The Dark Opens by Miriam Levine • 2007, selected by Mark Doty
The Song of the Horse by Samuel Hazo
My Life as a Doll by Elizabeth Kirschner
She Heads into the Wilderness by Anne Marie Macari
When She Named Fire: An Anthology of Contemporary Poetry by American Women edited by Andrea Hollander Budy

• winner of the annual Autumn House Press Poetry Prize

Design and Production

Cover and text design by Kathy Boykowycz
Cover art: "Signals" by Diane Itter
Knotted linen, 1989

Text set in Adobe Garamond, designed in 1989
by Robert Slimbach
Titles set in Univers 67, designed in 1957
by Adrian Frutiger

Printed by Thomson-Shore of Dexter, Michigan
on Nature's Natural, a 50% recycled paper